Love To Give

A Couple's Efforts to Become Parents

Denise E Johnson

Copyright © 2007 by Denise E. Johnson
Revised 2015

Edited by Abby Reiter

Because of the dynamic nature of the Internet, any Web addresses or links contained in this book may have changed since publication and may not longer be valid.

ISBN: 151432816X
ISBN 13: 9781514328163
Library of Congress Control Number: 2015910028
CreateSpace Independent Publishing Platform
North Charleston, South Carolina

Love To Give

A Couple's Efforts to Become Parents

This book is dedicated to my husband, Ron, who has been my rock through the many trials and joys in life. Thank you for being my partner, encourager, and best friend. Without you I would have never had the joy of being a wife or mother. You have made all my dreams come true. I will always love you.

Prologue

OUR MONTH-OLD SON Michael was asleep in the crib. There was such peacefulness about him as he sighed quietly. Everything about this room held such contentment and joy. The scent of baby powder, the layettes, music boxes, baby blankets, teddy bears, and the beautiful gifts we had received brought feelings of comfort and peace.

Michael was our long-awaited answer to prayer. After years of struggling with infertility, we finally had a baby. This was the child we had dreamed of and planned for since we married four years ago. In all our dreams though, we could never have imagined how one little baby could fill our lives and give us such a sense of completeness. What a joy to be parents finally. Our hearts brimmed with such pride and love as we looked upon our precious son.

Watching him peacefully sleep, our minds were crowded with so many thoughts; the love we felt for our son and the dread in what we must do. We wanted to savor this moment but it was impossible to ignore reality. Outside the nursery door, the unthinkable was about to happen. It was there that Michael's birth mother was waiting. Nancy had come to reclaim him, having decided to back out of the adoption.

Ron and I held each other as tears fell while we continued to watch our precious son. Nancy had given us this moment alone with Michael in order to say good-bye. We struggled to find the strength to do what we must. We tried to absorb this moment and imprint the tenderness of our son in our minds. Our hearts felt torn apart as if there were a hole in our chest a mile wide. Our home felt violated as if a thief was holding us at gunpoint. Meanwhile, our son peacefully slept. Thank God Michael did not know what was going on.

It seemed a shame to disturb him so we watched him for just a moment longer. He was such a beautiful baby. I wanted to get lost in this time, to stretch it and keep it going forever but then Ron pulled away. I put my arms around his waist as if to stop him. He kissed my forehead, loosened my grip, and then turned to the crib. It was time.

Ever so gently, Ron lifted Michael so he would not wake him. It was a picture I had seen so often this past month. Ron's obvious love for this little boy who had made him a daddy could not be hidden. Ron held Michael for a moment and then, attempting to stifle a sob, kissed our son. Turning to me, he placed Michael in my arms. My tears were uncontrollable. My lips trembled as I too kissed him good-bye.

As Ron moved to open the nursery door, it was all I could do not to cry out. I didn't want to leave the nursery. I didn't want to hand our baby over to Nancy. I just couldn't believe this was happening. What went wrong? How could such a beautiful and so well-thought-out adoption come to such a horrifying end? How could Nancy do this? How could she expect us to give up our son?

There had to be something I could do, something I had not yet thought of. Silently, I cried out to God. What could I say that would make Nancy realize what a horrible mistake she was making? My mind was racing as I thought back to where it all began...

Chapter 1

Seven months earlier:

Waking groggily from the anesthesia, I saw Ron looking down at me, his face filled with concern. My sister Colleen was there too. She had arrived while I was in surgery. To find out why Ron and I hadn't been able to conceive a child, I had undergone a laparoscopy. This procedure involved inserting an instrument called a laparoscope through a small incision in my abdomen to give the doctor a view of the outside of my reproductive organs. I had postponed this final step in our fertility testing process for over a year out of a fear of anesthesia. Finally, out of desperation, I had gone through with it. Perhaps now we would know what had caused us so much frustration and disappointment.

Ron and I wanted children more than anything. We had always planned to have them. Shortly after our marriage, we found a house with a fenced back yard where children could safely play. Then we bought a puppy. After all, every child should have a dog. The car we purchased had child safety locks—just in case. It was all here waiting. All that was missing was the child.

Even as a little girl, I dreamt of being a mom. After all, moms were the greatest people in the world. They could kiss a scratched knee and make it feel better and chase the monsters from the closet after a bad dream. They knew the magic that made cupcakes and games to fill up rainy days. As a child, I loved to pretend I was a mom and spent hours taking care of my dolls. If my dolls weren't enough then there was always my little sister Colleen to mother.

During my teenage years, I jumped at any chance to babysit. I loved children. In college, my world grew bigger. I learned there were many children who lived in less than desirable circumstances. It was then that I recognized a burning in my heart to do something good for children. I kept a picture that showed the sweet faces of children from a variety of races on my refrigerator. Perhaps someday I would be a foster parent or house parent in an orphanage. No matter what though, someday I knew that I would be a mom.

Becoming a parent was also important to Ron. There was a gentleness about him that I recognized from the moment we first met. Perhaps that is why it was love at first sight. Anyway, from the time we decided to get married, having children was a priority. It delighted me to watch Ron play with our nieces and nephews. "More, more," they would cry out, giggling, as he'd gently toss them in the air.

Several months after we married, we started trying to conceive. Years passed. Though I had a good job with the local utility company and the promise of future promotions, a career wasn't what I wanted. I wanted to be a mother. Parenthood, however, eluded us month after month. We began the long and sometimes painful ordeal of fertility testing. Initially there were general health examinations and blood tests. More complicated fluid tests and cervical examinations followed. Endocrine studies analyzed the pituitary gland in relation to hormone levels and ovarian functions. Dye was shot into my fallopian tubes to check for any blockages.

Ron too had undergone the personal probes with a sperm test to determine semen mobility and quality. Now it seemed as if the doctors knew everything about our lives. Our sex life had become a duty to perform around the time of the month when we were most likely to conceive.

The tests though, hadn't shown anything irregular. I felt inadequate, unable to accomplish the basic work of womanhood. Each month another opportunity passed. Someday the opportunities would run out. I felt this even though I was only twenty-nine years old.

All the while, our friends were having children. I was so envious. We confided our problem to only a few people. Others often teased us about not having children. "Don't you know what to do?" they would joke.

"I guess not," we would joke back. Inside we choked back our tears as emptiness knocked at our hearts.

I didn't want to admit that pregnancy might be impossible. Adoption sounded so complicated and costly. We had heard that some agencies set a maximum age. With Ron thirty-six years old, we were already out of the range. Besides, there were long waiting lists and social workers who would pry into our personal lives. After enduring the numerous fertility tests, I felt desperate to protect what little privacy we had left. I just wanted to have a baby and I wasn't willing to admit that we couldn't—not yet anyway.

"You have some scarring," Dr. Fellows explained shortly after I woke from the surgery. "I suspect it's a result of endometriosis."

"What's that?" I asked.

"Well, it's when tissue grows in abnormal areas such as on the ovaries or uterus. This could have caused your problems in the past but there does not appear to be any active sores at this time. That is encouraging."

I felt relieved that he hadn't found an insurmountable problem, yet upset that we still had no definite answer. The testing process had grown weary. I was tired of feeling like an experiment.

The doctor continued, "You'll have some discomfort and swelling from the gases we used to expand your stomach cavity. It may take up to six weeks for the swelling to go down. Once you're feeling up to it, I'd like to try a drug called Clomid to see if conception can be achieved."

"Clomid?" I asked, my spirits lifting.

"Yes. It increases the output of hormones by the pituitary, thus stimulating ovulation. Even though we know you're ovulating, increasing the hormone levels may help to achieve conception."

"Okay," I said, "let's try it."

Back at home, I had just put my feet up after getting the supper dishes washed when the phone rang. Moving slowly since I felt some pain from the surgery, I went to answer it. It was Nancy calling from California. She had been my college roommate and we had remained close through the years. Her parents lived only blocks from Ron and me. We usually had a chance to see each other whenever she came home to visit.

Immediately, I heard worry in Nancy's voice, but before I could ask her what was the matter, she pressed me with questions. I told her about my surgery since she was one of my few friends aware of our struggle.

"What did you learn?" she asked.

"There's a drug I can try so we'll start that soon. So, how are you?"

There was a long silence and then she said, "Denise, I'm pregnant."

I wasn't sure what to say. Nancy was unmarried and her current relationship was rocky. "Congratulations," I offered.

"No!" Her voice cracked as she began to cry. "This is not what I had planned. I always thought if this were to happen, Jim and I would get married but that's not going to be." She was talking and weeping at the same time. "Honestly, I didn't think I'd ever get pregnant. A gynecologist told me years ago that it was unlikely I would be able to have children. When I learned I was pregnant, I considered having an abortion but I'm too far along."

"How far along?" I asked.

"I think five months." She paused as if to gather her nerve. Then she blurted, "Denise, would you and Ron want to adopt the baby?"

I was stunned. I couldn't answer. Nancy filled the silence. "You don't have to tell me now. I know this is difficult, but somehow I felt I should call you, and I'll understand completely no matter what you decide."

"Nancy, are you sure?"

"Oh, yes," she stated emphatically. "I have no desire for a baby right now. The thought terrifies me. It is just not a good time in my life. I want to focus on my career. I don't want a baby!"

"What about Jim?"

"This isn't a good time for him either. He doesn't want the baby."

"Nancy, I just don't know what to say. We're still optimistic I'll get pregnant with the help of this medication."

"Oh, I know but it's okay if you have more kids." She sounded worried. "I don't know where else to turn. I do not want a child right now and I thought of how you want one so bad. I want this baby to have more than I could give, especially a mother and a father."

"Ron, you aren't going to believe this!" I cried out, bursting into the family room where he was watching television. "Nancy is pregnant and she asked us to adopt the baby."

He looked up from the television program with an expression of disbelief. "What did you say?"

"Nancy wants us to adopt her baby."

"After all these years—just out of the blue—you pick up the phone and—this is unbelievable! Honey, do you suppose God meant this baby for us?"

"I don't know but I already love this baby."

Tears welled up in his eyes. "Is she serious? I mean has she thought this out?"

"It sure sounds like it. She said she doesn't want a baby right now."

"Why not?"

"She and Jim won't be getting married. She didn't tell me why but I had the feeling that she didn't want to talk about it. She sounds serious about giving us the baby though."

I sat down next to Ron. The room was quiet as we each thought our own thoughts. Finally, he broke the silence. "I've never felt so excited and scared at the same time. I don't want to get my hopes up but how can I help it?"

"I know," I said, biting my lip.

"When is the baby due?"

"She thinks around the end of February."

"Do you suppose she'll let us be part of the delivery?"

"I'll have to ask. That would be wonderful."

"Amazing, isn't it?"

We were silent again. Then Ron introduced a somber note. "You know, she may feel differently as the due date approaches. As much as I would like to have this baby, I think we need to let her know that we will support her no matter what she decides. This could be the answer to our prayers but we should make sure it's what she really wants."

"You're right," I answered, suddenly feeling sad.

There was another pause. "Besides, adopting her baby could change your friendship with her," Ron added.

I had not thought of that. For a moment, I imagined what it would be like for Nancy to visit us and hear her child call me mommy. I tried to imagine how I would feel with Nancy watching us raise her child and perhaps judging our parenting skills. "How many friends get to share a child?" I said. It sounded a little lame.

After a while, Ron said, "We don't know much about adoption."

"How difficult could it be," I asked, "particularly in these circumstances?"

"I'll make some calls tomorrow."

"That's a good idea."

"What a great way to start our family," Ron said.

"This could be our only chance for a baby," I mused.

"Don't worry honey; everything will work out just fine."

"I'm sure it will," I agreed, hoping with every thread of my being that he was right.

After speaking with Nancy, our long-standing friendship was on my mind. It made me think of a special time that happened years earlier…

It was a chilly Tuesday evening in November, just a month before college finals. In addition to upcoming finals, I had entered a sewing and modeling contest called "Make It Yourself with Wool." I had struggled for hours to bind the buttonholes and finally threw up my hands in frustration. I wished I were home in Helena, especially since it was election night. Dad was running for his third term in the Montana State Legislature. Our home would be full of people awaiting election results. I was so proud of my dad! I hated missing the excitement of his possible re-election.

"Well, let's go to Helena then," Nancy said when I expressed my frustration. "We can surprise your dad and get buttonhole directions from your mom at the same time."

Oh, how I loved Nancy. She was so spontaneous and full of fun.

All the way to Helena, we talked and laughed, making a "congratulations" card for Dad, confident of his victory. When we pulled in, Dad opened the front door, expecting to greet more of his friends. His big arms embraced us both at the same time. He was so pleased to see us! We stayed up well into the early morning hours. Finally, it was official—Dad had been re-elected. By 5:00 the following morning, Mom had given me directions on the buttonholes and we were back on the road, intent on making 8:00 a.m. class.

Nancy's and my friendship had many such special memories. I remember sitting on Nancy's bed, crying together when she learned of her grandmother's death and Nancy's tears when we learned that my dad had cancer. Then on my wedding day, Nancy came looking for me several hours early. She couldn't wait to see me dressed as a bride. We both cried a little then too. I really treasured our friendship.

As much as I cherished Nancy's friendship, the night her phone call came would prove to be the first of many nights when I lay awake for hours, tormented by "what ifs." They grew more preposterous as minutes slowly ticked by, and yet I was unable to rid myself of them.

This Jim who wouldn't marry Nancy, what if alcoholism or other addictions ran in his family? What if he were a hustler and would think up some way to blackmail us? What if he persuaded Nancy to keep the baby at the last minute? On the other hand, maybe he would marry Nancy after all and decide to become a family. Or what if his family started coming around bothering us?

What if Nancy married and then couldn't have more children? Would she regret her decision? What if she married a lawyer who knew some loophole for taking the child back? What if she became rich and bought expensive presents for the child, making us look stingy or like failures? What if she insisted on having visitation rights at her discretion? What if her family wanted the baby?

By one in the morning, I'd thought of a million things that could go wrong.

Ron was pacing back and forth across the kitchen. My hands were sweaty as I sat at the table. I'd promised we'd call Nancy back with our answer tonight. We had to wait until 6:30 p.m. before she would be home from work. Ron rehearsed with me our response until it was finally time to call. Trembling with excitement, I dialed Nancy's number.

She answered promptly as if waiting by the phone.

"Hi there," I said. "How was your day?"

"Oh, pretty good." Her voice was apprehensive as if nervous about my answer.

She'd barely finished her response before I burst out, "Nancy, first off, Ron and I want you to know that we care for you no matter what."

"I already knew that," she said, sounding disappointed.

"If you want us to adopt your baby, we would be honored."

By now, I was crying and Nancy started to cry too.

"Oh, Denise, are you sure? Does Ron want to?"

"This is definitely what we both want as long as it's what you want."

"Oh, it is," Nancy said emphatically. "You know, last night after hearing about your surgery, I almost didn't tell you about my pregnancy but deep down I knew that everything would be okay. Just hearing your voice made me feel so much calmer. After I hung up, I knew I had done all I could. It was now in God's hands."

She seemed to have many words she needed to get off her heart. "I've been so upset and confused about what to do. One morning while I was lying in bed, trying to think things out, I heard a voice distinctly state your names. At the same time, a bright light suddenly illuminated your names on my wall. I know it sounds strange, but that is what happened. Anyway, after that, I just felt I should call you. I truly believe that God was giving me an answer to my prayers by telling me to call. Even so, I was really nervous!"

"Well, we feel very blessed to be asked," I assured her as my tears continued. "You think the baby is due around the end of February?"

"I think so but I'm not sure. My cycle has always been irregular. I had felt sick for some time but I thought it was the stress of my job. In fact, I even quit my job I was feeling so lousy. I will be starting a new one at the end of the month. It wasn't until just a few weeks ago that I found out I was pregnant. Anyway, I'll make an appointment for an ultrasound to get a better idea of the due date."

"You certainly have a lot going on in your life."

"I've been looking for an apartment too, closer to my new job." Then rather timidly, Nancy asked, "Could you be here for the delivery?"

"Definitely. We had hoped that you would want us there."

"Oh, yes. I really do not want to go through that alone. By the way, I'd like to keep this between us."

"What do you mean?"

"I don't want my family to know."

"Why?" I asked.

"They wouldn't understand about giving the baby up for adoption. Besides, if my parents knew that you had adopted my baby, they would always want to be at your house acting like its grandparents. You have a wonderful family and I don't want mine to interfere."

"This seems like a terribly big secret to keep," I pointed out. I hoped she would reconsider. I could not imagine how she was going to keep this from her family but decided to drop the subject for now.

"Tell me more about Jim," I said.

"He reminds me so much of your family, Denise. He is built big across the shoulders like the men in your family and has blondish brown hair and blue eyes. He is very athletic. And my family is like Ron's."

That was true. Although Ron's mom had passed away, there were many similarities between her and Nancy. They both were tall and thin. Even their hair color was similar.

"Well, I think this baby will really fit in with your family," Nancy went on. "And with my family being Norwegian like yours, that will be neat too. Oh, it is such a relief that you want to adopt the baby. I'm just so glad that I don't have to go through with that!"

"With what?"

Nancy hesitated before she responded. "Well, I found a doctor who was willing to do an abortion. It was scheduled for tomorrow."

I caught my breath. Her confession caught me totally by surprise. The very thought of destroying this baby that we already loved turned my stomach.

As if reading my mind, Nancy said, "I didn't feel I had many options. I don't want a total stranger raising my child but I don't want to raise it and neither does Jim. Now that you have agreed to adopt it, I know it will be loved and taken care of. I have a feeling that this is a very special child, and I want it to have all it deserves. Thank you so much, Denise."

That evening, Ron and I turned our thanks to God. For the first time, we were thankful we didn't have children. If we had, perhaps Nancy wouldn't have called us and this child would have been denied life. Now this baby, our baby, would live.

Suddenly, we felt at peace as we realized that we had been given the opportunity to save this baby's life. If the years of frustration and turmoil in trying to have children were for this purpose, they had been worth it. This one baby's life was worth it all.

Chapter 2

"WE'RE GOING TO have a baby," I announced to my sister Colleen.

"Are you sure?" she asked, puzzled. The surgery had been just last week.

Without even thinking I blurted out, "Nancy is pregnant. She wants us to adopt her baby."

Then I realized what I had done. "Oh, Colleen, I wasn't supposed to tell whose baby it is. Promise you'll keep it a secret." I felt horrible for disclosing Nancy's identity but knew that Colleen was trustworthy. Through all our years growing up, she had been my closest confidant and as adults, we were best friends.

"You know I will. I am glad you slipped, though. Knowing it's Nancy's baby makes it all the more special."

"We are so excited but we've decided not to tell anyone else right now. It is still so early and Nancy may change her mind. But I couldn't keep this secret from you."

"You'd have been in big trouble if you had," she laughed as tears filled her voice. "This already feels like it's meant to be," Colleen continued, bubbling over with joy. "Remember how last week while I was there for your surgery, I asked if you had given any more thought to adopting? It's been tearing me up to watch you and Ron go through so much."

"I know, isn't it amazing? God already had this in the works. So now we'll have a baby next year too."

"Our children will be close in age just like we always hoped," Colleen said. She and her husband, also named Ron, had a two-year-old son Anthony and were expecting their second child in early March.

"It will be so special. I can hardly wait."

We called Nancy the day she had the ultrasound. Hearing my voice, she said, "I was hoping it was you."

"Before you say anything, I have a confession to make. I accidentally told Colleen that you are the birth mother."

"That's okay. I was afraid you were going to tell me that you'd changed your mind."

"You don't have to worry about that. But I feel horrible that I didn't keep your secret."

"Don't worry. It's nice that Colleen is in on it." Nancy always had a fondness for Colleen. "Besides, I told my sister Diane too," Nancy confessed.

"I'm so glad! I must admit, Nancy, it really bothered me that no one in your family was aware of your pregnancy." That was another of my 1 a.m. worries: what if something happened during the pregnancy or delivery that made it necessary to involve her family? It would have been so awkward for Ron and me to break the news to them. With her younger sister aware of her situation, there would be a family member we could contact if necessary.

"So how did Diane take the news?"

"She's very supportive of both my pregnancy and my plans to give the baby to you."

"Have you given any more thought to telling the rest of your family?"

"No, I don't want to tell them. My older sister with children would never understand why I'd give my child to a friend before family."

As I listened to Nancy, I knew that she would not change her mind, at least not then. Besides, what if her family talked her out of the adoption? The thought filled me with fear. I wanted this baby so much. If keeping a secret was the price, I was willing to pay it.

"The ultrasound was really interesting," Nancy was saying. "I saw the baby move. The doctor said everything looks good. The baby is due close to the end of March, though. See how little I know about this stuff? I couldn't even calculate the date right."

"Oh heavens, I wouldn't know how either. So what's the exact date?"

"March 28th."

"You've got to be kidding. That's my grandma's birthday!"

"Oh, isn't that neat? Wouldn't it be something if the baby was born on her birthday?"

The later due date was disappointing, though. Already I was feeling impatient and didn't want to wait any longer.

Nancy filled me in on every detail of her pregnancy. Then she said, "Denise, thanks for being so interested in my pregnancy."

"It makes me feel so much more involved," I said. "I almost feel like I'm the one who is pregnant."

"I truly do feel that this is your baby. I am simply carrying it for you, and your interest only makes me more comfortable with my decision. It is so nice to have someone to share with. Besides, if the baby should ever have any questions about the pregnancy, I want you to be able to tell it as much as possible, just as if it were your own pregnancy."

Because of Nancy's continued assurances, we decided to go ahead and tell our family but we wanted to tell them in person. The three-and-a-half hour drive to Helena was beautiful as the last of the fall colors clung to the trees. Pulling into Mom's driveway, we looked around at the apartment complex. She had recently moved, having sold the ranch where my brother, sister, and I had grown up. Selling it had been hard on us. It was like giving up a piece of our life but the ranch was too much work for Mom now that Dad was gone. Besides, she needed a new start.

Thinking of Dad's absence, I suddenly felt sad. He had been a gentle person despite his massive size, six feet two inches and 240 pounds. His embrace had made us feel safe. Even as adults, Colleen and I loved to sit on the arm of his recliner where we could put our arms around his neck and savor the closeness to him. He had a way of making everyone feel important. Although greatly respected by his peers and fellow statesmen, no one respected him more than his own family. I missed him so much, especially today.

I could almost see how he would have grinned at our news. He would have struggled to keep from crying, not one to show such emotion. In his effort, however, his throat would have been making a sort of clicking sound and, filled with pride, his chest would have puffed out as his hug swallowed us up.

"Hurry up and get married so I can have some grandchildren," he used to tell us kids jokingly. "If you don't, I might have to adopt one."

Now Ron and I were going to adopt one, but Dad wasn't here. I wiped away tears as I quietly wished things could have been different.

Once in Mom's apartment, I felt the familiar warmth of home despite the unfamiliar surroundings. The apartment was much smaller than the ranch house but it was cozy. Immediately I noticed the wedding pictures of us three children on the wall. What a year that had been! Colleen married her husband Ron right after Christmas, followed by Ron and me in early May, and my brother Dave and his wife Brenda in mid-September. Three days later Dad passed away as cancer took his life. So much joy, yet so much pain! We were thankful that Dad had been able to see us all married.

Glancing around the apartment, I saw the round coffee table that Mom had refinished as well as the old player piano on which Colleen and I had learned to play. The walls held the familiar needlepoint pictures Mom had made through the years. She was a talented person, never without a project. It seemed as if nothing was too large or too difficult for her to undertake.

Colleen, Ron, and their son Anthony had already arrived. I could tell from the smile on Colleen's face that she was dying for us to get our news out so she could talk about it. Mom was fixing dinner. We chatted in the kitchen and set the oak table she had also refinished years ago. Although worn from the years, it was still very inviting.

Dave, Brenda, Granddad, and Grandma finally arrived. Mom was in her glory. Her children were together again! She loved having us all under one roof.

When I couldn't stand it any longer, I blurted it out. "Ron and I have some news. We're going to be parents."

Mom was instantly in tears.

Brenda gasped, "Really?"

"Yes, really," we answered. "We're adopting a baby."

Dave, a bit of a jokester, remained quiet while a big grin spread across his face. Finally, with complete joy, he reached over to hug me. "Congratulations," he said, expressing more emotion than usual.

I glanced across the room to where Granddad and Grandma were sitting. Both were beaming as tears rolled down their cheeks. Granddad's lip quivered as he struggled with his emotion. To them, we grandchildren, and now great-grandchildren, meant everything in the world. Ron and I were so happy to add to their joy with a child of our own.

Then the questions began. "How did you learn about the baby?" Mom wanted to know.

"A friend of ours called and asked us to adopt her unborn child."

"What friend?" Mom asked.

"Well, we've agreed not to disclose her name."

Then questions came from all directions.

"Why does she want to remain anonymous?"

"Why does it have to be such a secret?"

"How well do you know this person?"

"Is this one of Ron's friends or yours?"

"Where did you meet?"

"Are you sure about this?"

It felt like I was on trial. Mom looked worried. Brenda was biting her nails. Dave frowned out the picture window. Only Granddad and Grandma remained calm.

"Wait, wait," I pleaded. "We can't tell you more than we already have. I'm sorry. It is not unusual in adoption cases. Some information can't be revealed."

The questions stopped for a minute, but then, hesitantly, they started up once more. I had assumed my family would understand how sensitive the arrangements were, but I couldn't blame them for their concern. They obviously feared that we could be hurt or disappointed. They loved us. Keeping the secret was going to be far more difficult than I'd imagined. When Nancy expressed her desire to remain anonymous, I had only thought of what she was hiding from her family, not what we would have to hide from ours. We were not a family who kept secrets from one another. I felt deceitful and frustrated.

Making our way to the kitchen for dinner, Grandma came over to me and tenderly patted my arm. "Honey, I know there is only so much you can tell us. We understand."

As I hugged her, I whispered "thank you." I so admired my grandparents. It seemed they always understood and came through, saying or doing just the right thing. I wanted to emulate them in my life.

The office where Ron and I worked, having met there six years earlier, was buzzing with excitement as we shared our news with coworkers. I had brought cupcakes decorated with pink and blue booties. Fortunately, the cupcakes told the news since I could not get through our announcement without crying. Unexpectedly, our happiness was soon mixed with feelings of frustration. Everyone seemed to assume that we couldn't have children and, despite our years of infertility, I wasn't ready to admit that yet.

"Just wait, now that you're adopting you'll have your own," folks stated cheerfully. I felt on the defensive.

"We aren't adopting in order to get pregnant. The only reason we are involved is because we love this baby and the woman who carries it." The implication that we would meddle in one infant's life in order to become pregnant with another was downright offensive to Ron and me. We would not have dreamed of using a new little human being for our own ends like that.

Further, people's speculations about our infertility felt like a horrible invasion of our privacy. We still believed we would have children. Besides, it was no one else's business.

Comments such as, "How wonderful that you can give this child a home," also irritated me—not so much the words as the tone, as if we were heroes for taking in a stray animal!

We started to see how little most people understood adoption. This wasn't a matter of charity. We were not giving an unwanted, undesirable child a home. We were giving OUR child a home just as we would one born from my womb.

Although we hadn't conceived this child, that didn't change the way we felt about it. We loved and prayed for our little one from the moment we learned of its existence, just like any other parent.

I constantly felt pressured to justify our love. It was as if we had been segregated into a separate class—one for those who would never experience the exalted feelings of a birth parent. I felt as if we were being pitied for having to settle for someone else's child. How was it possible that human beings could not understand love for a child simply because it was a child?

Worst of all was, "I'm sure you'll love it like a real mother." I was mad at myself for being affected by something as stupid as that. Yet to console myself, I thought about my own mother. Did I love her because she gave birth to me, or because she was there for me as I grew up?

I didn't have to think long to know to the answer. Certainly, I loved my mother for giving me life, but I loved her more for the things she taught me *about* life. I loved her for being there when I needed her, for patiently teaching me to sew and to cook, for looking out for my best interests even when I argued with her. That was a real mother—not just someone who could have babies.

As time went on, I decided that once we had our baby home, I wouldn't tell anybody else it was adopted. This was our child! I didn't have to justify its importance in our life. My love was as worthy as a birth parent!

"How does that look?" Ron asked, stepping back from the crib he'd just set up.

"Perfect!" I said reaching to hug him. "I can hardly believe we're actually going to have a baby in there."

Our whole life had taken on a new look. I had been sewing maternity dresses for Nancy, making things for our baby, and preparing the house for an infant. Mom had been down to help me make a crib set, complete with bumper pads, comforter, and matching sheets. I had chosen primary colors with teddy bears and balloons, wanting the room to be bright and cheery. Bottles of baby lotion and powder sat ready on the dresser. The room was definitely transforming into a wonderful nursery.

In addition to all the physical things that indicated a baby was about to enter our home, there was a newness about our marriage. Our love and respect for one another was growing. The rest of our lives no longer seemed important—just our love, just our baby.

The holidays were approaching. Ron suggested we drive to California. "I think it would be good for the three of us to sit down and really talk things over, face to face."

"Great idea," I said and headed for the phone.

When I told Nancy, she said, "Oh that would be wonderful! I was really feeling blue about the holidays since I cannot go home with my pregnancy being so obvious. If you guys could come here, it would make my Christmas!"

As we continued to talk, Nancy told me about a TV program she had seen which covered adoption ceremonies. "It reminded me of a marriage but in this ceremony the baby is given to the adoptive couple. It would be a wonderful way to officially close our adoption. What do you think?"

"That would be beautiful, Nancy."

"Perhaps we could have it at the hospital chapel."

"Oh, I love it and I know Ron will too."

"Okay, I'll talk to the hospital. Oh, and I was wondering," she added timidly, "could you stay a few days after the baby is born? I would really like to have some time with the baby. It's all I'll have until the baby's older and can meet me as its birth mother."

"If that's what you'd like," I responded, feeling a bit hesitant. I was anxious to please her, yet something about this new development left me very uneasy.

Filled with disappointment once again, I recognized the signs. I had been taking the Clomid for several months and it hadn't worked. Although the pressure to have a baby didn't seem as intense now that we were adopting one, it hadn't changed my desire to get pregnant. Besides, the adoption could fall through.

I poured out my frustration to my doctor.

"Don't worry," Dr. Fellows said. "Sometimes it takes a few months."

A few months, I thought to myself. That was easy for him to say. It seemed like a lifetime away.

He sensed my disappointment. "Let's give this another month and then we'll increase the dosage. If that doesn't work, there is still another drug we can try."

Deep down, I was feeling stressed out. We were nearing the end of our options. I didn't like taking this medication because it made my emotions spike from one extreme to the other. Taking an increased dosage didn't sound like a good plan. My patience was wearing thin. Yet, I still did not want to give up.

When I opened the mailbox that evening there was a note from Nancy. Quickly I opened it. She wrote: Merry Christmas to two people who have become even more special to me. I love you like family. So what do you think of our baby?

Included with the card was a picture of the latest ultrasound. As I looked at it I thought to myself, *Yes, our baby*. The prospect was becoming more and more real every day. I could hardly wait.

The letter continued: I saw Jim this week. Things didn't go so great. He talked about everything except the baby and made sure he never touched my stomach. I really wanted to talk about my feelings and his but couldn't bring myself to confront him. Instead of feeling better after seeing him, I felt worse.

Nancy was getting no support from Jim and I wondered why. I was glad we would be there soon. Perhaps we would find out what was going on with him.

Chapter 3

THE SUN HAD barely stretched its rays above the horizon when we loaded our car and headed out. We had spent Christmas Day with my family. Now we were anxious to see Nancy and hoped to reach St. George, Utah by tonight.

We rode in silence for a while. Finally, I shared what was on my mind.

"You know, being friends with Nancy makes this hard. I should be thrilled if Jim married her and they could raise the baby. Selfishly though I am glad that he's not supportive so we get our baby. I know that sounds awful. At the same time, I'm also angry with him. Nancy deserves better. I feel torn apart with these emotions. I want to take care of Nancy so that she doesn't have to depend on him."

"I know what you're saying," Ron said. "For us to have the baby, Nancy has to be unwilling or unable to provide. It's a difficult position!"

"It's like walking a tight rope, balancing my role as Nancy's friend and my role as the baby's mother. Like last week when Nancy asked if we would stay a few days after the birth. As her friend my response is yes, but as the mother, I'm not sure it's a good idea."

"It's hard, all right," Ron agreed.

"I feel so vulnerable, like we don't have any control. Our world feels like it revolves around this baby but in one second it could be taken away from us. I don't like being so dependent on someone else for the fulfillment of this dream, a dream that means so much to us. Our whole life could tumble down and there's nothing we could do about it."

"I agree. It's very scary."

Arriving in California, the green grasses and chirping birds were a delightful contrast to the snow and ice we had left behind in Montana. Somehow, I expected Nancy to drive a sports car, not the Dodge Shadow but it did fit her practical side.

As Nancy drove into the parking lot having arrived from work, I immediately got out of our car. I could not wait to get my arms around her. It had been over a year since we'd seen each other and so much had changed. As soon as her car came to a stop, Nancy too jumped quickly out and we embraced. Then she pulled back and patted her stomach.

"Well, here it is," she proclaimed.

I put my hand to her stomach as tears spilled down my face. This was our baby and oh, how I loved my dear friend who carried it.

Making our way to Nancy's apartment, we chatted excitedly. The apartment was light and airy. Her furniture was simple and charming yet sophisticated. The decor included a rocking chair and contemporary sectional couch. A cookie jar shaped like a Jersey cow matched the kitchen towels and was a taste of the farm in the middle of the major city. I smiled thinking of how Nancy had always loved things that had Jersey cows on them.

Since Nancy had recently moved, there were boxes stacked behind the couch. The apartment was neat and tidy. However, with few pictures or other personal items, there was a sense of vacancy.

"So how is your new job going?" I asked.

"It's been hard. There is a lot to learn about the computer business. I had no idea there was so much to this industry."

"I'm sure you'll be up to speed in no time."

"I hope so. It's certainly different from what I expected though."

As we continued to visit, Nancy prepared a shrimp salad for dinner. "I don't have much of an appetite lately so I thought we'd have something light. Will that be okay?"

"No problem. Is that going to be enough for you, though?" I asked, privately questioning if she was eating adequately for our baby.

"Yes, this will be fine. I bought some wine if you'd like it."

"None for me but I'm sure Ron would enjoy a glass. Can I help set the table?"

"Sure, the dishes are in this cupboard," she said, pointing.

Opening it, I noticed prescription prenatal vitamins as well as generic one-a-days. I hoped Nancy was taking the prenatal vitamins.

As Nancy poured herself a cup of coffee, I thought of the caffeine and said, "I see you still love coffee."

"Yes, but I'm trying to drink only decaffeinated since I'm pregnant."

Glancing at the coffee can I could see that it was. "Are you still exercising?"

"Yes, every morning. Would you like to go along tomorrow?"

"Sure," I answered. I could use the exercise. Besides, it would give me an opportunity to observe how hard Nancy exerted herself. I was concerned she might be overdoing it.

Suddenly I realized I was analyzing everything Nancy did; what she ate, what she drank, how she exercised. Immediately I was ashamed for being so critical but all these issues were imperative to the health of our baby. If only this were my pregnancy, I wouldn't have to worry or question someone else. It would be my responsibility. This was not my pregnancy though. This was beyond my control. However, even though I fretted, I trusted Nancy and knew she would be very careful.

Throughout dinner, we continued to enjoy catching up with each other as friends. With the dishes done, we settled down to serious conversation.

"Nancy, how are you feeling about the adoption?" I asked.

"I truly believe that God intended for this to be your baby. I am simply carrying it for you."

Tears filled my eyes. This was the assurance Ron and I wanted and needed.

"You don't know how happy you have made us," Ron said.

"I'm happy too. This baby is very lucky to be a part of your family."

"Well, thank you," he responded humbly.

"So what about Jim?" I asked. "Will we be meeting him this weekend?"

"He has other commitments and besides, I haven't been too anxious to see him. That last visit was hard. I don't have the energy for another one like that, but I probably have a picture of him around here I could show you." She promptly changed the subject. I wondered why she seemed so anxious to direct the conversation away from Jim.

While Nancy was at work on Friday, Ron tried to check out California's requirements for adoption proceedings.

That evening when Nancy arrived home, she burst in the door and cried out, "Quick, come here. Our baby is moving." We rushed to her side and she pressed our hands to her stomach. "Can you feel it?" she asked with excitement in her voice.

"Yes, I can," I said. Ron had a big grin on his face as he too nodded.

"It's an active little one," Nancy told us. "It even gets the hiccups occasionally."

I felt such pride and anticipation. Then the baby settled back into its slumber and we sat to relax while Ron summarized our day for Nancy.

"We called several adoption agencies today and learned that we either have to go through an agency or an attorney. It seems somewhat silly to pay an agency since part of their cost includes finding a baby or adoptive couple. I got the feeling that they weren't really interested in us anyhow."

"Well, let's just go through an attorney," Nancy said.

"That's what we thought too. The yellow pages are full of lawyers who handle adoptions but how do you know who would be good? This is so important. I hate to just pick somebody from the yellow pages."

"Maybe I could do some asking around," Nancy offered.

"Or we could call the Bar Association. They might help us."

"Either way—just let me know what I can do to help."

There were so many issues and concerns to discuss. We needed to be certain that Nancy understood that this baby would be ours. Ron and I wanted a normal family but would she allow that under these circumstances? Would Nancy go through with the adoption? Then once she did, would she intervene in our child's life forever?

Trying to get a feel for this, I shifted our conversation. "How would you like to be known to our baby?"

"I think I'd rather be known as a friend of the family. After all, that is what I am. It is hard enough for a child to grow up in this world without confusion over who its parents are. Someday I'd like for the baby to know I'm its birth mother, but only when it's older and only if it asks."

"We want the baby to know early that it is adopted," Ron stated. "Learning about its adoption later might destroy its trust in us."

"I agree. You guys have really thought this out haven't you?"

"One of my cousins is adopted," I said. "He has always known and his folks presented it in a way that made him feel special, not different. We want our child to feel the same way, only in our case; we know who its mother is. Our child will always know how much you love it. Because of that, I'm sure that someday it will want to know you and we will welcome that."

Nancy's eyes moistened. "Oh, I hope so."

"Nancy," Ron said, "do you think it will be hard for you to hear your child calling us Mom and Dad?"

"Well, it's hard to say but I know that you will be the real parents."

"One thing is for certain," I said. "We will do our best. We won't be perfect but it won't be for lack of effort."

"I know," Nancy replied.

I took a deep breath and went to the heart of the matter. "Our biggest worry is that you may change your mind. But if you do, please tell us right away."

"Don't worry. I won't be changing my mind."

"Well, just remember that we'll love you no matter what happens," I replied.

"Thank you," Nancy said, "but if I do change my mind, please remind me of this conversation." Turning to Ron she said, "I don't know you as well as Denise. I'm concerned that you might be having doubts about all this."

"I am very excited about being this child's father," Ron stated.

"I just didn't want you to think this was some crazy idea between us girls. I am really serious about the adoption," Nancy said. "Since you will be the parents, I want to ask you some things like, what are your feelings about discipline? It's something that I think is really important."

"We agree," Ron said. "Children need a loving environment where boundaries are set for them."

"I'm glad to hear you say that," Nancy told him.

The conversation continued, almost as if we were in a duel as we tried to pinpoint our concerns. It was awkward, yet it was important to discuss these issues.

Finally, Nancy smiled. "We seem to agree on the critical issues. I feel comfortable with my decision. I know this will be your baby but I want it to grow up happy."

The next day was Saturday. Nancy wanted us to meet her aunt and only other relative that knew of her pregnancy.

"I've asked Lynn to join us for lunch. Since it is possible that you will not be here in time for the delivery, I thought I should have a backup plan for a labor coach. I've asked Lynn to be my coach." Nancy explained. "Besides, she'll be able to attend childbirth classes with me," she continued.

"What a great idea," I said. I was so pleased that we would get to meet Lynn on this trip.

Pulling up in front of Lynn's house, we noticed the wealth and prestige of the neighborhood. Immediately Lynn greeted us and then warmly hugged Nancy.

"Come in," she said enthusiastically while apologizing for the disarray of the house. "We've been remodeling for over a year but I'd love to show you around."

"That would be wonderful," we responded. Ron and I loved house tours. We often wandered through open houses just to see the layout. As we followed Lynn through the house, it was apparent no expense had been spared. Expensive, hand-made tiles had been selected for the bathrooms. Paint and carpet had been specially ordered in the just the right shade of gray. Oak trim was rampant.

"This is going to be beautiful," Ron said.

"I hope we get to see it completed when we return in March," I added.

"I hope it's done by then too," Lynn said emphatically.

After the quick tour, we drove to a quaint little restaurant. The atmosphere was casual, with tile floors and rough wood walls. After ordering our sandwiches, Lynn said, "So tell me about yourselves."

The tone of her question led me to believe we were in for some detailed questions, like an interview. Feeling nervous, I wondered if there wasn't more to Lynn's role than Nancy had described. Was this questioning part of Nancy's plan or something spontaneous by Lynn? Glancing at Nancy, I noticed her watching Lynn. It was apparent that she respected Lynn. Perhaps Lynn's impression of us would play into the events.

"What would you like to know?" I asked.

"Tell me about your backgrounds, where you met, how long you've been married." Courteously, Ron and I answered. The questions continued but soon the tone softened.

"You seem to have a lot in common with Nancy," Lynn concluded.

"Yes we do. But most importantly, we love this baby."

"What do you plan to name the baby?" Lynn asked.

We hesitated. This was not something we'd discussed with Nancy yet. However, looking to her, she indicated with her eyes that she too wanted to know.

"If it's a boy," I explained, "we'd like to name him Michael William. Ron has always wanted to name his first son Michael and William would be in memory of Ron's much loved grandfather."

"What a distinguished name," Lynn commented. "Wouldn't that be a wonderful monogram?"

Her remark surprised me, wondering what a monogram had to do with selecting a name. Again, I thought of Lynn's obvious wealth and suddenly I felt inadequate. I did not even own a monogrammed item. I pushed the thought away.

"If it's a girl," I continued, "we'd like to name her Amy Colleen. Amy is a name that we've always liked. Colleen would be after my sister."

"My middle name is Colleen," Lynn said with delight. "That would be a lovely name."

"I like the names too," Nancy agreed. The interview seemed to be over as the conversation lightened. Even Nancy seemed more relaxed.

"So what about you?" we asked Lynn. "You're Nancy's aunt?"

"I'm actually Nancy's father's cousin."

"But I think of her as my aunt," Nancy said fondly. "When I first moved here over a year ago, Lynn took me under her wing. We immediately hit it off.

It was like we'd always known each other even though we'd only met at a few family reunions."

"Yes, I never had a daughter so I'm enjoying having Nancy here."

"And she spoils me rotten. She's always buying me clothes or taking me to lunch."

The two of them continued telling us about their relationship while Ron and I enjoyed watching the exchange between them.

Turning to us, Lynn said, "I hope you didn't mind all my questions. Nancy has said many nice things about you but I couldn't help but check things out for myself. I know now why Nancy has been so happy with her plans to give the baby to you."

Nancy needed to pick up a few things before we headed back to her apartment. As we walked through the mall, we noticed a maternity clothing store.

"Let's stop," I encouraged Nancy.

"I do need some things but—"

"Come on, I want to see you in these billowing clothes. Besides, Ron and I want to buy you an outfit." I wanted to do something special for Nancy.

"But you've already made me two dresses."

"And I'd meant to make more but ran out of time."

In the store, Nancy picked out a few items and went to the dressing room to try them on. "This one is too large," she called out over the dressing room door.

Ron and I went back and forth from the racks, getting different sizes and picking out more outfits. As Nancy tried them on, she came out to model them for us.

"You should have been a model," I said. "You look terrific in everything."

Nancy blushed, obviously pleased with the special attention she was receiving. Finally, she narrowed her selection down. With the packages in our hands, our spirits were light as we headed back to the apartment.

It was late when we got back. Nancy went to her room to put away her new clothes. After giving her a moment, I tapped on her door and she invited me in.

As she hung one of her new dresses in the closet, Nancy said, "You might need these someday too, Denise, but I hope not too soon."

Her remark caught me by surprise. I felt a twinge of irritation rise up inside. *Hold on a second*, I thought to myself. *Now she's telling me when to get pregnant. Is she going to want every detail of my life oriented to what she thinks is in this baby's interest?*

"God seems to be in charge of the timing of that," I replied, trying not to show my annoyance. "We'd gladly accept any child he gives us at any time. And as you know Nancy, we haven't stopped trying."

She was quiet before responding, "It would be nice for this child to have siblings. That would mean that you and Ron would finally be able to get pregnant. Oh, that would be so wonderful!"

The next day we decided it was time to make a trip to the hospital, hoping to become familiar with the route.

"Turn off here," Nancy instructed Ron, and he maneuvered the car towards the exit. The freeways were much different from the highways of Montana.

Ron told Nancy teasingly, "It sure would be nice if you would have this baby during the night so I don't have to contend with rush hour traffic."

"I'll see what I can do," Nancy said, smiling back.

When we arrived, we were impressed with the warmth and spaciousness of the hospital. The receptionist directed us to the maternity ward where a nurse met us and briefly showed us around. We had hoped to meet Linda, the hospital social worker Nancy had been working with, but she was not in. Instead, we decided to look for the chapel. We were anxious to see if it would be a good place for our adoption ceremony.

"Here it is," Nancy said as she pushed the door open slightly. Inside we found a small but very serene room that seemed to radiate with God's presence. We sat silently in the stillness of the room as if to soak up its energy.

I closed my eyes. The peacefulness seemed to wrap itself around me. The apprehensions of the past days seemed to melt away. A quiet voice reminded me that God was in charge.

Suddenly I thought of the New Year's resolution we had made last year. We had resolved to either get pregnant or adopt a baby by year-end. Gratitude filled my heart as I realized God's power. Who would have ever dreamed His answer would come in this manner?

Back in the car, Nancy said, "By the way, at the last ultrasound, the doctor asked if I wanted to know the sex of the baby."

"Do you?" I asked.

"In a way— deep down, I have a feeling that if the baby is a boy, I'll have a tougher time giving him up. He would be my parent's first grandson. If it's a girl though, it is definitely yours. I cannot imagine me with a girl. Do you guys want to know the sex?"

Though she'd laughed as if what she'd said had been a big joke, I was troubled. Ron must have been too. "No," he said flatly, "it makes absolutely no difference to us."

"I don't want to know either," I said. "It doesn't even matter to us if it's perfect. We want this baby regardless."

"You wouldn't have to take it if there was something wrong with it."

"We wouldn't turn our backs on this baby any more than one we'd given birth to."

"I just don't want you to feel obligated."

"It's not obligation," I said, trying to remain composed. Inside I felt angry and concerned.

Nancy sounded puzzled as she changed the subject. "The doctor asked if I would want to have the baby circumcised if it's a boy. I told him that was your decision."

"We've discussed that," Ron said, "and we'd like to go ahead with a circumcision."

"I'll let my doctor know."

"By the way," Ron said, "would you feel comfortable with me being in the delivery room?"

Nancy was quiet for a moment. Then she said, "You know, I felt a little uncomfortable with that when I first thought about it but now that I've gotten to know you better, I'm sure it will be fine. It seems right that you should be there."

"Thank you, Nancy. I know it may feel awkward for you, but I would love to be there for our baby's birth."

"Well, thanks for not pushing me. I'm one of those people who, if I feel pushed, will push back."

I felt a bit of a threat in that. "We want this adoption to be the best thing for all of us."

"I appreciate that," she said.

Monday arrived. It was time to return home. We had so enjoyed the time with Nancy and our baby. The feelings of strain and worry from the past few days seemed to fade. Instead, all I felt was sadness at the prospect of leaving Nancy and our baby. It seemed we were leaving all that was important behind.

We sat at the kitchen table for a bite of lunch before we left. Nancy was quiet. Suddenly she said, "I have something I need to tell you." Tears welled up in her eyes. I felt a lump rise in my throat. I wondered if she had changed her mind.

"What is it Nancy?" I asked. I thought my heart would pound right out of my chest.

"It's Jim."

"What about him?" I asked tentatively.

"He's married."

I reached to take Nancy's hand. I felt more torn than ever between my relief and my sympathy for her. Her words tumbled out. "I didn't know he was married until after I found out I was pregnant. He is separated from his wife but I need to tell you this because he has two other children, a boy and a girl. I felt you should know that this baby has a half-brother and sister."

"Oh, Nancy," I said. "So that's why you won't be getting married to Jim?"

"Yes. He has a successful business. He tells me a divorce is out of the question."

I felt a huge surge of anger. *What a line!* I thought to myself. I wondered how many other women had received that same explanation.

"We still keep in touch but part of the reason I took this new job and moved was to get farther away from him. I was hoping it would help to end the relationship. I'll continue our friendship because I want this adoption to go smoothly and it will be easier if we are still friends."

By now she was crying. "That is why this adoption is so important to me. I want this child to belong to a family with a father and mother. When it gets down to the legalities of this adoption, I want everything wrapped up so Jim cannot later come and take this baby away from you. I don't expect any problems since he obviously does not intend to leave his wife. It's just that I don't want him to later regret how he handled this and then try to take the baby away from you."

"We appreciate that as well. How did you find out he was married?" I asked.

"It was really odd. I was telling a friend how crazy our schedules were, and that many times our dates didn't work out and we ended up talking on the phone instead. She casually asked me if he was married. I laughed and told her I would have to ask him. Well, the next time I talked to him, I jokingly asked him. The phone got very quiet and then he told me he was. I about dropped through the floor."

"How did Jim react to your pregnancy?" I asked.

"He wanted me to have an abortion but I kept thinking of you guys who so wanted a baby. He said he'd go along with the adoption."

Ron had gone outside to load the car. Alone with Nancy in the apartment, I reached to hug her. She suddenly looked so frail, having exposed her sad secret.

"Once the baby is born," Nancy said, "I am going to start over."

"Yes, and you'll meet a man who's really good to you. I know you will."

Her eyes moistened again as she said, "Denise, thank you for not judging me."

"Oh, we love you so much. Please let us know if we can help you at all. It really hurts to see you in so much pain."

"I'll be all right. It's just such a relief to have told you."

As we walked to the car arm in arm, neither of us spoke. Finally, we kissed each other on the cheek and hugged one last time. Then I climbed into our car.

Tears were streaming down our faces as we waved good-bye. Watching Nancy as we drove away, I thought of how different we were from our college days. It had been such an innocent time. Never would I have dreamed of all the pain and disappointment that lay ahead for both of us. Never would I have imagined Nancy so little in command, her life in such disarray. Gone were the days of innocence and what lie ahead was beyond what any of us could imagine.

Chapter 4

THE DOORBELL RANG. Ron and I glanced nervously at each other. Mrs. Madsen had arrived. She was here to conduct the home study required by the state of Montana in order to complete our adoption. Although we knew our home was adequate and our marriage sound, the thought of someone analyzing it was nerve-wracking. We had been preparing for this visit all week, having cleaned every corner. We wanted to make a good impression.

Answering the door, we greeted an attractive, grandmotherly type woman.

"Come in," I invited.

"Thank you. What a lovely home." Mrs. Madsen sat at the kitchen table. "Now, let me tell you a little about the process and then we'll begin."

As she described what lie ahead, Ron and I began to feel anxious. We had so much to do and so little time to accomplish it.

"Tell me about your adoption plans," Mrs. Madsen inquired. "Where did you meet the birth mother?"

Talking openly about the adoption was difficult. After all, we'd gone to great lengths to keep Nancy's identity and the details of the adoption a secret. Now we had to tell all. I sensed, however, that Mrs. Madsen was trustworthy.

"Have you hired an attorney yet?"

"Yes," Ron answered. "Nancy was able to obtain the names of two attorneys from the hospital social worker. We contacted Mr. Roger Miller and he has agreed to handle our adoption, pending Nancy's first visit with him. We want to make sure she feels comfortable with him before we commit."

"Will Mr. Miller handle the entire adoption?"

"No, an attorney friend of ours will take care of things from this end. He has two adopted children so is very sensitive to the importance of our adoption."

"It sounds like you are on track. Tell me more about yourselves, like how did you meet? What was your courtship like? How long have you tried to have children? Those sort of things."

We shared the details of our relationship with her. She quietly wrote things down as we talked. I wondered what she was thinking.

"What about your financial situation?"

Wow, this is in depth, I thought to myself. *My own family doesn't even know that.* Now it would become a matter of record in order to adopt our baby.

Inside I shuddered, feeling vulnerable, but I told myself it would be worth it. As I answered the questions, I wondered how many birth parents would pass this analysis. It seemed so unfair that we had to go through such an ordeal to have children while others had them without even trying. For the next two hours, we answered many personal questions. Mrs. Madsen's caring tone helped to lessen our anxiety.

"I'd like to look around your home now before I go," she said, ending our visit.

"Certainly, let's start at the nursery," I suggested.

Mrs. Madsen was complimentary as we showed her around. Finally, she said, "I am most impressed with how you are handling this adoption. In all my years as a social worker, I have never seen one handled so well. You have shown remarkable sensitivity to the birth mother and discussed many important issues. Although we need to meet one more time, I see no reason for not proceeding with the adoption. I will process the paperwork, giving you a strong recommendation."

After Mrs. Madsen left, Ron and I were giddy with excitement. We were one step closer to getting our baby.

A few days later, we were visiting with Nancy. She'd had her first visit with the attorney we'd hired in California.

"How did your appointment go today?" I asked Nancy.

"Good."

"What was he like?"

"He was very pleasant and easy to talk to. I had to laugh though. He seemed a bit surprised when he met me. I don't know what he expected."

"What do you mean?"

"He kept complimenting me on my professionalism. Maybe he is used to seeing teenagers or something. Anyway, as our conversation progressed, he told me that there are many people who would love to adopt my baby. With the drug and alcohol problems of today, evidently there aren't many babies in the adoption pool not affected by these problems. I think he was surprised I was giving up my baby."

I felt an uneasiness come over me. "Do you think you'll be comfortable working with him?"

"Oh yes."

"So what did you do?"

"He had me fill out some of the papers. Those sure made the adoption feel real."

"I bet. Do you still want to proceed?"

"Certainly! By the way, I checked into some counseling options this week. I called an adoption agency but learned that since I wasn't one of their clients, the fee would be $80.00 an hour!"

"You've got to be kidding!"

"No. Then on top of that, the social worker tried to encourage me to work through them rather than continue with our private adoption. She kept trying to get me to come in and go through their list of prospective couples." Nancy's voice was shaking as she continued, "Naturally, I wouldn't even consider it since I want you to raise my child."

It was obvious Nancy was upset. I was angry, feeling as if she had been taken advantage of.

"Don't worry though," Nancy continued. "I told them I was happy with my plans and would look elsewhere for counseling. It was disheartening though."

"It's disgusting," I said. "So were you able to find someone?"

"Yes, I met with a woman named Connie yesterday. I really like her. I think I'll feel comfortable working with her."

As we hung up from our conversation, it felt like everything was coming together. The home visit, the attorney, and the counselor; it was really going to happen.

We had signed up for a newborn parenting class, another requirement of the adoption. As we walked into the room, I immediately felt out of place. All the other women were pregnant. As we settled into our places, the instructor asked each of us our due dates.

"March 28th," I answered. Everyone did a double take, their eyes seeming to scrutinize me. I couldn't help but laugh a bit though I felt left out.

The discussion teetered back and forth between newborn care and pregnancies. Again, I was reminded of what was yet to be accomplished—conception.

Driving home that night, I said to Ron, "I'd like to try going on the Clomid again."

I had stopped taking it, discouraged as another month passed with no success. Besides, we were consumed with the many details that had to be considered regarding the adoption.

"Sounds good with me—I know what that means," he said with a wink.

I smiled. I so appreciated his ability to lighten my mood. "I know we could have two children within a short period of time but I don't want to give up. Time could change the factors and if we wait too long, we may have to redo some of the fertility testing. I don't want to go through that again."

"I agree. We've come too far to stop now. Besides, we want more than one child. If we happen to be blessed with two this year, it would be fine with me."

Opening the mailbox, I was thrilled to see another letter from Nancy. In the past weeks, she had written often. We loved getting her letters, reading them over and over. I knew they would be a special treasure for our little one someday so I safely put them away.

Our phone conversations were also frequent. I craved each visit, anxious to hear how Nancy was feeling. Our friendship seemed to blossom. Our trust and commitment in one other intensified. It was wonderful sharing so much together again, just as we had in college.

Later that night I tried to call Nancy but she wasn't home.

"I hate it when that happens," I said to Ron.

"What?"

"Nancy's not home. I got her answering machine. It drives me crazy, wondering what she is doing with our baby. I know it is really none of my business but I can't help it. I just want to know where our baby is. I wish it were inside me; then I would know. I miss that part of this baby so much. I guess deep down, I'm envious that Nancy gets to share this time with our baby."

Ron pulled me close and gently kissed my cheek. "Honey, you'll get pregnant too. We can't give up yet."

It was the next day before I was able to reach Nancy. As usual, we were sharing the details of the past days with each other.

"I picked up an extra set of bumper pads for the crib today," I told her on the phone. "We'll need a spare when it's laundry time."

"I can't believe the details you've thought of Denise. That wouldn't have crossed my mind," she said as her voice dropped, almost as if apologizing.

"Well, why should it? After all, you're planning for a delivery and we're planning for a baby."

"Yes, I guess that's true," she said as her voice lightened again. "I'm buying books that deal with pregnancy and delivery."

"And I'm purchasing ones that pertain to child rearing and adoption."

We both chuckled as we continued sharing notes. Nancy was attending childbirth classes and meeting with the attorney while we were at parenting classes. As she purchased hard candy for labor and warm socks for the hospital, we bought layettes and receiving blankets.

"It is funny, isn't it? It's as if we are planning for two completely different events," Nancy said.

In a way though, we were, for at one critical moment Nancy's role as the nurturer would end and ours would begin. I could hardly wait!

Nancy called us a few days later. "Oh, Denise," she exclaimed. "Thank you for sending me a copy of the birth announcement you've selected. It brought tears to my eyes. I had to call you and tell you how much I like it." Her voice was quivering.

"I'm so glad," I answered. I had sent Nancy a copy of it earlier in the week.

"I love the drawing, the large hand with the baby's hand in it. And the wording, 'A new hand in ours'— I really admire the way you guys are handling the adoption. This is going to be a very lucky baby."

Hearing Nancy's pleasure, I felt warm inside. Her approval meant so much. I wanted her to be happy with our plans.

"By the way," Nancy said. "I finally told my coworkers about my pregnancy."

"How did they react?" I asked.

"They pretty much knew. After all, I have been showing for some time. I keep a picture of you and Ron on my desk. I showed it to them when I shared my plans for the adoption. Everyone was so supportive and offered their help. All except one anyway."

"Why was that?" I asked curiously.

"Well, after I made my announcement, one of my co-workers asked me to come into her office. She told me she had given her baby up for adoption many years ago. She said it was the worst thing she had ever done. She wanted me to reconsider!"

I felt a cold chill run down my spine. Quietly I took a deep breath and then said, "How did that make you feel?"

"Our situation is so much different," she answered confidently. "Adoptions were handled differently then. This woman doesn't even know what happened to her baby. I will know throughout my child's life how it is doing. I will even be able to watch it grow up. There's just no comparison!"

Her assurance was music to my ears. I was angry though, that a stranger would try to intervene in our very private and beautiful process.

The following week Nancy's sister Diane had stopped by our house. She had just returned from a short visit with Nancy. On one of their shopping trips, they had selected a teddy bear for the baby's room. Nancy had asked her to bring it by. Diane visited briefly as she shared news of Nancy, including that Nancy had just lost her job. After Diane left, I immediately called Nancy.

When she answered, I blurted out, "Diane just told us about your job—that your entire department is being laid off. What a shock! What are you going to do?"

"I'm trying to get some things worked out here so I can make it through these last months of the pregnancy. The placement agencies aren't too encouraging though. No one wants to hire a pregnant woman."

"Would you consider coming to Montana? Ron and I would love having you here with us. I know I could get you in with my obstetrician. He is very good. And the adoption would be much simpler if we were all in the same state."

"I appreciate it but I just can't come. It is too close to my parents. I am afraid I would run into them. I don't want to hide out for the remainder of my pregnancy. It's best I stay here."

"But how you will manage?"

"The company is going to keep my insurance going throughout the pregnancy so that will help a lot. I will apply for unemployment. That should get me through until after the baby is born."

"Well, there would be some real advantages to being together here."

"That's probably true but I want to stay put. I am going to talk to Jim about helping me too. After all, he is equally responsible for this pregnancy and certainly has the means to help me."

I was disappointed that she wouldn't consider coming but could understand her perspective. "As long as you'll be all right but promise you'll let us know if we can help. And don't worry about the medical bills. Ron and I will certainly take care of any that your insurance won't cover."

"I appreciate your offer but if I need any financial help, I feel it's Jim's responsibility before it's yours."

Silently, I wondered why he had not offered without her asking but remained quiet. Nothing could be accomplished by attacking his obvious lack of responsibility. I sensed that Nancy still loved him.

Despite Nancy's confidence though, I knew the months ahead would be much more difficult without the security of a job or income. I worried for Nancy and what the future held.

A week passed. Nancy continued to fill my thoughts with concern. Then she called, sounding excited and upbeat.

"I've finally decided what I'm going to do after the baby is born."

"What?"

"I'm going back to school to finish my master's degree." Nancy had been working on a master's in business but had left school with only one semester remaining. At the time, she had needed a change from the tediousness of her studies.

"You know," Nancy continued, "it's almost as if God had me postpone that semester so I'd have a place to start over again."

"What made you decide to go back to school?"

"My counselor Connie. She's been encouraging me to think about my life after the baby is born." Nancy's enthusiasm pleased me. For the first time in months, she seemed to have a sense of direction. "Connie has really helped me," she continued. "She also suggested I look into volunteering at a local home for unwed mothers, a place called St. John's. She thought it would be good for me to visit with other women in my situation. I stopped in there today after our session."

"What was it like?"

"I think I'll really enjoy it. It was fun meeting the other women. In fact, I got into a discussion with a young woman who is planning to keep her baby. She asked me if I thought it odd that, at age 29, I was placing my child up for adoption while she, only 18, was keeping hers. It did make me feel strange, but then we talked about how it is important to do what is best for the babies. I think it will be a good experience for me and hopefully for them too."

"Oh, I'm sure it will."

"But most exciting is that the staff has asked me to help them develop adoption procedures for the home. To date they haven't advocated adoption but after hearing about ours, decided it might be time to take a closer look at it."

"Wonderful."

"Yes, isn't it amazing how our adoption interests those who hear about it? I am really thrilled about sharing our experience."

Nancy continued. "Oh, and I spent over an hour working with the attorney, trying to determine what financial assistance Jim should provide."

I cringed, thinking of Roger's hourly rate of $175. It wasn't that we were cheap but we needed to keep costs to a minimum. We didn't exactly have a bankroll stored away and the adoption was rapidly becoming much more costly than we had imagined. I did not want to worry Nancy however, so I didn't say anything.

As if sensing my concern though, Nancy said, "I asked Roger to bill me separately for that time since it has nothing to do with the adoption. You guys shouldn't have to pay for that."

"Oh don't worry about that," I replied, trying to sound nonchalant.

"Roger made an odd comment though. He said he would not charge you for that even though it would be cheaper than paying my living expenses as is done in many private adoptions. Doesn't that seem like an odd thing to say?"

I felt stunned. I didn't even know how to respond.

Nancy continued, "Anyway, we did come up with a solution. Roger called it a release agreement. With the agreement, Jim relinquishes all rights to the baby. At the same time, he pays me a specified sum of money. The payment would also release him of any future responsibility to the baby or me. This gives him an added incentive to sign. He'll be assured I will go through with the adoption since I can't count on his help to raise the baby."

Nancy was bubbling over with excitement, obviously pleased with the arrangement. I was horrified. This sounded more like blackmail than a legal document. After all, according to Nancy, Jim was more than willing to sign the release of parental rights. Based on his complete lack of support to date however, it was obvious he was unwilling to help her financially. I wanted Nancy to get some help from Jim. I just did not want our adoption being tied to it. It could jeopardize our adoption. This was our baby, not a playing card in a poker game.

I was livid at our attorney but Nancy continued, unaware of my anger. "I was also thinking that Jim should provide a trust fund for the baby. Would you think about what you feel is appropriate?"

"Sure," I said. Anxious to get off the phone so I could talk to Ron, we said our good-byes and promised to call each other soon.

Bursting into the family room where Ron was relaxing, I blurted out our conversation. "You won't believe what Roger and Nancy came up with today," I said.

As he listened, I could see that he too was angry as his face began turning red. "What do payments between Nancy and Jim have to do with the adoption? Talk about a conflict of interest. Roger is our attorney. How can he possibly represent our best interests if he is negotiating a financial arrangement for Nancy by using our adoption? Any consultation regarding that should have been treated as a separate issue. In fact, he should have referred Nancy to another attorney."

"Well, not only is he handling it but you can bet we'll get the bill for that session."

Ron didn't seem to hear me as he continued. "And to suggest to Nancy that we pay her living expenses? We have already offered but Nancy refused. Who does he think he is, meddling like that? Is that what he considers appropriate representation of us?"

"I agree. This really upsets me."

"Things suddenly seem really complicated."

"I know. We thought this adoption would be so simple. Now I feel like we're being taken for a ride. I wish I understood more about the legalities. Maybe this is on the up and up but this does not feel right. Perhaps we should terminate our arrangement with Roger and seek other counsel."

"That's my first reaction too but we don't have much time to start over."

"Well, let's think it over and pray about it. By the way, Nancy also mentioned that she wants Jim to provide a trust fund for the baby!"

"A trust fund?" I don't think I had ever seen Ron so upset as he continued, "Why would we want a trust fund? We wouldn't have agreed to adopt the baby if we couldn't provide for it."

"That was my thought but I promised Nancy we'd discuss it."

"It's almost insulting. Doesn't she think we can handle this without Jim's money? I do not want his money. I will be this baby's father and can certainly take care of it without Jim or Nancy's assistance."

"I know honey," I said, trying to calm him.

"This is our baby and once the adoption is finalized, it will be our responsibility, one that we're more than willing to accept. The last thing this child or we need is a big bank account from its birth father. Besides, we hope to have more children. How could we treat them all equally if one of them had a trust fund? If this baby had one, we would need to provide one for all our children. But would it be fair to give our other children a trust fund and not our adopted child?"

"You're right. This whole thing is so unsettling. I just want to bring our baby home, no strings attached."

Silently, we tried to sort out our thoughts.

Ron broke the silence. "Although my instincts tell me to drop Roger, doing so might only prolong the process and increase our costs. Besides, it may upset Nancy and thus make things awkward. We'll just have to trust everything works out."

A week passed. A letter arrived from Nancy:

> Thank you for the beautiful flowers on Valentine's Day. As usual, Jim didn't remember me.
>
> I saw the doctor today. He seemed less rushed and took a moment to ask about our adoption plans. We talked awhile. He then told me about a patient who placed her baby with an obstetrician friend. Three months later, the birth mother took it back. Dr. Thomas said it was one of the most heart-wrenching, cruel things he has ever seen—where people stopped thinking about the baby and only thought about themselves. Awful.

Reading Nancy's letter, I was grateful that her doctor had shared the experience. Somehow, just the fact that she told us about it seemed like a message: She understood the cruelty in taking a child back. She would not do that to us. From that moment on, I knew that regardless of anything else, once she gave us her child, it would be ours.

Her letter continued,

> I saw Jim and we had a long talk. I asked him if he wanted to meet you but he didn't commit. I was encouraged though that he was taking more interest in the adoption. I was able to share my feelings and frustrations about the pregnancy. It was good for him to hear what I have been going through.
>
> I also talked to him about the release agreement. He didn't sign it but agreed to if that is what I want. He said he doesn't want it to turn into a legal thing, as if he had to be 'bought off'. He did tell me that he would give me any money I ask for and would provide a trust fund for the baby. I asked him to think about the amount. I am curious as to what he will come up with.
>
> He also called my bluff on the agreement—you know, the fact that it would assure him I will go through with the adoption. He said he knows the type of person I am. He's trusted that I would go through

with what we agreed upon and what is best for everyone. Sometimes I wish I had a more questionable character! Anyhow, I think I will talk with Roger again before I decide what I am going to do.

Regarding the maternal release of rights form, it states that all rights are relinquished forever, as if no blood connection exists. My request is that somehow we modify it; in case something should happen to both of you, I would like to have the right to custody or determination of what happens to the child. Roger said it is a separate issue and can only be dealt with by means of a will. I don't want to feel like I gave up my child twice and don't want the child to think I rejected it twice.

I want to respect your wishes too, though and would always want to do what is best for the child. Roger suggested a joint custody/guardian clause where a party of your choosing and I would decide custody together. Please think about it and let me know.

After reading Nancy's letter, I knew we needed to respond to her requests. I felt nervous though as I called. These were such sensitive issues.

"Nancy," I said, "regarding the trust fund, Ron and I have decided we don't want one."

"Why not?" She sounded surprised.

I told her what we had discussed. After hearing my explanation, Nancy was apologetic. "I'm sorry," she said. "I hadn't even thought about how disruptive it could be for your family in the long run."

"No problem," I continued. "I'm glad you understand. Regarding your concerns for the baby's custody, I can certainly appreciate your feelings. If it would make you feel better we could include you in our will."

"You don't mind?"

"Absolutely not but regardless of the will, I know that Colleen would make sure you were included should a decision of that nature have to be made. But I hope you understand it would be very cruel to pull this child out of our family, especially if we both died."

"I do. I just want to make sure the baby's always taken care of."

"That is our priority too."

As our conversation ended, I was relieved to have aired these issues and, at the same time, grateful that Nancy and I could be so honest with each other.

March finally arrived as our countdown continued. Nancy's due date had been changed to April 7th. Ron and I were beside ourselves with excitement. We would be parents soon. As if that weren't enough though, Colleen's due date was also nearing. We planned to take care of Anthony while she and Ron were at the hospital delivering their second child. We felt like we were on pins and needles as we waited for her call.

On March 7th, the call finally came. "The baby is getting too big," Colleen said. "The doctor wants to induce tomorrow. Can you come over tonight so you are here when we leave for the hospital?"

She didn't have to ask twice. Ron and I threw our things in the car, stopping only to call Nancy so she would know where we were in case she should need us.

Jacob Eugene was born the next day—a whopping 10 lbs. 5 oz. It's a good thing the doctor didn't give him any more time to grow. Anthony was anxious to see his new brother so Ron and I took him to the hospital.

Jacob was beautiful and we all enjoyed having a chance to love on him. Watching Colleen, Ron, and their sons, my heart was full. We were so blessed to have this dear family as part of ours. What fun to witness their joy as a family during this special moment.

Quietly, I slipped my arm around Ron's waist. "Just think honey," I whispered, "the next one will be ours."

"I was just thinking the same thing," he answered. "And I can hardly wait."

With only two weeks before our scheduled flight to California, I began feeling extremely anxious. I couldn't sleep. Although everything seemed to be going as planned, I felt obsessed with worry. Desperate to find some relief for my worries,

I called Linda, the social worker at the hospital where Nancy would deliver the baby.

When Linda answered, I spilled my thoughts, "Nancy continues to be very adamant that this baby is ours," I told her. "Deep down though, I'm feeling a lot of fear that things may not turn out as we've planned. Adding to that are many friends who continue to ask about the possibility of Nancy changing her mind. I guess it is all coming down on me. I'm feeling a bit edgy," I confided.

"How do you answer your friends?" Linda asked.

"Well, I know that once the baby comes home with us, it will be ours so that is generally how I respond. That is the one thing I am absolutely certain of since I know I can trust Nancy to keep her word."

"That's my feeling about her too," Linda agreed.

"Then why do I have this nagging doubt? Is she just going through the motions and telling us what we want to hear or am I just being crazy?"

"Denise, it's not unusual for adoptive parents to be nervous as the birth draws near. Quite honestly, I'd be concerned if you weren't."

Hearing Linda's assurance, I felt better, realizing that my feelings were very normal. Then I thought of my other concerns. "Linda, a while back I promised Nancy that Ron and I would stay with her for a few days after the birth so she could have time with the baby. I have a feeling that was a mistake. I am afraid that staying will make it more difficult for Nancy to give the baby to us. She could get extremely attached. Besides, the wait is already feeling long. Once the baby is born, we'll be anxious to bring it home and share it with our family."

"Staying could be awkward for you," Linda agreed. "Have you discussed this with Nancy?"

"Just briefly but she's pretty adamant about us staying."

"Perhaps you should bring up your concerns with her again. She might reconsider when she understands how difficult it could be for you."

"You're right. I will. There is one other thing. Due to Nancy's history of allergies, it has been suggested she breast-feed. I am really uncomfortable with this. I have heard so much about the bonding that takes place. Would there be any alternatives that might be more comfortable for all of us?"

"The hospital doesn't encourage or discourage breast-feeding in adoption cases but pumping might be a good compromise. That way the baby gets the benefits of the mother's milk but it's not quite so personal."

"Would you be willing to talk to Nancy about it?"

"Yes, I will. And listen, Denise, I cannot make any guarantees but Nancy has given considerable thought to the adoption. She appears to be comfortable with her decision and from what I observe, all seems to be going as planned."

It was Monday. We would be leaving in one week. I was at the office working out the final details before we left. As usual, the phone was ringing non-stop, making it impossible to get anything done.

As it rang once again, I answered it. Holly from Dr. Fellow's office responded. "Congratulations Denise. Your test came back positive. You're pregnant!"

"Are you serious?" I asked. I could not believe my ears. After four years of trying, three years of testing, and months of disappointment, I was finally pregnant. Tears were streaming down my face as I stammered, "Wh..what do I do now?"

Holly laughed, "You'll need to make an appointment for an exam. Would next week be okay?"

"Actually, no. We will be in California waiting for our baby. Can I call you when we get back?"

Holly giggled. "Oh, that's right. What a year for you. Yes, that would be fine. Just call me when you get back. Congratulations again. I am so happy for you. And have a great trip."

Hanging up the phone, I reached to dial Ron's extension. Then I remembered he was out of town for the day. Shaking with excitement, I left the office, hoping the fresh air would help to calm me. Somehow, I would have to control my excitement until I could share our news with Ron.

Once outside I fought the urge to scream for joy. Noticing the gift store, I decided to buy a card for Ron. Then after a walk around the block, I felt a little more under control.

Back at the office, I tried to force myself to concentrate but it was no use. All I could think about was the baby—the life that was finally growing inside me, a sibling for our baby that was due soon. This was more than I could ever have dreamed possible. We were going to have two babies this year after all.

Opening the card I had purchased for Ron, I wrote:

Dear Ron,

    Thank you for all the happiness you have brought me. Most especially, thank you for being the father of our children. Our second is due November 17th.

After work that evening, before Ron could even take his coat off, I thrust the card into his hands. He gave me a curious look as he opened the card. As he read it, I could see him struggling with tears as he reached to hug me.

"Is this for sure?" he asked.

"Yes, Holly called today."

"This is more than we had ever hoped."

"I know. We're going to have an instant family. From my calculations, our children will be about eight months apart."

Ron began laughing. "Can you imagine the looks we'll get when people see your pregnancy as well as our newborn baby?"

I started to laugh too. "Yes, they'll probably think you couldn't leave me alone!"

Both of us were howling with laughter as we visualized how people might react, particularly once we had both babies.

"Well, do you think we can handle it?" Ron asked more somberly.

"I have no doubt. We have been waiting for children for a long time. There are going to be some major changes in our lives but it's what we've wanted."

"It will be like having twins!" Ron said. "We'll need two of everything."

"And don't forget the thousands of diapers and bottles as well as a double stroller."

Ron was shaking his head. His face was radiating with a smile. "What do you think we'll have?" he wondered, "boys, girls or one of each?"

"Any combination would be great. It would be fun to raise one of each though. They'll have so much fun playing and discovering the world together," I said. Already my mind was whirling as I thought of our children growing up together. I could hardly wait for Christmas. This year would be so special with two babies. Our dreams of a family were finally coming true.

"I hope they'll be good friends, being so close in age like Colleen and I are," I added.

"Speaking of our family, what do you think they are going to say?"

"There won't be a dry eye for miles," I said. "They'll be so happy for us."

"We'll have to sign them up for shifts to help us with the babies, especially after you come home from the hospital."

"I have a feeling we won't be short of assistance. We'll probably have to force everyone to leave when we get tired of them."

"That's probably true. When should we tell them?"

"I don't know. I was thinking about that. In a way, it would be nice to wait until after our first is born so we don't take any of the excitement away from it. I don't know if I can keep this quiet though."

"Me either but that's a good point. What about Nancy? Should we tell her?"

A nervous feeling crept into the pit of my stomach. "I don't know. How do you think Nancy will take it? Do you think it would change her feelings about the adoption?"

"Why should it? It hasn't changed ours. Nothing has changed except that her child will now have a sibling."

"I know but what if it did?"

"Oh, I can't imagine...," Ron said, his voice drifting off.

The excitement of our news seemed to have dissolved. Suddenly I felt irritated. All we ever wanted was children. Now we were expecting two and, instead of being overjoyed, I was terrified.

"I think we need to tell her," Ron finally said. "After all, this baby will be her child's sibling. Everything we have done to date has been based on trust and honesty. We don't want to change that now. Besides, Nancy will find out eventually. If our news causes her to change her mind, it would be better to know now."

Tears sprung to my eyes. "You're right. I am just so scared. I love both these babies so much. It's as if they have always been in our lives. I can't imagine not having both of them."

Ron pulled me close. "Don't worry honey. We'll just pray that Nancy sees our pregnancy as a blessing rather than a change in the plans."

It was the night before we were to leave for California. Five months had passed since the night Nancy had called asking us to adopt her unborn child. It seemed unbelievable that the time had finally arrived.

I couldn't stop thinking about Nancy. I wondered what she was thinking. Although we had already discussed the details of our arrival, I called Nancy to go over them again. Actually, that was just an excuse. I knew that despite all that we had done to get to this point it was worthless if Nancy didn't want to proceed. I also knew that once we arrived in California, if Nancy had any reservations, it would be more difficult to express them. For us, once we got there it would be heartbreaking to leave without the child we had awaited for so long. Therefore, before leaving for California, I wanted to be sure.

There was a sense of excitement in the air as Nancy and I chatted about our pending arrival. Finally, I took a deep breath and then asked. "Nancy, do you still want to proceed with the adoption?"

She laughed a bit as she answered. "Yes, Denise. This is your child. I can hardly wait for you to get here."

As we said good-bye, we both choked on our tears. The time had finally come. Soon we would be together awaiting the child that we would always share.

Chapter 5

It was raining as the plane touched down. I was glad to be on solid ground, having battled nausea the entire flight. Perhaps my stomach would now settle.

Glancing around the terminal, I saw Nancy. She was waiting by the stairs outside the secured area. Dropping my bag in the middle of the floor, I rushed to her and we both began crying. It was so good to be together again. Instinctively I reached to touch her stomach as if to tell our little one that we were here. I had missed them both of them so much.

"Let me look at you," I said, pulling away. Nancy looked terrific. There was no hiding her pregnancy now.

"I'm so glad you're here," Nancy said.

"So are we," Ron said as he caught up with me. He had stopped to pick up my carry on. "I didn't think this time would ever come."

"I've been so nervous the baby would be born before you could get here, especially since I've felt sick all week."

"Have you really?"

"Yes, but I was told that you often feel sick just before the baby is born."

"Well, now that we're together, it can come any time."

"Let's get your bags," Nancy said. "I have a doctor appointment in a half hour. I wanted you to meet Dr. Thomas. You can tell me about your trip on the way."

"So these are the Johnsons," Dr. Thomas said as he entered the waiting area.

"Yes, this is Ron and Denise, the parents of my baby."

I was so pleased with Nancy's introduction.

"We're all relieved you're here," Dr. Thomas said.

"So are we," Ron and I said simultaneously.

"Would you like to hear the baby's heart beat?" Nancy asked.

"Oh, could we?"

"Yes, just let me get a gown on and then I'll have the nurse come and get you."

Moments later, the nurse called us back to the examining room. Hearing the rapid pounding of our little one's heart, I started to cry.

Dr. Thomas interrupted our thoughts, "It doesn't appear this baby is in any hurry. It still hasn't dropped. There are no signs of dilation. I'd say it will be at least another week."

Leaving the doctor's office, Nancy stated, "We have one more appointment. Reverend Birch would like to meet with us about the ceremony. I thought we should get as many details as possible wrapped up so we're ready when the baby arrives."

"That's a great idea," we agreed. I was getting so excited. Everything was finally coming together.

Entering the hospital, Rev. Birch greeted us. After Nancy introduced us, Rev. Birch showed us to his office. It reminded me of the serenity of the chapel.

"Before we begin," Rev. Birch said, "I would like to tell you how honored I feel to be included in your special adoption. I admire what you're all trying to accomplish."

"Well thank you for agreeing to perform our ceremony," Ron said.

"My pleasure. So what would you like included in the ceremony?"

Nancy spoke up first. "I'd like to say something to Ron and Denise just before I give the baby to them."

"We've prepared something to say to Nancy as well," Ron said.

"That's a beautiful idea. Anything else you can think of?"

"Yes, we'd like to include this song somewhere too," I said, handing Rev. Birch a copy. "It's sung during baptism ceremonies in our church. I thought it would be fitting."

"One other thing," Nancy said, "during the ceremony, I would like to give my baby to you, Rev. Birch. Then you can give it to Ron and Denise. I want it to symbolize giving my child back to God so it can be given to Ron and Denise."

"Oh, Nancy that would be so beautiful," I said as tears threatened to spill.

"Well, I truly believe I have been given this child in order to give it to you."

Back at the apartment, we prepared dinner. Settling around the table, we chatted happily, discussing our day. Then out of the blue, Nancy said, "Denise, are you planning to continue your fertility testing?"

I glanced at Ron. This was the moment we'd anticipated, the moment we'd dreaded. It was time to tell Nancy.

I took a deep breath before answering. "No, it doesn't look like it. I'm pregnant."

"What?" Nancy said in a startled voice as she jumped to her feet. Her arms were around me as we both began crying. "Oh, Denise, I'm so happy."

"Are you really?" I asked, my voice almost pleading.

"Oh, yes. When did you find out?"

"Just last Monday."

"I can't believe it."

"Neither can we. We still feel like we're in a dream."

"How are you feeling?" Nancy asked still wiggling with excitement as she settled back into her chair.

"Great until our flight. I do feel a bit more tired than usual though."

"That's to be expected."

Ron was anxious to get to the root of our concerns. "Nancy, our pregnancy obviously doesn't change our feelings about adopting your baby. We wouldn't be here if it did. However, we realize our news may not be what you expected. That is why we decided to tell you right away. If you want to talk out your feelings with anyone, please do."

Nancy looked blankly at Ron.

I continued, as if giving a sales pitch. "We still believe this adoption is what is best for all of us, especially the baby. There will never be any difference in our hearts between the child you are carrying and the one we are carrying. If for some reason though your feelings about the adoption change, please let us know. All we ask is that you be honest with us."

Nancy was shaking her head as she responded, "No, this doesn't change my feelings. This is still your baby. Your pregnancy only makes me more excited. My child should have siblings. How special that they will be your children."

Several days later, Easter morning arrived. It seemed fitting that Nancy and I were together on this holiday. During college, she had spent several Easters with my family. It had become somewhat of a tradition as my family looked forward to having my roommates home for the Easter holiday. This year was even more special though as we awaited our child.

Lying in bed, I thought of the fun the three of us had dying Easter eggs the previous evening. I hadn't done that in years. It was like being a kid again.

"Write Mom on this one," Nancy had said, handing me an egg. She then gave one to Ron and asked him to write Dad on it. Her request had touched our hearts, hearing her once again refer to us as the baby's parents.

My thoughts were interrupted as Nancy emerged from her bedroom. "Happy Easter," she said, handing me a card.

"Can I open it now?"

"Of course, it's for Easter."

Inside I read:

Dear adopting parents & baby,

Never again will an Easter pass when I will not think of the days we spent together, preparing for and anticipating the birth of our child; the fun we had coloring eggs, talking of God's blessings in our lives.

I am filled with such happiness when I think of Easters you will share as a family—the egg hunts, baskets from the Easter bunny, gathering with close family members, watching spring come to life in Montana. Spring is such a wonderful time to bring a new life into the world. Happy Easter. Happiness always!

Love, your birth mother.

During the first week in California, we contacted our attorney. The paperwork was complete except for Jim and Nancy's signatures on the relinquishment papers. Nancy said that Jim was planning to come in and sign them any day. Nancy, however, wouldn't legally be able to sign until after the baby was born. So with the legalities in order and the adoption ceremony planned, we settled into enjoying our time together as we waited.

At Nancy's next doctor appointment, Dr. Thomas expressed his desire for the baby to arrive since we were finally here. He hesitated to induce but did order an ultrasound. He wanted to make sure the placenta was still healthy. As the technician moved the device over Nancy's stomach, I could see our baby's form moving around.

"Oh, look," I gasped as tears sprung to my eyes. "There it is."

"I know, isn't it amazing?" Nancy said.

"Here's the head," the technician pointed out. "And here's a foot." Slowly she continued to look over the baby and the placenta. "Everything looks healthy," she said. "I'll get the results up to the doctor. Would you like to take pictures with you?"

"Yes, I would," I answered.

"Take them out and show them to Ron," Nancy added

"Oh, he'll want to see them too," I agreed.

With pictures in hand, I headed to the waiting room as Nancy got dressed.

"Look honey," I said, holding out the pictures. "Can you believe this is our baby?"

Ron grinned as I pointed out the different body parts of our child.

"It's feeling more real all the time. I can't wait to hold that little one," he said.

"Me too but it sounds like we'll have to continue our wait. Everything appears healthy so I doubt the doctor will induce. I'm glad all is well but I don't know if I can stand waiting much longer. I'm just so anxious," I said.

"But with each day, we're that much closer," Ron reminded me. Then with the pride of a typical father, he put the ultrasound pictures in his wallet.

Days continued to pass. The apartment seemed to be closing in on all of us, and we longed for some space. Ron suggested we go to Universal Studios.

"Would you like to go along?" he asked Nancy.

"No thanks. I was just there a few months ago. You go ahead though. I'm sure you'll enjoy it. I'll just hang around by the pool and work on my tan."

We hated to leave Nancy alone in case she went into labor. She insisted we go though, assuring us that she felt comfortable. Just in case, we made plans to call her. If she went into labor, she would leave a message on her answering machine.

It felt good for Ron and me to get away together alone. The highway seemed to fly by as we talked. I was feeling so impatient.

"I love this time with Nancy but I'm just so anxious to have our baby and get on with our lives," I shared.

"I know but the wait will seem insignificant once we have our baby," Ron said with a smile. As usual, his perspective was more patient than mine.

Noticing a road sign, I commented, "That must be the exit to the community where Uncle Don and Aunt Peg live. I guess I didn't realize we were this close to them. Wouldn't it be nice to be able to visit? But we wouldn't dare."

"True," Ron said. "Since Nancy's privacy is our first priority, we can't visit or we'd violate that. It does seem a shame though. Then again, our purpose for this trip was not to visit. We would not be here if it weren't for our baby. We'll just have to stay focused on that."

Once at Universal Studios, we had a wonderful time taking in the sights and attractions. It was hard to relax though. Our minds were constantly on Nancy, wondering if she was all right. Several times we called but since there was no change on the answering machine message, we resumed our activities. All the same, I felt like a mother hen as I worried about her.

Several more days passed when we received a call from Nancy's relative Lynn.

"Why don't you come up to visit me?" she asked over the phone. "I'll get you rooms at the hotel near our home so you can enjoy the pool."

Lynn's invitation was just what we needed. Time was dragging as day after day passed without signs of labor. Eager for a change of scenery and some space from the apartment, we headed out Saturday morning.

Arriving at the hotel, we quickly unpacked and headed for the pool. After several hours in the sun, it was time to get ready for dinner. Lynn and her husband would be picking us up.

They treated us to one of their favorite restaurants. We had a wonderful evening. It was fun getting to know Lynn and her husband better. She was such a sensitive and caring woman. We felt like we'd known her for years. I felt in awe of her sense of strength. She was so supportive of Nancy. I could feel her concern for us too. It was as if she had taken us all into her care, trying to be there for each of us.

Back at the hotel, Ron and I crawled into bed. Although tired from the day, we felt renewed and ready to continue our wait.

The following morning we went for a bicycle ride on the beach, a first for us. Then we joined Lynn and Nancy for some shopping. Arriving back at Lynn's house with packages in hand, Lynn found a message on her answering machine for Nancy. Janet, the owner of a dress shop, had called and asked if Nancy could come back in. We'd been there earlier shopping for an outfit for Nancy to wear home from the hospital. Perhaps she had left something there by accident.

"Why don't you go down now," I suggested. "Ron and I will visit with Lynn while you're gone." Nancy agreed and was off.

An hour later, she was back. She looked flustered and upset.

"What did she want?" Lynn asked with concern.

"She wants to adopt my baby!" Nancy said bluntly. "She told me that she and her husband couldn't have any more children and asked me to consider letting them adopt mine."

Ron and I were stunned, unable to believe what we were hearing. Nancy had introduced us to Janet and told her we were going to adopt this baby. How could she be so brazen?

"What did you tell her?" I asked. There was a quiver in my voice.

"That I was happy with our arrangements."

Lynn was upset but Nancy remained quiet, seeming to be lost in thought. I wondered what she was thinking.

Days continued to pass slowly. Nancy arrived back at the apartment after doing some volunteer work at St. John's.

"I stopped by the hospital and talked with Linda today," she said. "She asked me what my plans are as far as breast-feeding. She suggested I consider pumping rather than nursing. She thought it might be more comfortable for all of us."

I seized the opportunity. "I must admit Nancy; I've been a bit uneasy with the thought of you nursing. I have heard so much about the bonding. I'm afraid it will make giving up the baby harder on you."

"That's what Linda said. Pumping might be best under the circumstances."

"I'd feel more comfortable with that as well," I added.

"Linda also asked me about my plans after the baby is born," Nancy continued. "When I told her that you would be staying a few days, she mentioned that it might be awkward for you. She said it's difficult enough to be new parents in your own environment, let alone in someone else's. You may feel like you're in a fishbowl with everyone watching you."

"You know Nancy, that's one of the reasons I've been reluctant about staying. I'm afraid it will be hard for all three of us to parent the baby at the same time."

"I guess I hadn't thought about that."

"I'm also concerned that you'll get further attached, which will make giving the baby up more difficult."

"Oh, don't worry about me. I'm prepared for that."

"Nancy, just three weeks ago I spent four days with Colleen and my nephews when Jacob was born. When it was time for me to go, I had a tough time and they aren't even my children."

"I can handle it," Nancy said firmly.

"Are you sure?"

"Please allow me this time with my baby," she said in a pleading tone.

"I just don't want this to be any harder on you than necessary."

"Don't worry. I fully intend to give you my baby."

I knew from her tone that it was time to drop the subject. Deep down though, fear had again found a foothold in my heart.

Eighteen days had passed since our arrival. Stirring awake, I noticed the light under Nancy's door. It was still early. Quickly I got up and knocked. Nancy was sitting up in bed.

"I think this is it," she said. "I've been having contractions most of the night." Her eyes were wide with anticipation.

"Oh, I can't believe it," I said, squealing with delight as I hugged her. "We're finally going to have our baby. What do we do now?"

"I don't remember," Nancy said with a giggle.

Waking Ron, we found the childbirth manual and studied it again. Following the instructions, we timed the contractions and determined it could be a while yet.

"Let's get dressed so we're ready to go to the hospital once it's time," I suggested.

By the time we were ready, contractions were coming a little more often. Finally, at 10:00 a.m., we called the hospital. Nancy explained what was happening.

"You probably have some time yet," the nurse said. "Why don't you wait a little longer?"

Nancy was disappointed as she hung up the phone. So were we. None of us wanted to wait any longer. We tried to keep our spirits up though as we continued timing the contractions while practicing the breathing techniques with Nancy.

By noon the contractions had completely stopped. It felt as if we had been teased unmercifully. At least there had been some signs. Perhaps it wouldn't be long now.

Several days passed with no further activity. The three of us were relaxing in the apartment, trying to stay cool. I was experiencing constant waves of morning sickness and it seemed less severe if I stayed out of the heat. Nancy was in a talkative mood.

"I really appreciate you guys keeping my secret. I know my family would be so disappointed in me if they knew. Besides, I have always wanted them to like Jim. I've even told them things about him that weren't completely true just so they'd like him."

"Like what?" I asked, surprised at her confession.

"Remember my short vacation up the coast? I told them Jim paid for that in order to give me a break after losing my job. They were so impressed at his thoughtfulness. But if I told them about my pregnancy, not only would they dislike him but they'd question my judgment in getting involved."

"Perhaps they wouldn't be as hard on you as you imagine."

"Well, even if they weren't, the people from my hometown would never let me live it down. Most of them already think I am an old maid. What would they think if they knew I'd gotten pregnant?"

As if realizing she had exposed some dark secret, Nancy quickly changed the subject. "When the baby is born, are you going to call your family from the hospital?"

"I don't know. We might wait until we're on our way home."

"Why?" Nancy asked.

I hesitated but then I said it. "In case we don't bring the baby home. It might be easier on our family if there isn't all the excitement of hearing of its birth."

Nancy looked at me as if I were crazy. "Denise, this is your baby and you will be taking it home. That's final."

I started to laugh, realizing how silly my comment must have sounded to her. However, I wanted her to know that even now, despite having waited almost three weeks with her in California, if she wanted to keep the baby that was still her option. It would be a painful option for us but still an option.

"Besides," Nancy added with a laugh, "can you imagine the temper tantrums this child is going to have in public? The challenges will be never ending. You are the ones who should raise this child."

By now, all three of us were laughing as we visualized the things children do that invariably embarrass their parents.

"And once you take it home, you can't give it back!" Nancy said.

"Well, you can't take it back either," I added with a tone of seriousness.

"Don't worry, I won't! This is your baby. Trust me."

Once again, my worries dissolved as we enjoyed sharing our thoughts and dreams of our much-anticipated child.

Nancy was getting nervous. So were we. There were still no further signs of labor and time was becoming an issue. Nancy's sister Diane would be here within the week. She hoped to give Nancy moral support after giving up the baby and help Nancy pack for her move. Summer session would begin the end of May. Nancy needed to move in less than a month.

Our time was also becoming more precious as Ron's vacation and my maternity leave continued to dwindle away. Furthermore, I worried that our time together was working to our disadvantage. Ron and I were beginning to feel under scrutiny as if we had to be the perfect couple, free from disagreements. The week after week of waiting combined with the stress of the situation did not make that entirely possible. It was somewhat awkward sharing Nancy's small apartment even though we were grateful to be able to spend this time together. Although we had adapted fairly well, the wait was wearing all of us down. We all longed to have our own lives back. We were anxious to have this behind us and to move on to the futures we had planned.

Adding to the strain was my morning sickness that was becoming more of a bother every day. The California heat wasn't much comfort with my queasiness. I longed to be in my own environment. Nancy seemed overly concerned about how I was feeling. I wondered if she questioned if I could handle her baby. I, on the other hand, was trying not to linger on my pregnancy. This was Nancy's time. I wanted her to feel special, not as if she were sharing the spotlight. There would be plenty of attention for me later.

The long vigil continued for our family in Montana as well. I knew this was difficult for them too. They didn't know where we were due to Nancy's desire to remain anonymous. Our phone calls home were seldom since it was so hard to keep from saying something incriminating. Colleen tried to ease our wait by organizing mail drops from our family since she was the only one who knew our whereabouts. Their cheery messages and words of encouragement reminded us that the wait would have to end someday even though it seemed it never would.

For Nancy, our presence was a constant reminder that we were still waiting. I think she felt under pressure to have the baby even though it wasn't in her control. We tried to make the most of the time by enjoying long walks, relaxing by the pool, and taking in the sights. Occasionally we would go out to eat, have a picnic at the beach, or see a movie. We even made a day trip to the San Diego Zoo. Nancy hoped a good walk would encourage labor.

Our most critical concern, however, was Nancy's parents. They planned to arrive within a month in order to move Nancy back to school.

"How am I going to do this?" Nancy said in frustration one afternoon. "I've got to have this baby, get my body back in shape, get rid of all the baby evidence, and pack. I'll never make it."

"Is there anything we can do to help?" I knew the answer to my own question but somehow asking seemed the only thing to do.

"No, not really. I cannot do anything until the baby is born and you are gone. I still need the maternity clothes, the childbirth books, all this—." She waved her hand around the room. There was evidence of her pregnancy and our extended stay everywhere. "I'll never be able to pull this off!" There was desperation in her voice.

We tried to calm her but she was right. The best thing that could happen was for the baby to come so we could leave. Only then could she get on with the life she had planned. Tensions were mounting. It felt as if a time bomb had been set.

That evening after we cleared the dinner dishes, Nancy began crying. "I'm going for a walk," she stammered as she headed out the door.

I didn't offer to go along as I usually did, sensing she wanted to be alone.

As she left, she slammed the door. The apartment was quiet as Ron and I looked at each other, filled with questions.

"What brought that on?" Ron asked.

"I don't know."

"Do you suppose she changed her mind?"

I started to cry. "No, it couldn't be. Not after all this!"

"This is unbearable," Ron said as he too struggled with tears.

"I'm so scared," I said, burying my face in his shoulder.

"Me too." He was trying to be brave as he continued. "We always knew this was a possibility, but I had no idea it would hurt this much."

"Maybe that's not it," I said, trying to be optimistic.

"What else could it be?"

I shook my head, unable to imagine.

"I'm just so tired," Ron said. "This has been so emotionally exhausting."

"I agree. It reminds me of when Dad was dying. Only this time we're awaiting birth rather than death. What an emotional roller coaster."

"I don't know about you but I'm to the point where I just want it to be over. If Nancy has changed her mind, then I want to know so we can go home and try to put our life back together."

"But how could we go home without our baby?"

"I don't know, but we may have to," Ron said. Tears were brimming in his eyes. "Our next baby is coming soon. Somehow, we'll just have to focus on it. We really don't have any other choice."

Some time passed and we continued to talk. Ron nervously glanced out the window. "It's starting to get dark," he said with worry. "Perhaps we should go find Nancy."

"I'll go," I said. "She might feel more comfortable if it's just us girls."

Ron hesitated. He did not want me to go alone, but neither of us had the energy to argue. "Okay, just tell me which direction you're going in case I need to come looking for you too."

Heading towards the busier section of town, I kept my eyes peeled for Nancy. Finally, I saw her in the distance. She was coming my way. I could see she was still crying.

I had no idea what to say. I feared the worst but was equally concerned for Nancy. I loved her so much, I didn't want her to be hurting.

Reaching one another, we embraced. We were both crying as we stood on the sidewalk hugging.

Finally, Nancy took a deep breath. "Denise, I feel so guilty."

I didn't say anything. I was afraid I would fall apart.

She continued, "What kind of a mother am I that I don't even feel bad about giving up my own child?"

"What?" I asked.

"I know the adoption is the best thing. I know it's the right choice but I feel so guilty for not feeling bad about giving up my baby."

"You mean you haven't changed your mind?"

"Oh, no. Is that what you thought?" Realizing the reason for my tears, Nancy hugged me again. "I'm sorry I left so abruptly. I just had to think things out."

"It's okay. I am just so relieved. Ron and I thought it was over."

"Not at all," Nancy said.

We walked on in silence, arm in arm. Finally I said, "Nancy, perhaps you don't feel bad because you believe you're doing the right thing. Why should you feel guilty about doing something so good?"

"That's true," she said thoughtfully.

I continued, "You're the kind of mother who loves your child enough to give it more than you alone can. You have made a very loving and courageous choice. Don't ever feel guilty about that."

"Thank you, Denise," Nancy said, her eyes again filling with tears.

"Lynn just called," Nancy said. "She's decided to come and stay with us, baby or not."

Word of Lynn's arrival was music to our ears. Twenty-two days had passed since our arrival and our spirits were worn. We all needed a distraction, and Lynn would certainly help. She had a way of calming any situation.

As promised, Lynn arrived the next day. Her car was loaded down with gifts for Nancy and the baby, including five beautiful pictures for Nancy. She hoped Nancy would find one pleasing to use as a focus picture during labor. The first four were beautiful scenery pictures, but the fifth in particular caught my eye. It was a black and white photo of two children holding hands. They appeared to be entering a garden as they left behind darkness that resembled a cave. The tallest child was a boy, the shortest was a girl.

"I tried to find a picture with just one child but I couldn't," Lynn explained. "I kept coming back to this one. It makes me think of children leaving the womb and entering the world."

A chill ran down my back as I caught Ron's eye. We hadn't told Lynn of our pregnancy. She could not begin to know the appropriateness of the picture.

At the doctor's office the following day, Dr. Thomas said, "The placenta looks as if it's being taxed."

Nancy had been in for another ultrasound. The doctor was keeping a close watch, particularly since the baby was now past due.

Dr. Thomas continued, "I won't be at the hospital until Thursday, so let's schedule you for inducement then."

"That's the soonest we can do it?" I asked. Thursday was three days away.

"Well, unless someone else delivers it."

"No," Nancy said. "I would prefer you."

My mind raced as concern consumed me. If the placenta is being taxed, why wait? What if the placenta failed before Thursday? What if there were complications? I just wanted our baby delivered safely, no matter who did it. I also wanted our baby to arrive so we could get on with our life. I knew Nancy would not be pushed though so I remained quiet.

Leaving the clinic, I was disappointed. I tried to think about Thursday. At least there was a deadline now. Our baby would be born this week, no matter what. Even so, there was a sense of conflict and disagreement in the air. The end was so near, yet why did it seem so far away?

"Let's celebrate," Lynn suggested, trying to cheer us. "How about dinner out?"

"That's a good idea," Nancy said. "What about Marie Calendar's? I craved their strawberry cheesecake during my first trimester. It seems fitting to have a piece now that we're at the end."

Arriving, we ordered dinner and chatted. Our moods lifted as we discussed plans for the last few days of our wait. Suddenly, I noticed Ron looking at me. He had an odd expression on his face.

"What is it?" I asked quietly.

He motioned his head toward the window. My eyes followed his nod. I gasped. My Uncle Don and Aunt Peg were sitting at a table ten feet away!

"Denise?" Aunt Peg cried out. "Is that you?"

There was nowhere to hide. I leaned over to Nancy. "We'll go over and say hello. Why don't you try to sneak out?"

Nancy's face had gone white. Tears were in her eyes. "Do you think they've recognized me?"

"I don't know."

Quickly I rose, not wanting them to come to our table. Ron followed me as we met them halfway. Hugging them, I glanced over my shoulder. Nancy and Lynn were leaving.

"I can't believe this," Aunt Peg was saying. "I didn't recognize you, Denise, with your short hair cut but I kept looking at Ron, unable to believe how much he looked like your Ron. I told Don there truly must be doubles in this world."

"So have you been in California this whole time?" Uncle Don asked.

"Yes," Ron said. "We wanted to call but didn't dare since the birth mother wants to remain anonymous." Although they knew of the adoption, they had no idea that the birth mother was someone they knew.

"Was that the birth mother? Wasn't that your college friend Nancy?" Aunt Peg asked.

"Yes, but it's very important to her that we respect her privacy. We have tried very hard to honor that."

"We understand. We won't say a word."

"Thank you so much," I said. "I'm just sorry that now you'll also have to watch every word you say so as to not slip."

"It's all right. We'll keep your secret."

"I just talked to your mom today," Peg said, shifting the conversation. "I wondered if there was any news. It has been so long since you left Montana. We knew you were somewhere out of the state but had no idea you were here."

"That was the idea," I said. "I can't we believe we ran into you. What are the odds of this happening?"

"Very slim," Aunt Peg said with a laugh.

"So how are you doing?" Uncle Don asked.

With his question, all the pent up emotions and feelings came pouring out like water from a spillway. It felt so good to completely open up about all that had been occurring in the past weeks. As we talked, the tensions seemed to dissolve.

Love To Give

We felt energized again. God must have known how much we needed our family right then, for only He could have arranged this unlikely coincidence—the same restaurant, at the same time, while far from home in Southern California. Our God truly is amazing.

Although we wished we could have visited longer, we kept our conversation brief. We didn't want to keep Nancy and Lynn waiting, especially knowing Nancy was upset.

As we departed, Aunt Peg called out. "Don't forget to buy lottery tickets tonight," she said with a chuckle. "With our odds in seeing each other tonight, there's a good chance we could win."

Nancy was crying as we got in the car. Lynn was trying to calm her.

"I know they will keep our secret," I assured them. Our words seemed to offer little comfort though as Nancy continued to cry.

"I just can't believe what bad luck," she said.

I felt as if I had been slapped as anger rose inside. This unlikely encounter, although unplanned, had been so good for Ron and me. I was hurt, feeling as if Nancy had attacked my family just because she had been discovered.

Silently I seethed, *This isn't just about you. You have been babied and pampered by everyone from the moment you made this decision! For a change, someone was here for us. Why don't you grow up and think beyond yourself?* Thankfully, though, I kept my thoughts to myself, and the expression on my face could not be seen in the darkness.

In silence, we drove home. The sense of celebration of moments ago had dissolved, leaving the air heavy with tension. Nancy seemed angry with us, as if the encounter had been our fault. I was angry with her for making such a big deal out of something over which none of us had any control. Then again, what was new? Our whole life felt out of our control. It seemed Nancy had more control of our lives than we did. I felt resentful. I missed my family, my home, my life. I just wanted this to be over!

Back at the apartment, Nancy sulked. Consumed in her misery, she checked her answering machine. There was a message from Jim.

"Nancy, I fell off my horse today. I am in the hospital with a broken collarbone. I know I told you I would sign the papers this week but it looks like I will not be able to make it. Talk to you soon."

She began sobbing. It was as if the last straw broke as she cried out, "Oh, everything is falling apart!"

Chapter 6

THURSDAY MORNING FINALLY arrived. Ron drove us all to the hospital with great anticipation and excitement. Nancy went to the registration desk. She had red hair today—one of her adventures yesterday had been a stop with a hair stylist to get her hair colored. The woman at the desk told her we would have to wait for a bed to become available. An early morning call from the hospital had delayed the inducement time by two hours due to a shortage of beds. Now we were here and we still had to wait! Impatiently, the four of us settled into the waiting area.

Suddenly, Lynn cried out, "Oh, I can't believe it! We forgot the focus picture."

Nancy sighed with exasperation. The morning had gotten off to a shaky start with the delays and now we had left the picture! What else could go wrong? Lynn and Ron decided to head back to the apartment to retrieve it. I didn't want them to go. It would take them at least an hour and a half to make the round-trip drive depending on the traffic. I didn't want them to miss anything. However, since we were waiting anyway, it probably would be fine.

After they left, Nancy and I continued our wait in silence. Two women who were obviously in labor checked in. Nancy and I looked at each other without saying a word. We knew the wait would be longer now. It felt like we would never have the baby.

Time seemed to drag. In an awkward silence, we fidgeted. An hour passed. Finally, a nurse called Nancy's name. Our spirits immediately lifted as we made our way to the maternity ward. We were directed to a small room.

"Would a birthing room be available?" Nancy asked timidly. She hated to push her luck but this room was so tiny. There wouldn't be room for all four of us as well as the staff during delivery.

The nurse acted put out but left to check. Moments later, she was back. "One just opened up."

I was glad Nancy had asked. The birthing room was much more spacious and private, decorated in soft pinks. It was warm and inviting. This would definitely be more comfortable. Nancy put on a gown as instructed. She had barely settled on the bed when Ron and Lynn returned with the focus picture in hand. I was relieved. Now we could get on with what we had all been waiting for.

All morning a steady stream of nurses and technicians came and went, administering the IV and medications. As each new staff member arrived, Nancy introduced us as the baby's parents. Everyone seemed to be in awe of our arrangement. An external monitoring device was placed around Nancy's stomach to track the baby's heartbeat as well as her contractions. With inducement underway, we visited. The steady sound of our little one's heartbeat filled the room. It was mesmerizing.

A lactation nurse arrived. "I understand there is an allergy history in your family," she said.

"Yes," Nancy responded. "My brother has some food allergies."

"Oh, that's it? I had assumed it was much more serious," the nurse said.

I wondered what she meant. Perhaps breast milk wasn't as critical as we had been led to believe. Before I could inquire though, she continued. "Regardless though, breast-feeding is the most desirable method. That way the baby receives the colostrum from your milk. You could pump but it is not as efficient. I think you are wise to nurse."

I was dumbfounded. The hospital social worker had assured me that the lactation nurse knew of our concerns. Nancy had just introduced us as the adoptive parents, but the nurse seemed completely unaware of the sensitivities of our adoption.

I wanted to point out that the baby would have to be comfortable with a bottle too. I wanted to reiterate that we had agreed pumping would be best. The nurse, however, rattled on, intent on promoting breast-feeding as if it was the only option.

"You're not as likely to be uncomfortable with engorgement if you nurse. Besides, it's much more natural."

I was feeling anxious. Clearing my throat I tried to interrupt, but Nancy spoke up.

"I agree," she said. "I would prefer to nurse. As you say, it's more efficient."

"But Nancy," I started.

"I might not have any other children. This may be my only chance." Her tone was firm and definite.

Ron was standing quietly by the wall. His face was red, and I could tell he was angry. He quietly slipped out of the room. I followed him, feeling as if I would burst into tears. Hastily, we walked down the hall, not saying a word. Then, turning the corner in the hall, Ron unloaded his anger.

"Can you believe it? We had this issue resolved but in a matter of minutes, a so-called specialist blows the whole thing!"

"She seems to have a one-track mind," I agreed. "But I can't believe she hasn't considered how nursing could impact an adoption."

"Well, if Nancy's going to nurse, we might as well go home. She won't be able to give up the baby after nursing it."

"But why is Nancy so adamant despite knowing our concerns? And to change her mind without even talking to us about it? I don't understand."

"If it was so important to her, why didn't she just tell us to begin with?"

"I don't know. I feel betrayed. How could she back out on what we've agreed upon?"

"What else do you think she'll back out of?" Ron asked.

His question hit like a bomb. I knew what he was implying. We walked on in silence as the all-too-familiar sense of fear again swept over us.

"Maybe we should cut our losses now and head home," he said. "I can't bear to see the baby and then not take it home. Besides, it's pretty apparent she isn't interested in our feelings or concerns."

I remained quiet. I felt torn. I knew Nancy didn't want to go through labor alone, yet I didn't want us to experience further disappointment.

"On the other hand," Ron continued, "we have everything to lose if we leave. After all, this is still Nancy's baby. I guess she has the right to make this decision."

"True, but don't our feelings and concerns count for anything?"

"Well, this is obviously what she wants. I doubt there is any sense in discussing it further. But I admit I feel discarded." Then with a sigh he added, "But we've come this far. We might as well see it through."

Hours later, Nancy was beginning to feel uncomfortable. The anesthesiologist had started the pain medication through an epidural. Although it relieved the pain, it was also numbing her legs. Ron and I took turns rubbing her calves and feet, trying to help her get some feeling back. With labor finally progressing our spirits were light again as we set our worries aside.

Afternoon wore into evening. At 11:00 p.m., the nurse checked her. It looked like we were in for a long night. Ron encouraged me to rest, thinking of my pregnancy but I was too excited to consider resting.

At midnight, Nancy said she felt uncomfortable. I summoned the nurse who poked her head in the door.

"I feel pretty uncomfortable," Nancy said.

"Well, you can expect that," the nurse said unsympathetically. "Just try to relax. It will be a while longer." She then departed without any further interest.

Nancy tried to relax but, within moments, again expressed discomfort. Once again, I called the nurse.

"Please check her this time," I said firmly.

"I'm sure you have some time," she replied bluntly but checked on Nancy anyway.

Suddenly, the nurse flew into action. "The baby's head has crowned," she said. "I'll call the doctor!"

The room filled with tension as the nurse hustled around, gathering various instruments. Nancy's eyes were wide. She was about to deliver, but the doctor had not arrived.

"I have to push," Nancy said with panic.

"No, just pant like you were taught in childbirth classes," the nurse ordered.

Nancy looked around frantically. I didn't know what she'd been taught but took her hand. "We'll pant together," I said.

Nancy fixed her eyes on mine and together we panted. She was struggling as she tried to stay focused. Finally, Dr. Thomas rushed into the room. Sharply, he ordered the nurse around. He was obviously unhappy for not being called sooner. The anesthesiologist arrived and gave Nancy more medication.

At last, the doctor was ready. "Push with your next contraction," he instructed.

"I can't feel them," Nancy said with frustration. The latest dose of anesthesia had evidently numbed her. I put my hands on her stomach, trying to feel them for her but lacked experience. The nurse took over, telling Nancy when to push.

Everything was a blur. Ron and I stood at the end of the bed. We could see the top of our baby's head, covered with just a little bit of hair. Time seemed to stop as we watched in awe.

The first sounds of our baby filled the room as its slippery body emerged. "It's a boy," Dr. Thomas announced.

Ron and I were in each other's arms. Tears were streaming down our faces. We had a son. He was beautiful and absolutely perfect. The nurse noted the official time of birth— April 19th, 1:14 a.m.

"What's his name?" Dr. Thomas asked.

"Michael William," Ron replied, swelling with pride. There was a glow about him like I'd never seen.

"Are you getting pictures?" Nancy asked, stirring us from our state of awe.

We grabbed the cameras, wanting to capture the moment forever. Dr. Thomas cut the umbilical cord and then handed our little Michael to the nursery ward nurse. She measured him—7 lbs. 5 oz., 21 inches long. Then it was time for his bath. Michael obviously was not impressed though as he cried loudly.

Ron and I giggled while tears flowed as we watched, observing every detail. Michael had fair skin like us and even had a slight cleft in his chin like Ron. Although he didn't have much hair, it was light brown in coloring. I couldn't help thinking how much he looked like us. It didn't matter what he looked like though. He was ours and we loved him so much.

"It's good we didn't wait any longer," Dr. Thomas said, looking Michael over.

"Why?" I asked.

"Can you see how wrinkled his skin is? The protective coating is gone. This little guy has actually started to lose weight. He wouldn't have survived another week in the womb."

My stomach turned at the thought. I quickly pushed it out of my mind as I sent a prayer of thanks heavenward. Our son was safe. That's all that mattered.

Suddenly, I thought of Nancy. I had been so absorbed in our son that I hadn't even checked on her. Glancing in her direction, I noticed her watching us with a slight smile on her face. Torn between staying with our son and being with Nancy, I pulled myself away and quickly walked over to her bedside.

"How are you feeling?" I asked.

"Fine," she said, her smile broadening. "This is what I wanted for my baby—a loving family. I am so happy. Now go be with your son."

She didn't have to tell me twice. I kissed her cheek and hurried back to Michael. Our little son was finally all cleaned up. I wanted to hold him, but we thought Nancy should have the first opportunity. After all, she had done all the work.

The nurse placed Michael in Nancy's arms. She smiled sweetly down at him. "Isn't our baby perfect?" she said. Then looking at Ron, she asked, "Would you like to hold him?"

"Oh, would I," Ron said as he gathered his new son in his arms.

Ever so gently, Ron sat in the rocking chair and rocked Michael. There was an intense sense of peace in the room as he talked to his little son. "We have been waiting a long time for you Michael. We are so happy you are finally here. You can't imagine how much we all love you."

Michael eyes were wide, looking up at Ron as if understanding every word. Tears again fell as I watched my husband transform into a father. Never could I have imagined what joy and love I would feel, seeing the man whom I admired more than anyone holding his newborn son.

By 4 a.m., Nancy was resting in her room, and Michael was asleep in the darkened nursery. It was time for the rest of us to get some sleep. Kissing Nancy good-bye, Lynn, Ron, and I left to drive back to the apartment. Although we had been awake for over 24 hours, we felt exhilarated as we chatted about our beautiful little Michael.

We dropped Lynn off at the apartment and then drove to the hotel. Lynn had reserved a room and then graciously offered it to us in order to give us some privacy. How would we ever be able to thank her for all her thoughtfulness?

It was 5 a.m. by the time we got to the hotel. It would be 6 a.m. in Montana. We started making calls to announce the arrival of our new son. Tears were flowing on both sides of the phone as we shared the news. Mom had been up all night, pacing, knowing inducement was scheduled for the previous day. Finally, the wait was over and for the first time in months, there was a sense of peace and fulfillment. Our family now included a little boy of our own. Soon we would be home to share this long-awaited blessing.

Allowing ourselves just two hours of sleep, we quickly showered, dressed, and rushed back to the hospital. We were so anxious to see Michael. Passing the nursery, we noticed his bassinet gone. He must be in Nancy's room. Our pace quickened.

Nancy smiled as we entered. She looked radiant. Her sister Diane was there too, having flown in the previous night. I placed the flower arrangement we'd had made for Nancy on the table and then looked at Michael asleep in Diane's arms. I felt a tinge of jealousy as I observed the scene.

"Why don't you hold him?" Nancy suggested.

Without hesitation, I lifted Michael and kissed his precious little head. Finally, I was holding my son. In all the excitement of last night, I had missed out. In a strange way, I had felt like the odd man out, uncertain where my role as a mother began. Now though, he was in my arms and I felt complete. Nothing else in the world seemed to matter as I held my newborn son and savored the feelings of motherhood.

"All his bodily functions seem to be in order," Nancy said, interrupting my thoughts.

"Wonderful," I said. "Has he eaten?"

"I nursed him this morning."

I felt a twinge of sadness with her answer but didn't look up from gazing at Michael.

"By the way," she said, "I've named him Michael Barrett, after his birth father."

"That's a nice name," I said, trying to sound positive. Linda had told us that birth mothers often choose a different name for the initial birth certificate. Once the adoption became final, a new birth certificate would be issued with the name we had chosen. I was grateful Linda had prepared us for this.

"I hate to bring this up already," I said, changing the subject, "but Ron and I need to finalize our return flight as soon as possible. Would Tuesday be a good time for our departure?" That was four days away.

"That sounds fine," Nancy replied. Much to my surprise, she sounded confident. I had expected her to be noncommittal.

"I bet you'll be so glad to get home," she added.

"Yes, we will!" We were so homesick, especially now. We just wanted to take Michael home and start our life together.

"I suppose we should also contact the attorney," Ron said.

"Good idea," Nancy agreed. "Would you ask him when I should come in to sign the papers? Or maybe he will bring them here. Oh, and let's not forget to call Rev. Birch to arrange for the ceremony." Nancy's willingness to move forward with the arrangements made me relax again. Things were going as planned despite all our concerns.

The morning passed enjoying our son and one another's company. It was time to return to the apartment to get Lynn. She had opted to sleep in and had mentioned that she wanted to get a few things done at the apartment. I think it was just an excuse to give us time alone with Michael though. Since she was didn't like driving the freeways alone though, we'd promised to pick her up after lunch.

"When you come back," Nancy said, "why don't you bring the gifts that are in my night stand. I picked up some things for you and the baby. We can have a baby shower when you get back."

Parting seemed unbearable as we left Michael once again. Kissing him goodbye though, we were off.

When we arrived back at the apartment, Lynn was busy cleaning. Everything looked so neat and tidy. I smiled, remembering how particular Nancy had been about cleanliness in our apartment during college. I knew she would appreciate it.

Since Lynn wasn't quite ready, Ron finished vacuuming while I dusted. Then we loaded the packages that Nancy had requested into the car. Finally, we were in the car headed back to the hospital. It felt like we had been gone all day. We were anxious to get back to Michael.

Arriving at Nancy's room, we found the bed empty. We inquired at the nurses' station. Nancy had moved to a private room. Lynn, in her usual sensitivity, had arranged it.

Nancy, her sister Diane, and Nancy's friend Joann were there. Joann was holding Michael. Once again, feelings of discomfort rose up in me. I felt out of place as I observed this gathering of Nancy's family and friends. They were here admiring her son. Meanwhile, our family and friends were denied this special time with us and our son. Everything felt so backwards. I felt like Michael's mother, yet in this room I felt more like a guest.

Joann seemed to have read my mind as she asked, "Do you want to hold Michael?"

I desperately did but instead responded, "It's okay. You go ahead. I suppose I have to share." I laughed, trying to be nonchalant, but inside I felt torn. I wanted to grab our son and flee. He should be in Montana with our family. There he would be our son and I wouldn't feel like the outsider. We couldn't leave though. Trapped in Nancy's world, we graciously visited. I wanted to be considerate of Nancy and her guests. This was her time with her son and I wanted it to be special for her, even if it was painful for me. Inside, I fought back tears.

"Let's open the gifts," Nancy encouraged.

I was glad to have something else to focus on.

"Here, open this one first," she said, handing me a package. Inside was a handmade baby blanket. "I made it for Michael. I wanted him to have something from me."

"Oh Nancy, it's beautiful. It will be a treasure. I'll make sure he knows you made it for him."

Opening the next package, I found a blue sleeper and bib with the word "boy" written across the front. Suddenly, I realized that Nancy must have known the sex of our baby even though she told us she didn't. "You knew it was a boy?" I asked in a shocked tone.

"Yes, I hope you don't mind my finding out," she said rather apologetically.

"Of course not but why didn't you tell us you knew?"

"I didn't want to blow the surprise, but I knew it would be harder for me to give up a boy. I wanted to make sure I was prepared."

Despite her logical explanation, feelings of betrayal once again crept in. It was a small matter but she had not been honest with us.

Opening the rest of the gifts, I felt dazed and full of confusion. The concerns of the past weeks seemed to come into focus once again, and the big question stuck in my mind: Had Nancy truly prepared herself to give up her son?

Michael's first few days of life passed quickly. Nancy didn't seem in any rush to leave the hospital. We, on the other hand, were very anxious to get him and Nancy checked out. It was one step closer to taking him home with us. Finally, on Sunday we prepared to leave.

While Nancy showered and got ready for the day, I watched as Ron dressed Michael. What a challenge it was to get those little limbs in those little openings. We were both enjoying the challenge as we talked to our little Michael. Finally, Nancy was ready to go as well. Just as we were leaving, a nurse trainee appeared at the door.

"I hope you don't mind but when I heard about your adoption, I just had to stop."

"No problem," I said.

"I won't keep you but I wanted to tell you how much your adoption has affected the staff here. It has really touched us all. I also wanted to share with you that I was given up for adoption at birth. My adoptive parents are wonderful people, and I love them very much. I feel so lucky to be their daughter."

Looking directly at Nancy, she continued, "I recently met my birth mother. I have not met my father yet, but I love them both for what they did for me. I know it must have been hard, but I am so grateful that they gave me to my adoptive parents. Your child will love you for what you're doing too."

Tears filled our eyes and voices as we choked out a "thank you." Then, as abruptly as she came, she left. It was almost as if an angel had visited.

Back at the apartment, the afternoon passed quietly as we all admired our precious son. Bedtime was approaching.

"Let's put the bassinet next to our bed," Ron and I suggested to Nancy. "That way you can get some extra rest." We were so anxious to begin parenting our son.

"No, it would be much easier for me to nurse him if he were in my room."

Unsure what to say, I remained quiet. I had just assumed that he would sleep in the room with us and that we would be the primary caregivers. Nancy, however, was taking charge, making it clear that Michael was still her son. Furthermore, it disturbed me that she would use nursing as an excuse, especially knowing our displeasure. It was as if she was rubbing it in our face. This was not what we had visualized when we had agreed to stay after Michael's birth. There seemed to be no consideration for our feelings, needs, or concerns.

Once again, feelings of conflict rose up inside. I was finally a mother yet even now, it seemed it would never happen. I fought back tears.

With Michael asleep in the bassinet in Nancy's room, I covered him with a blanket and kissed him goodnight. Tears close to the surface, I silently left Nancy's room and shut the door between her and Michael and us. Nothing felt more unnatural.

Tossing and turning, I tried to sleep as the "what ifs" again filled my mind. If only we had not agreed to stay. If only we had been clearer in what we expected to begin with. Had we known this was Nancy's intention, we would have stayed in a hotel and left Nancy with Michael. At least then, we wouldn't have to bear with this conflicting situation.

I wondered what Nancy was thinking. Had she intended to keep Michael all along? Was our only purpose for coming to help her through these initial days as a parent? Had she only wanted us here so she wouldn't have to go through labor alone?

Deep down though, I knew it was too late to question any of this. We were stuck here until Tuesday. Somehow, we would have to get through this horribly uncomfortable situation.

Finally, I feel asleep, but during the night, I woke to hear Michael crying. Immediately, I got up and knocked on Nancy's door. She had already picked him up. In the dark, I retrieved a diaper from our suitcase. Then the two of us quietly changed him. Trying to make conversation, I watched Nancy nurse him. I felt so inadequate, seeing our son at her breast. It was a painful reminder of the one function I could not perform for him. Finally, though, the agony was over. Michael was asleep. Nancy carried him to his bassinet.

Several hours later, Nancy woke me. "Where are the diapers?" she asked.

"Did Michael wake? I never even heard him."

"Oh, he just started to stir. I picked him up before he cried."

I didn't respond, feeling like this was a contest to decide who had the best maternal ear. Quickly, I retrieved a diaper and then sat quietly as Nancy nursed him. Again, sadness and anger welled inside. There were one too many mothers in this scene.

Back in bed, I held back my tears. "Oh, God," I silently prayed. "Please give us the strength and grace to get through this too."

At last, we were alone with Michael. Nancy and Diane had gone shopping. They needed some time alone as, did we. It was wonderful to be able to hold our son without anyone else around. We enjoyed the chance to become familiar with him. All too quickly though, our solitude was over and Nancy and Diane arrived with packages in their arms. Immediately Nancy prepared to nurse Michael. I couldn't take it anymore.

"Ron and I need to get a few things at the store," I said abruptly. "We'll pick up formula while we're there so Michael can get used to it."

"Good idea," Nancy said without much enthusiasm.

It was good to get away from the apartment for a while. We loitered a bit, giving Nancy time alone with Michael and Diane.

Back at the apartment, I began sterilizing the bottles. I felt like I was being bullied and I was tired of it. At the next feeding, I took charge and warmed a bottle. Ron fed Michael for the first time. It was wonderful to be allowed this one small privilege of parenthood. Michael seemed unaware of any difference as he devoured the bottle.

Nancy, however, quietly watched with a sad expression on her face. My frustration overrode any compassion though as I said, "Perhaps you should pump in the future and fill bottles with your milk. That will give Michael the benefits of colostrum while allowing him a chance to get familiar with the bottle."

Nancy nodded in agreement without saying a word.

Later that evening Nancy was again preparing to leave, this time to join Diane and her boyfriend for dinner. Turning to go, she looked back at Michael, asleep in Ron's arms. She began to cry.

"Don't worry. We'll take good care of him," I said. My heart felt a tug though. She was looking at him so longingly. It worried me.

She closed the door but then poked her head in again. "Would you guys leave tomorrow so I can have some time with Michael?" Her voice was cold and harsh. She did not wait for our answer as she pulled the door closed.

I started to cry. I felt under attack. What did she expect? This was our son too. Besides, we thought we had been as accommodating as possible. If she wanted to spend time with him, she could. We were not making her go shopping or out to dinner. The tension was building and I could not think of any way to release it except to leave.

Taking Michael in my arms, I rocked him as tears fell. We had longed for this child all our lives. He was the answer to our prayers. By staying though, it felt as if we had forfeited the opportunity to be his parents. Nancy was growing more attached. We knew this would happen, especially if she nursed. Now, instead of this being her only time with him, it felt like it would be our only time. If only we had followed our instincts.

Chapter 7

The next morning I woke to see Nancy standing next to our bed with Michael in her arms. She smiled at me and then laid Michael between Ron and me.

"Didn't Michael wake last night?" I asked.

"Yes, but I just took care of things. After all, it will be months again before you will get a full night's rest. I thought I'd give you a break." With that, she went off to take a shower.

Her remark caught me by surprise. There was such certainty in her voice, despite the tensions of last night. Watching Michael sleep, our worries seemed to melt. He was so precious. Peacefulness seemed to surround him. I could have watched him all day but that could not be.

We had promised Nancy this day alone with Michael. Although the thought of leaving Michael hurt me to the core, it seemed easier than spending another day together at the apartment. Kissing our son good-bye, it felt like we were leaving our heart behind.

Away from the apartment, Ron and I spent the day talking out our feelings as tears frequently erupted. Michael was at the top of our thoughts. We wondered what today would bring. At the mall, we bought "it's a boy" golf balls for Ron to hand out to his friends back home. We hoped we would have the privilege of celebrating in this way. The day seemed to drag. We were mentally and emotionally exhausted. Several movies provided an outlet for us to just rest. Finally, around 7:00 p.m., we headed back to the apartment.

As we entered the apartment, Nancy looked up from her magazine. She looked irritated. Perhaps she was angry we had been gone so long. I decided to ignore it. I could certainly be overly sensitive myself.

I looked in on Michael, asleep in the bassinet. Then turning to Nancy, I asked about her day.

"It was quiet. My friends from church were over. They brought this for Michael," she said, holding up a cute romper. It was thoughtful of them but again I felt a horrible conflict. I didn't know these people. Their gift was for Nancy's baby, but this was our baby. A personal gift for Nancy would have been more appropriate.

Nancy continued, "It was odd today trying to go about my routine with Michael here. Even the simplest tasks were more difficult. I can't believe how time-consuming a newborn baby is." She sounded frustrated.

I was relieved. She had gotten a taste of what it would be like raising a baby alone. The experience may have been good for her. She seemed to recognize how difficult it would be.

As we settled into bed that night, there was only one thing on our minds. Tomorrow we would be going home.

As the morning sun peered through the window on April 23rd, Ron and I woke with excitement. Today was the day. Michael was now four days old. We'd been in California twenty-eight days. We were so ready to get home.

Once again, I hadn't heard Michael during the night. Nancy had continued to nurse him despite our encouraging her to pump. I didn't care anymore though. One way or another, it would be over today.

Ron and I showered and dressed. Nancy was also getting ready. She had planned to meet with our attorney to sign the final adoption papers. Michael was asleep, for which I was grateful. It gave us some time to pack.

As Nancy was eating breakfast, I laid a gift on the table. She looked surprised.

"Oh, you shouldn't have," she said.

"We wanted to leave you something as a thank you. Although nothing we could ever do can compare to your gift, we hope this will be a special treasure to you."

"Can I open it now?"

"Please do. We thought this might be the best time. The rest of the day could be a bit busy."

Inside the large package were several smaller packages. Nancy seemed pleased as she opened each gift. One contained small cedar acorns, a dresser drawer freshener. Another was bubble bath. Nancy loved taking baths. Next, she opened a friendship plaque that had special significance to both of us.

Nancy's eyes moistened as she read it. "This is so appropriate."

"It makes me think of the times you've told us that you believe it to be God's plan for us to raise Michael," I added.

"I agree. It's beautiful. Thank you so much."

"There's one more gift," I said. We had shopped the longest for this gift. It was a gold necklace and pendent that held a Montana Yogo sapphire and Michael's birthstone, a diamond. Nancy began crying when she saw it.

"Whenever you wear it," I said, hugging her, "think of the little diamond that is living with us in Montana."

"Oh, would you put it around my neck for me?" Nancy asked with delight. Then with one last hug, Nancy left for the attorney's office.

Several hours later, Nancy arrived home.

"How did it go?" Ron asked Nancy.

She hesitated before answering. "I noticed the papers were incorrect when I started to sign them."

"Incorrect?"

"Yes, Michael's name was listed as William Michael rather than Michael William."

"How could that be?" Ron said. "I carefully gave Roger that information over the phone. How could he get that goofed up?"

"I don't know but, before I can sign them, Roger said he'd have to correct them. He asked me to come in another time."

I felt like I was going to be sick. "You didn't sign the papers?" I asked in disbelief.

"No, but I will!" Nancy added emphatically.

Looking to Ron, I saw that he was equally upset about this latest development. My mind was reeling as a million thoughts went through it. What could Roger have been thinking? He knew it was critical that Nancy sign the papers. In fact, that was the only reason we had hired him to begin with—to make sure our child was released before we left the state. There was simply no excuse. Besides, we knew from previous conversations that the documents were on his computer. It would not have taken him long to correct them. They probably could have been corrected in the time Nancy was there.

Nancy continued, trying to reassure us. "Roger and I talked for quite a while. He suggested I seek further counseling before signing the papers since I am feeling somewhat overwhelmed. He said it is a normal feeling but thought it might be easier for me to wait until another time. With you leaving today as well as the ceremony, it's already an emotional day."

I could understand her feeling overwhelmed but it wasn't fair to hold up the paperwork. Besides, she was the one who decided that today would be the best day to sign them rather than attending to it yesterday. It was by her choices that there was so much going on. Was she now simply using all this as an excuse? Besides, when did she think it was ever going to be "easy" to sign them?

I was so angry. It was as if she just wouldn't let go. By not signing, she could continue controlling the adoption, the baby, and us. I was so tired of feeling controlled.

Nancy disappeared into the bedroom. Ron and I talked in a whisper as we tried to sort out this latest twist.

"Is Roger deliberately trying to foil our adoption?" Ron asked.

"It's almost like he's giving Nancy any excuse for not signing."

"Maybe we should all go back to Roger's office and tell them both that either they are signed or it's over."

"But what purpose would that serve? I know Nancy. She won't be pushed. If she feels like she is, we'll be the ones who lose."

"I'm not sure we haven't already, but you know her best. Do you think she'll eventually sign them?"

"Yes," I answered, not feeling as confident as I sounded. "She gave us her word. Besides, at this point, the papers are meaningless. Since California law allows a six-month grace period, even if Nancy signed them, she could change her mind and take Michael back within six months. It isn't laws that have gotten us this far though. It's our relationship with Nancy and the trust between us. The true test will be the ceremony. Nancy specifically asked for the ceremony as a way of officially closing the adoption. If she goes through with that, I know she'll sign the papers," I concluded.

"Well, one thing is for sure. No matter what happens, we are leaving today, with or without Michael. I can't take another day like this."

"I agree honey. We need to know, one way or another."

As we continued to talk quietly among ourselves, the doorbell rang. It was Lynn. After Michael's birth, she had gone home for a few days to give us time together. As we opened the door, she reached to hug us both.

"How are you doing?" she asked cheerfully.

"Good, except Nancy didn't sign the papers," I said bluntly.

Lynn gasped. Worry came across her face. Just then, Nancy came out of her room. She gave Lynn a warm hug as she showed her the necklace we had given her. The conversation quickly shifted to Nancy's summary of the previous day alone with Michael. "It was so challenging. I can't believe how much work he is," Nancy concluded.

Lynn was sympathetic but I could tell her mind was still on our announcement.

"Let's fix some lunch," I said, hoping to lighten the mood.

"I'd like to nurse Michael first," Nancy said. "I'm feeling rather uncomfortable."

"He just had a bottle before you got home from the attorney's office," I said. "Why don't you pump and we'll put it in a bottle for later." Nancy looked unhappy but went to get the pump anyway.

With the sandwiches ready, Nancy remembered the non-alcoholic Cold Duck that she'd bought for this occasion. "Let's have a toast," she said, sounding more upbeat and happy.

"To Michael and Nancy," Ron said.

"And to Lynn," I added. "Thank you for being here for all of us. We appreciate you."

"And to you, Michael's parents," Nancy added, smiling.

The anxieties of the morning seemed to have passed. Happy again, we enjoyed sharing this final moment together before heading to the chapel. Then it was time to go. I picked up Michael from his bassinet and fastened him in the infant seat we had brought all the way from Montana. As I carried him to the car though, my thoughts were miles away. Would Nancy go through with the ceremony? Would she be able to give her son up for adoption? It all came down to this one moment.

Rev. Birch and Linda were waiting in the hospital chapel when we arrived. Soft, peaceful music filled the chapel. Ron proceeded to set up the video camera. We had purchased it just before leaving Montana since we wanted to videotape the ceremony. It would be a treasure for all of us but especially for Michael when he was older.

Linda came over to greet me as I set Michael's infant seat down. "How are you doing?" she asked.

Without notice, I erupted into tears, unable to respond. I felt so many different emotions. How could I ever answer her question? I was happy that Michael had been born safely, relieved that it was almost over, afraid it would end differently than planned, excited about taking our son home, and yet sad. Yes, despite the tensions of the past weeks, parting was going to be very difficult. I knew Nancy would have a tough time in the weeks to come. I wished I could save her from the sadness but knew I couldn't. It was something she would have to go through.

Quickly, I composed myself, knowing we needed to keep moving if we were to stay on schedule.

Rev. Birch instructed Nancy, holding Michael, Lynn, and Linda to sit on one side of the aisle. He then asked Ron and me to sit on the other side.

"Before I begin," Rev. Birch said, "I need to thank you once again for allowing me the honor of being a part of your adoption. I can't begin to tell you what it has meant to me. Now, if you're ready, let's begin." Nancy nodded.

Clearing his throat, Rev. Birch said,

This is a tender moment, a time that none of us will forget, for here this afternoon we have come together to witness and to bless the adoption of baby boy Michael William into the home of Ron and Denise Johnson. The circumstances that brought you all to this moment have now passed. There is no reason to reflect on what has happened. I can only say that you, Nancy, and you, Ron and Denise, have been in a unique process of open, honest, and transparent dialogue about all the ramifications of what is to happen here today and have come to the settled belief that this is to be. None of us can add to that process, because you all have accomplished such good work in establishing the foundation for the adoption today. This is also a powerful moment, for our feelings are surely on the surface shouting to us. It's a time of incredible ambivalence too. It's a time for the ultimate good-bye and ultimate hellos—a time of receiving, of loss and joy, of pain and healing, of endings and new beginnings. Therefore, it is right and proper to acknowledge those feelings, hold them up to the light of God's presence, and ask him to be near us and speak to us in this moment. In thinking about today, I searched the Scriptures for what would be appropriate to confirm and affirm what we are doing. I would like to read the following for our admonition: I Corinthians 1:3-4: 'Blessed be God and the Father of our Lord Jesus Christ, a gentle Father and the God of all consolation, who comforts us in all our sorrows, so that we can offer others, in their sorrow, the consolation that we received.' And Lamentations 3:21-23: 'This is what I shall tell my heart, and so recover hopes: the favors of Yahweh are not all past. God's kindnesses are not exhausted; every morning they are renewed; great is God's faithfulness.' And in I John the 3rd chapter in talking about love He says, 'Dear children, let us not love in words or tongue but with actions and in truth. This then is how we know that we belong to the truth...'

As Rev. Birch spoke, I felt peacefulness like never before. The anxiety and stress of the past days suddenly seemed to melt away, leaving only serenity. It was as if God had wrapped His arms around the whole room, filling it with love and holiness beyond words.

Tears were streaming down my face as Rev. Birch continued. Turning to look at Nancy, he said,

> Our words will be brief, but we need to say how much your courageous act has affected us all today. We hold you in deep respect for the ultimate act of giving that is transpiring here. You have bravely processed this letting go of Michael William with both grief and joy, motivated by your unselfish wish for his ultimate benefit. We honor you today. You, in a sense, are surrendering your needs in this act of love. Surrendering walks hand in hand with letting go. To surrender is to give over to God, to give up your power. Now you will be moving on, ever opening yourself up to the mystery of life, to the risks of the future, and to the challenge of the unknown. We trust you to a loving God who is always saying 'yes' to our good and our happiness. We know that He will be there to guide you and sustain you through whatever hardships, heartaches, and joys that life will bring. As you begin to come to grips with your good-bye and begin the hard work of the grieving process, we remind you that there is now new country awaiting you, filled with new hope and new vistas. There will be new melodies to be sung. Please remember that even in the most desolate of days, there will be seasons of springtime and new hellos that will await you.

Turning to look at Ron and me, Rev. Birch said,

> Nancy is saying good-bye today. You are saying hello. I know your hearts are full of joy but you too are feeling ambivalent. That can only be expected under these circumstances, so those feelings need to be honored and processed too. This is a new beginning for you and beginnings are

rife with expectations and promise. You will be basking in the joy of a new life entrusted into your care. The days ahead will be filled with the blessing of Michael for whom you are responsible. There will be times of challenge and frustration, times of crisis and hope. As new parents your tasks will increase in the nurturing of little Michael William to see that he eventually comes to his full potential as God created him to be. The task is demanding, challenging, and not to be taken lightly, but reverently and with humility. Our prayer for you is that love and understanding will surround your dwelling. We pray that no matter what happens in the days ahead, this young boy will always know that he was so loved by his natural mother and by you, that he will never be in doubt about being loved. That is the powerful legacy that you all will pass on to this child. We bless you and honor you for your willingness to enter into this covenant of love.

With that, Rev. Birch paused as the hymn we had chosen was played. When the hymn ended, Rev. Birch walked to Nancy. She stood, placing Michael in his arms. He then returned to the podium. "Nancy, do you have something you'd like to say?"

Trembling and fighting tears, Nancy turned to us and began reading from a piece of paper she was holding in her hand. Her voice quivered. "I believe that children are not really our possessions, but that we are all children of God."

Nancy paused to catch her breath. For a moment I wondered if she was going to be able to continue, but then her voice steadied and she proceeded. "Michael William was God's gift to me, and I am now passing that gift onto you as I feel He intended for me to do. Not keeping this baby that I love so much is the most difficult and painful thing I will ever do, but I also feel joy in knowing I am doing what is best for all of us, especially Michael."

She seemed to be gaining strength and was no longer crying. "I could never go through with an adoption if I didn't know and love the people who would raise my child. God must have known that when he gave us you. I feel so privileged to be a part of turning you, a loving couple, into a real family. Don't worry about living up to my expectations. I am totally trusting and confident that you will raise Michael much as I would, only in a better environment with more time and stability. Just be yourselves and I will be more than happy."

Nancy's voice again cracked and she started to cry again. "As you take Michael with you today, you are taking a part of me. Please love him and guide him. And when you tuck him into bed at night, always give him a kiss from me."

By now, there wasn't a dry eye in the room, including Rev. Birch's. "Please bow your heads as we say a prayer for Michael," Rev. Birch said. Placing his large hand on Michael's head, Rev. Birch continued. "As I hold this little boy who just arrived on this earth, Father, we give thanks. God, our creator, cherish this child. Jesus, our savior, protect him. Holy Spirit, our comforter, strengthen him. Michael William, God be with you. God be in your heart. May God bless and protect you. Amen"

Rev. Birch then approached us. Ron took Michael in his arms. Then turning to me, Ron placed our son in my arms and then took out the paper that held the words we had written for Nancy. Cradling Michael in one arm, I put my free hand on Ron's knee, as if to give him strength.

Turning to face Nancy, Ron cleared his throat. Fighting tears, his voice trembled and his hand shook. "Nancy, we want you to know that we accept Michael as our first born child, a gift from God and you, with love in our hearts. Along with the joy we are feeling, we understand the responsibility to raise Michael to be a good man—one who loves God. We just want to say that we love you, Nancy, and respect the courage that you have shown through this whole process. Thank you for bringing this little life into this world. We love Michael and promise to take very good care of him."

Rev. Birch then said, "Before I pray, I want you all to know what this occasion has meant to me. Your gift of love and act of kindness reverberates around the whole community. Again, I thank you for the privilege of being with you during this powerful moment. Now would you please join hands as I read our closing prayer?"

> Father of us all, we thank you for your presence with us today. As we all journey onward in life, may this moment of love and loss, of joy and pain, of good-byes and hellos be forever etched on our hearts. We

pray for Nancy, and Ron and Denise. As they experience the pain of change and the insecurity of moving on, may they also experience the blessing of inner growth. As they walk through the good times and the hard times, may they never lose sight of the shelter of your loving arms. As they question their decisions and wonder about the fruits of their choices, may your peace reign in their hearts. We praise you and thank you, God of our journeys, for little Michael William who is soon to leave with Ron and Denise to his new home in Montana. We trust him into your loving care, always knowing that you are the faithful traveler and companion on our way. Shelter Nancy and protect her from all harm and useless anxiety. May her future be a source of many enriching and transforming moments. We pray in the name of our Lord, Amen.

As Rev. Birch concluded, John Rutter's hymn "The Lord Bless You and Keep You" came over the sound system. Quietly, we all stood listening as the song filled the chapel. The tears I'd shed throughout the ceremony seemed to have washed away the pain, the anger, and the fears of the previous months, weeks, and most especially the past few days. Gone was the strain. All that remained was a quiet. It was as if God had healed my heart.

Looking down at our new son, I continued to cry. Michael was so beautiful. We were finally a family. Everything that we'd been through had been worth it. We now had a son. Our lives would never be the same.

Arriving at the airport, we stopped in the loading area and pulled our luggage from the car. We were behind schedule, so Lynn parked the car while we went into the terminal. As we approached the door, a man sitting near the door rose to meet us.

The tears Nancy had shed during our drive suddenly vanished as she cried out, "Jim!" She seemed like a college girl again, light and happy as she greeted him.

Right away, I noticed his size. He was tall with broad shoulders and had a gentle face. He had a cleft chin like Michael. Jim had promised Nancy he'd be here but even so, I was surprised he had made it. Nancy had wanted him to see Michael. She planned to take Jim to the attorney's office after we left so he could sign the papers. I hoped Nancy would also sign them while they were there. Perhaps it would be easier for her with Jim along.

Nancy seemed engrossed in Jim, so Ron and I made our way to the ticket counter, allowing them time alone with Michael. As our seats were being assigned, I anxiously looked over my shoulder at Nancy. She seemed so happy now. The tears of only moments ago were gone.

Ron was watching them too. Under his breath, I heard him whisper, "I don't think we'll be taking Michael home."

I pretended I didn't hear. We had made it through the ceremony. She wouldn't change her mind now, would she?

With our seats assigned, it was time to join Nancy. She saw us approaching. Smiling, she introduced us to Jim. We politely shook hands. I wondered what he thought of Michael, and what he thought of us.

We didn't have much time before our departure but we tried to visit. Nancy seemed distracted though. "I'm feeling pretty miserable," she said. "Could I take a moment to nurse Michael?"

It was all I could do to keep my cool. Here was that nursing issue again. Although I knew Michael would be hungry soon since he'd slept through the entire ceremony, I didn't want him to wake until after we were on the plane. I had planned to give him a bottle then. I'd heard it would help a baby if they had something to suck on as the cabin pressure changed. Besides, Nancy had taken something to calm her nerves before leaving the apartment. I didn't want Michael to ingest it.

"There really isn't time," I said, glancing at my watch. Nancy seemed disappointed.

"Let me get some pictures of the three of you," I said. "I'd like Michael to have them some day." Nancy seemed pleased at my suggestion as she thanked me.

Then it was time to go. We wandered to the gate, and our feet seemed to drag. We were dreading this time when we'd have to say good-bye. Lynn was crying as she kissed Michael, then hurriedly hugged Ron and me, and rushed away. Parting was difficult for her too.

Ron, Nancy, and I were crying as we hugged each other. Jim quietly watched the three of us embrace. I felt somewhat sorry for him. He seemed unable to comprehend the impact of this moment. It was as if he were more of a stranger than the birth father.

Finally, Nancy kissed Michael and then laid him in Ron's arms. Pausing to look at one another, Nancy and I embraced each other one more time.

"Thank you," I said. "We love you so much."

Then turning to Jim, I hugged and thanked him too. "Take good care of Michael," he said.

"We will!"

As we made our way through the security gate, I looked back at Nancy and waved. Tears were flooding my eyes but even through them, I could see her tears too.

Chapter 8

THE PLANE WAS full as it landed in Billings, Montana that evening. Of all the people on it though, we were the most excited of them all. We were finally home. Although the flight was only about fifteen minutes late, it seemed like an eternity. We could hardly wait to be home with our family.

Dozens of people were waiting in the terminal, but right away I saw Colleen and Mom. Our eyes met. From the distance, I could see they were crying. We had the baby carrier. They knew Michael was with us. Until now, they really didn't know if we'd come home with him.

Above all the noise, I heard them call out our names. Within seconds, we were in each other's arms, clutching one another tightly as we sobbed with joy. It was a good thing Michael was in his infant seat, or he might have been thoroughly squeezed.

Unveiling Michael from under his blankets, both Colleen and Mom giggled and cried at the same time while enjoying the precious addition to our family. Mom was quick to take pictures, wanting to capture this special moment.

"I didn't know you had a baby," a woman said. I looked up to see an acquaintance. She must have been the only one in town who didn't know. We had told everyone, even total strangers about our upcoming baby.

"We just brought him home," Ron announced. "Isn't he handsome?"

It seemed as if everyone was watching us. They were all smiling, watching us while we all cried tears of joy. A sense of celebration was in the air.

Making our way to baggage claim, we talked a mile a minute. Mom and Colleen were busy trying to take in every detail of Michael. Once at the conveyor belt, we found some seats while we waited for our luggage. Mom and Colleen quickly pulled Michael's limbs from his sleeper, anxious to check out his fingers and toes. Michael began to stir; he was getting hungry. He didn't seem the least bit interested in being admired.

With luggage in tow, we headed to the car. During the short trip home Michael began crying, upset that we weren't immediately attending to his needs. I was crying too, only mine were tears of joy. Never in all my life had I felt so happy.

"Oh Ron, look at the blue ribbons," I cried out as we drove up to the house. Although it was dark, I could see ribbons tied to the trees. A big bow was on the mailbox. "Your neighbors decorated the trees," Colleen explained. "Mom and I added the bow to the mailbox."

"What a wonderful welcome home," I said, tears again falling.

As soon as the car stopped, I leaped out. It felt so good to be home. Just walking up our sidewalk and opening our front door felt like such a joy. The lights were on in anticipation of our arrival. Colleen's husband Ron and their sons were waiting for us inside. They too were anxious to meet this new member of our family.

Our dog Angel immediately jumped up on us, forgetting all her manners. She was so excited to see up. She probably thought we had left her for good. After all, we had been gone for 4 weeks.

Balloons, flowers, and gifts filled the house. There was even a box of malted milk balls on the counter; they were my favorite candy. A sense of contentment like never before enveloped me. We were so fortunate. We had a place to come home to, family and friends to greet us, and most especially, a child of our own. Life was complete.

Feeding Michael while we visited, we tried to be quiet to not wake up our nephews. It was such fun hearing about what had been happening at home since we'd left. Our family was also most anxious to hear about our trip. We could tell them so little though. Our outings to Universal Studios, the zoo, and especially our chance encounter with Uncle Don and Aunt Peg all had to remain a secret.

To share would have revealed our location and thus Nancy's identity. Those memories would have to remain between Nancy, Ron, and me.

It was close to midnight when we decided to go to bed. Although my adrenaline was still pumping, we all needed the rest. After all, Michael and my nephews weren't likely to sleep in just because we adults stayed up late.

Saying goodnight, Ron and I carried Michael downstairs. Laying him in his cradle, we kissed him goodnight. Then, arm in arm, we watched him as he slept. It was all we could do to pull ourselves away from him, but finally we headed to bed. At last, we were in our bed, snuggled together. Behind us lay the months of anticipation and worry. Despite the doubts and fears, everything had turned out as planned. Nancy had given us Michael. He was our son. We could now start our new life as a family.

Morning arrived with Michael's cry. It was time to eat again. He had woken at 4:00 a.m. and downed a bottle but heavens, that was three hours ago! Pulling on my bathrobe, I hastened to get him.

Upstairs, Colleen and Mom were already up, attending to Jacob. After warming Michael's bottle, I joined them in the living room. While Colleen breast-fed Jacob, I fed Michael his bottle.

Glancing at Colleen, we smiled at each other. No words were needed as tears again welled in our eyes. At last, we were sharing motherhood. We'd talked about this privilege since we were little girls. We always planned to have children close in age. Perhaps they would be good friends. We couldn't imagine it being any other way since we were so close.

Already, I could visualize the two of us sharing notes about our children, discussing our joys, frustrations, and worries. I could hardly wait until I could call Colleen for some advice on parenting. What fun it would be to load up all our children and take them to visit our family in Helena. None of this was discussed though. We'd already talked about it many times throughout our lives. Now it would finally happen.

Except for the sounds of two hungry babies sucking, the room was quiet. Mom too remained silent as she watched us feed our babies. Tears moistened her eyes too. I could tell she was proud of her two girls. As the day came to life that early morning, so did the dreams of our whole family.

Colleen and her family were going to go home. She wanted Ron and me to have some time alone with Michael, knowing we'd been sharing our son from the moment of his birth. Before they left though, Ron and I decided to tell them about our pregnancy. After all, I was two months along. I don't think I'd ever kept a secret from Mom and Colleen that long.

"I need some advice in the nursery," I announced. Everyone obediently followed us into the nursery, obviously uncertain why it was necessary for all of us to be there.

"I just can't figure out where to put the second crib," I hinted. "Any ideas?"

They stared at me with a blank look, completely missing the huge hint I had just dropped.

"We'll need another crib in November for Michael's brother or sister," I said.

Mom was instantly in tears as she kept repeating over and over, "When?"

Colleen was bombing us with questions. She thought we were kidding, while her husband Ron was watching us with a look of disbelief, trying to determine if we were serious.

"We found out just before we left," I explained. "We're going to have two babies by the end of the year."

"I can't believe this," Colleen said, still stunned. "This will be like having twins!"

Anthony was squealing with delight as I explained he was going to have another cousin. "Another one besides Michael William?" he asked.

"Yes. Uncle Ron and I are going to need your help with all these babies."

The next few days were hectic. There was a steady stream of visitors anxious to see Michael; flowers and cards also arrived daily to welcome him. Mom stayed a few days to help us get organized. Having been gone so long, there was much to do. It was so nice to have her help. She did the laundry, put Michael's clothes in the dresser, sorted mail, cleaned the house, addressed birth announcements, and helped me get bills paid. She even babysat one morning so Ron and I could get groceries and long overdue haircuts.

She was thrilled to finally spend time with her new grandson. Already she was visualizing the fun we'd have as a family. One afternoon, the ice cream cart went by playing carnival music. "Oh Michael," Mom said, holding him close. "We're going to have so much fun eating ice cream on the steps when you get a little bigger."

Mom expressed admiration to me as she watched us adapting to life with our son. "I can see so much love between you and Ron," she said. "And the love you have for Michael radiates from you."

"Oh, Mom," I said. "I've never felt anything like this. The love for your child is so different from anything else. And never would I have imagined that I could love Ron more than I already did. This must be why God intended children to be a blessing of marriage. With Michael, we've not only been blessed with his life but our marriage has deepened. We are the luckiest people. We love our Michael so much."

I needed to make doctor appointments for Michael and myself. Calling the clinic, I made one for Michael's two check-ups. I then asked for a prenatal appointment with Dr. Fellows' nurse.

"Do you mean postnatal?" the receptionist asked.

"No, this is for my pregnancy. I'm two months along."

The phone was quiet. She was obviously confused. I chuckled as I filled her in on our situation.

"Oh, how exciting," she said. "What a wonderful year you're having." It seemed that everyone was getting caught up in our excitement.

We had been home three days when Nancy called. She sounded content as she described what she'd been doing since we left.

"I had a long visit with my counselor Connie. I am beginning to feel like things are leveling out for me. Denise, I feel so good about my decision to give Michael to you and Ron. I know he will have a wonderful life with you. Now I can get on with my plans."

Relief swept over me. I wanted her to be able to go on and find the kind of happiness we now felt. "So when will you see Connie again?" I asked.

"She's left that up to me. She thinks I am doing really well so suggested I call only if I need. With my parents arriving shortly, I'm not sure I'll have much time so I didn't make another appointment."

It worried me that she had no plans to continue her counseling but I understood. She had so much to accomplish yet.

"How are things going for you?" Nancy asked. "How is Michael?"

"We're all doing really well. Michael is already on a schedule. Ron is taking turns with the night shifts in order to allow me extra rest. Just between us though, I think he's really looking for an excuse to spend time alone with Michael. Ron is a wonderful father."

"I knew he would be. That is what I wanted for Michael. By the way," Nancy added, "I found some things you left. I'll get them in the mail tomorrow. I need to get rid of the baby evidence!"

I wanted to ask if she'd signed the papers yet, particularly since she sounded so confident. I hesitated though, not wanting to appear pushy. Besides, I knew she would have to take care of them soon since she would be leaving the state.

"Just be patient," I told myself.

Later that afternoon a note arrived from Nancy. It was dated the day after we'd left.

Dear Ron and Denise,

Thank you so much for all you did for Michael and me. I cannot thank you enough for the gifts, flowers, and for just being there. As

you may have noticed, Michael's birth father didn't do anything. I know Michael will appreciate that you were so good to his birth mother during this time.
Love, Michael's birth mother.

I loved hearing from Nancy but upon reading the signature, I felt anxious. It almost seemed as if she was pushing her birthright in my face, as if to remind me. I wasn't going to forget though. I loved her for being Michael's birth mother but I wished she had signed the card "Nancy," just as she always used to. In time, I hoped our friendship could again resurface—the one between Denise and Nancy, rather than the adoptive mother and birth mother.

I had great intentions of being the perfect wife and mother. At home full time with our son, I planned to be showered and looking fresh as I served Ron breakfast before he left for work. Then, on his way out the door, I would have a kiss for him, one of those that would send him rushing home after work. What a dreamer!

Instead, after a 2:00 a.m. feeding, Michael was up at 6:30 a.m. Ron fixed his own breakfast while I fed our son and cleared my head of the cobwebs. Instead of the passionate kiss and fresh attire, there was a tired wife still in her bathrobe, hair standing on end. He didn't seem to mind, but how he hated to leave us. He didn't want to miss out on anything. Hanging around the house until the last possible moment, he found every excuse to delay. It was time to get back to real life though. One of us had to keep food on the table.

For me, between jet lag, new motherhood, and my pregnancy, I felt pretty worn out. I took advantage of Michael's naps and took one myself. On some days, simply getting showered and dressed seemed a big accomplishment. I couldn't have been happier though, as I savored each day with Michael.

Ron too was on top of the world. There was a new spring in his step. Each night he rushed home, eager to be with us. I always loved having him home. It was fun being together as a family. He helped with dinner and Michael's care. Neither one of us could seem to get enough of our little guy.

Even our dog Angel seemed to adapting to the newest member of our family. Whenever I fed Michael, she was so attentive, watching nearby. If his toes happened to poke out from under his sleeper, she would promptly lick them. She already seemed so protective and was right at my side whenever Michael cried. I couldn't help thinking of days ahead when Michael's giggles would fill the room as he and his dog played together.

A package from Nancy arrived, and I opened it, anxious to see what she had sent. Inside were some clothes, bottle liners, and a few envelopes with her handwriting. There was also a Xerox copy of a brochure.

"I found this in some of the information at St. John's. I thought you might want to subscribe," Nancy had written. It was a newsletter for adoptive families.

I noticed an article about a couple who adopted a child. When the baby was three months old, the birth mother told them she was taking it back. Suddenly I was nervous, recalling the long grace period. What if Nancy did something like that? A knot tightened in my stomach. I felt so vulnerable.

Then I thought of our endless conversations with Nancy. I knew I was being paranoid and scolded myself for even thinking about it. However, I finished reading the article anyway, noting the birth mother eventually left the baby with the adoptive parents after seeing how content it was with them.

Despite Nancy's suggestion we subscribe to the brochure, I thought better of it. Ron and I were adamant that there be no distinction between Michael and our birth children. Michael was an equal part of our family, regardless of how he came into it. A monthly adoption publication might only make him feel different. Perhaps I'd feel differently in time, but for now I just wanted to enjoy my son.

I turned my attention to a large envelope. It looked like it could be a card. Opening it, I was surprised to see a baby card with the same title and poem as the baby book Mom had given Michael. It was called "God's Masterpiece." I read the verse and then Nancy's message at the bottom:

I know this sounds like I'm bragging, but I can't help it. I know you'll understand! Remember looking at our newly born son in the delivery room and being so in awe of how delicately and perfectly God had created him? You do have a wonderful baby boy! Continue to love and enjoy him through all your years as you come together as a family.

All my love and best wishes, Michael's birth mother

Also included in the card was a typed letter:

Dear Denise and Ron:

Looking back on our entire story and the birth of little Michael, I think you probably agree that our little guy is one of God's most precious and beautiful masterpieces. I have loved Michael since the day I discovered I was carrying him. But as you know, that was also a very confusing and difficult time for me. I am so proud of my little guy; how he and I went through so much together and both came through it so well. God was surely with us. And I think Michael will be very much like me—a survivor and someone who would do anything for those I love.

I know that passing Michael into your care is the best choice I could have made for his well-being. In today's world, I feel it is so important that he have both a mother and father to love, guide and nurture him in a healthy, stable environment. You are such good, loving people and such a great "team." I admire you and your relationship so much. I hope you will continue to put your marriage first in your lives and to be each other's best friend. Your strong and positive relationship will also be best for Michael. Although you have accepted a blessing into your lives, you have also accepted a big responsibility—one I'm sure you, with God's help, will handle beautifully. You have my highest confidence and respect.

I look forward to our contact through the years to come. In fact, these thoughts are the only thing that get me through these difficult days when I am missing my child so much. I believe we will share much joy in the coming years. I realize you will be Michael's "real" parents and that he will love you in that way. But I also hope he will not forget me and my special love for him. My heart will always feel the pain of my separation from him.

Please always make sure Michael understands how much his birth parents wanted the best for him. We will always love him. We both hope that when he is old enough, he will want to meet us. Of course, we will always keep in touch with you and be willing to help with anything you may ever need from us. We can never adequately express our thanks for your love and care for our child. You are such a blessing in his life as I know you feel he is in yours. Best wishes for a wonderful life together.

In love and friendship, Michael's birth mother

I was crying. I felt such gratitude to Nancy for blessing us with Michael. Her words were such a comfort. They assured me that what we'd accomplished in the past months was what we all had desired.

Looking back in the box, I saw two matching purple envelopes. The first contained the words Nancy had said to us at the adoption ceremony. The other envelope had the following typed on the outside:

Ron and Denise:
    This note is for your family members, with special consideration for Grandma D. and Aunt Colleen. Please share my message with each of Michael's new loved ones.
Thank you! The Mother

Anxious to see she'd written, I opened the envelope. The note was dated April 26th, one week after Michael's birth:

Dear extended family of Michael,
    I want you to know how important each of you were in my decision to ask Denise and Ron to be the parents of my child. Besides wanting both a mother and father to love, guide, and devote time to him, I

wanted Michael to be surrounded by the love of aunts, uncles, cousins, grandmothers and grandfathers. I have heard about each of you, from the oldest to the youngest. You are each very dear to my heart, as I know you will be to Michael.

I am not sure if you can imagine how extremely difficult it is to pass on God's gift of a child. Michael is such a part of me and he has my deepest love. To me, he is the most beautiful and perfect child a person could ever be blessed with. To pass him into your family's care was a painful but loving decision. I have such high hopes for Michael and I want the best for him. I believe you are the best.

Thank you for your love and acceptance of Michael as a true part of your family and your lives. God bless each of you.

With love and gratitude, Michael's birth mother

We'd been home about ten days when Mrs. Madsen arrived to finalize the home study process. She was anxious to see Michael too.

"It's as if he knows how much he's loved," she said, looking in on him as he slept. "He seems so at peace with you." It warmed my heart to hear her comments. "How was your trip?" she asked.

"Long!" we both responded.

"But it was worth it," Ron added.

"I wish you could have been at our adoption ceremony," I said. "It was so beautiful." Tears welled in her eyes as we described it. She was such a loving Christian woman and understood the significance of our ceremony.

"So where is the paperwork?" she asked.

"Our attorney forwarded copies of Jim's relinquishment papers this week," Ron said as he pulled them from a file. "We're still waiting on Nancy to sign them."

Mrs. Madsen's face immediately clouded with concern. Seeing her concern, I promptly added, "She promised to sign them soon. I expect we'll get them any day."

My assurance seemed to offer no comfort. "You mean your attorney didn't secure the relinquishment papers before you left?" Mrs. Madsen asked in disbelief.

"No. Believe me, we're not too happy about that ourselves," Ron said as he described what happened.

"I can't believe this. The baby should have been released before you left. Furthermore, for him to suggest more counseling was beyond his professional expertise. That's for counselors to determine, not lawyers."

"That was our opinion too but we didn't feel there was anything we could do about it."

Still shaken, she ended our visit. "I'm sorry but we simply can't proceed any farther. Let me know when the papers have arrived."

Several more days passed. I couldn't take it anymore. I was angry. How could Nancy keep us waiting like this? Mrs. Madsen's words worried me. Besides, I was tired of feeling as if we were under a microscope. We had our son now. All we wanted to do was go on with our life like any other family. It was just so wrong of Nancy to keep us dangling. I decided to write her a letter:

Dear Nancy,

It was so nice to get your package with your very touching cards and words. We will treasure them always. Our social worker was here and she was disturbed to learn that the papers had not been signed. We cannot proceed without them. I know you're busy but we would appreciate your attention to them as soon as possible. We are so anxious to get on with our life and to be the family you intended. We believe we have met and honored all your expectations. Please allow us to fulfill our promise to you.

Love, Ron and Denise

I hoped my letter didn't appear pushy, but I could not remain quiet any longer.

Arriving at the doctor's office for Michael's first appointment, the nurse instructed me to undress him. *What?* I thought to myself. *After going to such efforts to have him in cute clothes, now you want me to take them all off?* The nurse didn't seem apologetic though so I did as she'd instructed.

It had been a wild morning getting ready for this first outing alone. I felt so clumsy carrying all the baby things along with Michael. I wondered if all new mothers felt so awkward at first. Arriving on time even felt like a victory.

Soon the doctor appeared. I told him of Michael's birth and gave him the records from California. The doctor looked him over. "He is really strong for only being two weeks old. And look how much he's grown; eight pounds, eleven ounces." Dr. Jones said. "You have a very healthy boy."

I smiled, feeling myself swell with pride. It was wonderful hearing such good things from the doctor. Leaving the office, I made another appointment for Michael's first immunizations.

When we were home, I called Ron. Upon hearing the positive report, Ron proudly said, "That's my boy!"

I then called Nancy. We'd been in touch often since arriving back in Montana and I knew she'd love to hear about Michael's growth. She wasn't home though so I left a message on her machine.

It was later that afternoon while I was napping with Michael when Nancy returned my call. Michael was snuggled next to me, so I answered the phone quietly. Nancy sounded frantic as she asked, "Denise, is everything all right?"

"Yes, everything is fine. Why?"

"When I heard your message, I thought something was wrong with Michael."

"Oh, no, he's doing great. He had his first appointment. The doctor was very happy about his growth. I just thought you'd like to know how well he's doing." For the life of me, I couldn't understand why my message had made Nancy think something was wrong.

Nancy still sounded upset though. I tried to reassure her, filling her in on the details.

"Are you sure he's not gaining too much weight?" she interrupted.

"No, Nancy," I said with exasperation. "Like I said, the doctor was very pleased. He wants us to continue exactly what we're doing."

Nancy continued to fuss, questioning every detail. I began to feel angry. It was as if she was questioning how we were caring for him. Didn't she think we could handle it? I wished I hadn't even called her.

"So how is the packing coming?" I asked, trying to change the subject.

"Fine. I still have lots of do though." Nancy sounded despondent. I could hear her crying.

"Have you been talked with Connie lately?" I asked.

"No, I haven't had time."

"Perhaps you need to make some time."

"My parents will be here soon. I don't think it will work out."

Her tone made me worry. Things were definitely coming down on her. There was so much going on between her parents' pending arrival, packing in order to move, and having to say goodbye to Jim, not to mention giving birth and placing her son up for adoption. It was no wonder she was feeling overwhelmed.

"Nancy," I persisted. "Your mental health is important too. I really think you need to see Connie."

"I'll try." Then gathering herself, she said, "By the way, I sent all my maternity clothes to you. I hope you don't mind. I had to get them out of here. Besides, I know you'll need them soon."

"Thanks Nancy. I appreciate it."

Distracted for the moment, Nancy again sounded composed as we ended our conversation. Then she started to cry again.

"I can hear Michael in the background. I miss him so much." Michael was cooing, having woken when the phone rang.

"I know you do Nancy. We miss you too," I said. By now, I just wanted to get off the phone. The whole conversation bothered me. As I said goodbye, I again encouraged Nancy to call Connie. I knew Nancy's emotions must have been like a roller coaster. As friends, particularly over the past six months, we had shared our closest feelings. Naturally, she was feeling sad and missing Michael. I knew she always would at some level but I also knew how happy she was with her decision to place Michael with us. Once she settled back into school and was busy with her new life, I knew she would find happiness again.

I said a quick prayer for Nancy and then turned my attention to Michael who was in need of a diaper change.

Michael was two weeks old the night we celebrated our fourth anniversary. Typically, we took a vacation day and prepared a special dinner at home. Since Ron couldn't afford any more time away from work we simply planned a special meal together.

As I set the dinner table, I began to laugh. In the past years, we had gone to great lengths to set the table with pretty place mats, our best dishes, and candlelight. Tonight was a huge contrast though. Instead of a neat, romantic dinner setting, a stack of unsorted mail as well as thank-you notes that needed to be mailed filled the table. In the middle of it all was our precious son, sound asleep in the infant seat. There simply wasn't room for place mats or romantic candlelight.

As Ron sat down to the table, I noticed he still had a burp cloth over his shoulder. He was completely unaware of his latest accessory. Despite the contrast though, we couldn't have been happier. Michael was the greatest blessing of our marriage. This 4th anniversary was truly an anniversary to celebrate. Finally we had a child of our own.

At 4:00 a.m. Michael started stirring. Ron got out of bed as he had done so many other mornings. Like many new parents, he was sounding tired.

"Thank you, honey," I whispered, trying to encourage him. It was so nice of him to let me rest. I was feeling tired. Thankfully, though, Michael was an easy baby. Besides, with my first trimester almost over, I'd been told I'd have more energy soon.

I heard the water in the kitchen sink running. Ron was warming the bottle. Moments later, Michael quieted as his daddy picked him up. I know I could have gone back to sleep, but I loved eavesdropping through the baby monitor as Ron tenderly talked to his son

"There, there. Daddy's here. I know you are hungry but let's get some dry pants first. You'll feel much better once we have that done." Ron's voice was tender as he gently talked to his son.

Michael continued to cry as Ron changed his diaper. Soon I heard Michael's noisy sucking sounds. I could almost see him looking up at Ron, his eyes wide, watching his daddy. My heart felt full. Already they were becoming such good buddies.

Michael was getting much more alert. I held him for hours, enjoying our time together. It was no wonder I was getting so little else done. Michael was just too much fun for me to be distracted with routine duties.

Time was flying by. Every day it seemed there was something to do. There was the baby shower the neighborhood women held, doctor appointments for my pregnancy, or lunch with Daddy. Ron and I were having so much fun, enjoying any excuse to show off our son. With each day, we were becoming more confident as we adjusted to our new life. Even the small things, like Michael's first bath, added to our confidence.

I called Colleen often, sharing the joys of our son. It was so fun comparing notes on the things our little boys were doing. She was so happy for us. Sharing motherhood was definitely the most fun we'd ever had.

When the phone rang that afternoon, I answered it to hear Nancy crying. Her counselor had warned her that she would experience grief, similar to the grief associated with death, because of the adoption. I knew she was there—it was inevitable, particularly combined with hormonal changes after giving birth.

Hearing Nancy's tears, I thought of when Dad died. Never before had I felt so torn apart. I would have done anything to have him back. In my selfishness, I would have chosen him to live again just so my life wouldn't have been so empty. That would have been unfair though. No one deserved to suffer as he did. His pain was over and he was living in glory with Jesus. I, in time, had to learn to live with my own pain and loss.

I tried to comfort Nancy. I knew she had never lost anyone that close before. She probably felt as if she would die, just as I did when we lost dad. She needed comfort and support, but I wasn't sure I was the person to help her. After all, the baby she grieved was now my child.

"Nancy, of course you miss Michael," I consoled. "Remember, Connie told you there would be times like this. You really need to see her. She can help you."

Nancy seemed exasperated by my response. "I don't have time."

"I think it would really help you," I offered.

"Well, I'll see."

Abruptly, she ended the conversation. My own heart was hurting as I hung up the phone, feeling her pain. I wished I could help her but how? Suddenly, I remembered that I had both Connie and Linda's phone numbers. Pouring through the stack of adoption papers, I located them.

Linda was in. Without even greeting her, I blurted out my conversation with Nancy.

"Could you call her and see if you can help?"

"Certainly, I'll call her right away."

Still feeling upset, I then called Connie. By now, I was crying. Stammering over my words, I spilled my thoughts. "I love Nancy so much. I just don't know how to help her."

"You just did by calling me. I'll phone her right away and set up an appointment, even if it has to be after hours."

"Oh, thank you so much. Please let me know if there is anything more I can do."

Hanging up the phone, I felt better knowing I had done all I could. I now had to trust that Nancy would accept their help.

It was Mother's Day weekend. We planned to take Michael to Helena to meet his family. He was already three weeks old and our family was so anxious to see him. We were excited to share him with them.

Michael was a wonderful traveler, waking only once during the four-hour trip. As we pulled into my grandparents' driveway, Grandma came rushing out of the house. Tears were streaming down her face.

"Where's the baby?" she cried. Then taking Michael into her arms, she swooned, "Oh, he's so perfect, so handsome." You certainly could never tell that she was his great-grandmother!

Granddad was standing at the door. Tears rolled down his cheeks as he admired his newest great-grandson. They already loved him so much.

It was so good to be with our family again. Granddad and Grandma's home always felt so comfortable. As I stepped into the house, I could tell Grandma had baked. The house smelled of homemade breads and cookies.

Michael was the center of attention as loving relatives held and kissed him. He seemed very unconcerned as everyone fussed over him. Once again, I was filled with complete contentment as the love of our family surrounded us. I was so grateful that Michael was a part of this wonderful group of people.

After lunch, a baby shower was on the agenda for Michael. The guests would be arriving soon. With Michael asleep on my grandparents' bed, I proceeded to freshen up. I would have loved to take a nap but there wasn't time. Besides, my pregnancy was still a secret. I didn't want to tip off the rest of my family. We had decided we'd tell them this weekend though. At three months along, I probably wasn't going to be able to hide it much longer. Besides, we wanted to tell them in person rather than over the phone.

Emerging from the bedroom, I noticed the pretty decorations now arranged around the house. Everything looked so nice. Soon the guests arrived. It was like homecoming. I saw friends I hadn't seen in years.

"What is the hardest thing about being a parent?" one asked.

Without hesitating, I responded, "Becoming one. From here on out though, everything will be a cakewalk. I'm just so glad it's over."

It's good I didn't know what lie ahead.

The sunshine streaming through the window at mom's house awakened me. I hadn't heard Michael during the night. Panicking, I jumped out of bed and rushed to his crib. He was peacefully sleeping. I took a deep breath as a sense of relief swept over me. Everything was fine. Michael had simply slept through the night.

What a perfect child, I thought to myself. *He let his mommy sleep all night. He must have known today was Mother's Day.*

Before long though, Michael was stirring, ready for breakfast. With his usual inquiring eyes, he watched us as we each took turns feeding him and prepared for the day.

Grandma had planned a Mother's Day brunch. When we arrived, preparations were already underway. I could smell Grandma's homemade cinnamon rolls from the driveway.

"Relax with the baby," Grandma encouraged us as we came through the door. "I have plenty of help." That was always Grandma's way, serving others first.

Eager to share Michael's baby book as well as Nancy's letter, I took advantage of the moment and shared her letter. Granddad struggled with emotion as he read her letter. Trying to compose himself, he cleared his throat. "She must be a very brave and courageous woman," he managed to choke out.

"She is! You would really like her." I already knew they did however for, unbeknown to them, she was the young woman who had spent several Easter weekends with our family. They loved her like one of us. It seemed so fitting that we could now love her child as such too.

"Time to eat," Grandma called out causing everyone to move to the kitchen. We all knew that food at Grandma's table was never a disappointment.

Gathering in the kitchen, I winked at Mom and Colleen sitting across the table. I had warned them that we planned to announce our pregnancy during grace since as usual I had the honors. Ron was standing away from the table trying to videotape our gathering discretely. Meanwhile, Colleen had secretly tucked a camera in her lap in order to capture the moment.

"Now, you aren't going to make me cry, are you?" Aunt Pat asked.

"Oh, no," I winked. I had a bit of a reputation for long and emotional blessings. Bowing our heads, I began, "Dear God, thank you for allowing us to be together on this special Mother's Day Sunday." As usual, I was already crying but I continued, "Thank you also for these wonderful mothers that provide such a beautiful example for us new mothers. Especially, thank you for our children and the upcoming blessing of Michael's little brother or sister in November. Amen."

I could feel Grandma's hand on my arm. "Oh, honey," she cried out. Tears were streaming down her face. Granddad was also crying, shaking his head in disbelief.

"Well, if Colleen is going to have two children, we aren't going to be outdone," I joked.

Needless to say, we spent a great deal of the meal discussing our children.

"Won't Christmas be wonderful with all the babies?" Grandma said, still crying.

"Yes," I replied, "and every day from now on."

It was time for us to get back on the road to go home. Before going though, Ron handed me a little box, neatly wrapped in pink paper.

"Michael asked me to give this to you."

I smiled at him. Ron was always so thoughtful. I loved being the mommy to his son.

Curiously, I looked at the package. It had a big yellow card attached. "MOM" had been crudely written across it. Reading the card, my heart warmed, seeing "Luv Michael" roughly printed at the bottom. Then turning to the box, I unwrapped it. A beautiful gold chain and pendant shaped in the letter J lay inside.

"It's a mother's necklace," Ron said. "The 'J' shape is for Johnson. Pointing to the diamond for Michael, he added tenderly, "There's room for a few more stones." Besides Michael's birthstone, there was also a sapphire that matched my wedding ring.

In typical form, I began crying. Gently I kissed Michael's head. Then turning to Ron, I hugged him. "Thank you honey. Thank you for helping me become a mother. I will never forget this day. You've made me the happiest woman alive."

"And so have you," I said, whispering to our sleeping Michael.

Chapter 9

MICHAEL WAS NAPPING. The house was quiet except for the sounds of a distant radio. Taking advantage of the time, I was writing thank-you notes for the baby shower. I felt such peace and contentment as I reflected on the events of the previous weekend. What fun we'd had sharing Michael and the news of his upcoming sibling.

The phone rang, stirring me from my thoughts. It was Nancy. I was happy to hear her voice. We chatted cheerfully about what she'd been doing—mostly sunbathing and packing. Since I knew her parents were there, I was careful not to ask anything that she would find difficult answering in front of them.

Suddenly, the conversation shifted. "Denise, I have to take Michael back!" Nancy blurted out.

I felt like someone had just knocked the wind out of me as a wave of nausea and panic swept through my body. "Nancy, you're grieving right now!" I responded in a weak whisper.

"No, Denise," she said abruptly. "I have to do this. I tried to call Ron at work but he was gone so I called you instead. I'll be there Wednesday at 2:00."

I tried to stay composed, but my mind was a blur. I could not believe what I was hearing. Nancy sounded adamant, like she'd made up her mind. I didn't understand. Just a little over a week ago, she affirmed her belief that the adoption was the right decision. The sadness she expressed on the phone during our last conversation was a natural part of the grief process.

"How could you do this to us?" I asked. "You're the one who asked us to adopt him, remember? You promised you'd never take him back."

"But you said I could change my mind."

"Yes, you could have at the appropriate time—before you gave him to us but not now. You gave us your word."

"I know," Nancy said as she started to cry. "I just can't live without him." Her words were tumbling out as she went on, her voice filled with tears. "Denise, you've got to understand that I've been taking drugs just to go on. I know you will never want to speak to me again but I have to take Michael back. I'm an intelligent and well-educated person and I can raise him." I wasn't sure if she was trying to convince herself or me.

"Nancy, that was never the question. I know you are intelligent and there was never any doubt you could raise him. But you're the one who wanted him to have two parents." Then it occurred to me, "You told your folks, didn't you?"

"Yes, but they didn't have anything to do with my decision." She sounded defensive as she added, "I've been seeing a *professional* adoption counselor who helped me see that I need to start thinking about myself rather than everyone else."

I gasped. Whom did she think she was kidding? Nancy had thought about herself throughout the process. In fact, such narrow-minded thought had caused incredible pain for us—her desire for anonymity, her desire to nurse, her desire for us to stay a few days after Michael's birth. The list went on. Now she was telling me that she hadn't thought of herself? It was simply absurd!

Besides, once she gave Michael to us she no longer had the luxury of just thinking of herself. Other people were now involved, namely Michael, Ron, our families, and myself. Where did she ever get the idea that she was the only one that needed to be considered?

And who was this so-called "professional" counselor? What about Connie who had been her counselor throughout the process? Or Linda at the hospital? My head was spinning as I tried to sort things out. Tears were streaming down my face. I searched for something brilliant to say—anything to convince her to change her mind.

I started to talk but she cut me off.

"Denise, when you're a mother and have a child of your own, you'll understand."

I began losing control as hysteria took over. Sobbing, I screamed into the phone, "How dare you tell me that I'm not a mother. Who do you think has been Michael's mother the past three weeks?"

"I mean when you have one of your own."

"Michael is our own child as much as the one we're carrying. If we didn't feel that way, we'd have never come to California."

Nancy was quiet on the other end of the phone as I continued crying. "We'll be calling our lawyer to see what we're going to do. I'll call you back tonight." With that, I slammed down the phone.

Trembling, I called Ron's office. I remembered that he was in a meeting that afternoon. His boss John would know where I could reach him. Mustering as much composure as possible, I asked to speak to John. He must have sensed my hysteria as he quickly looked up the location of Ron's meeting without asking questions. Calling the number, I explained to the secretary that I needed to get a message to my husband. She started to give me an excuse.

"This is an emergency," I blurted out. By now, I was crying again. "I'm sorry," I said. "It's just terribly important that I talk to him."

"It's all right. I'll try to locate him." She put me on hold. Soon she was back. "I'm sorry. The meeting just broke up. Everyone is already gone."

"Thank you anyway. I'll try back at his office."

Again, I called the office. Ron had not arrived so I left word for him to call me immediately. Hanging up the phone, the house suddenly seemed deadly quiet. I paced in a state of numbness, waiting for Ron to call. Finally, after what seemed like an eternity, but was only minutes, the phone rang.

Hearing Ron's voice, I broke down. Completely out of control, I choked out Nancy's call. I could hear Ron struggling, trying to keep himself together.

"She sounded so definite," I explained, "like she won't be changing her mind."

"I'll be right home," he said.

The house was again quiet. As if by reflex, I began angrily gathering everything that even reminded me of Nancy. Picking up each item, I sobbed. The picture she had given me for my birthday, childhood and college mementos, the teddy bear she'd sent when Dad died, the items we'd brought back from California, absolutely everything that brought thoughts of Nancy I stuffed into a grocery sack. If Nancy was going to take our child, I wanted nothing left to remind me of her. She had betrayed our friendship and our trust. If that was the kind of person she was, I wanted her out of my life.

Going in and out of the nursery as I gathered items, I couldn't even look at Michael as he slept in his crib. I felt as if my heart would virtually rip out of my chest at the sight of him.

As I picked up Michael's silver cup, I hesitated before putting it in the bag. The cup had been a gift from Lynn; it was engraved with Michael William Johnson. I knew it would be of no use to Nancy the way it was engraved, but it would be so painful for me to keep so I put it in the bag. "Perhaps this will remind Nancy who this child is," I said aloud.

Before long, I heard Ron drive up. When he entered the house, we clung to each other, sobbing. After some time, Ron called our Montana attorney. We hoped he'd know what to do, but he wasn't in so Ron left a message.

Within moments, our attorney returned the call. "I just heard," he said. "Roger called from California."

"What can we do?" Ron asked.

"Quite honestly, since Nancy never signed the papers, there is nothing you can do."

"What about the papers we signed at the hospital, the ones giving us responsibility for his medical care and custody? Do they mean anything?"

"No, unfortunately they don't. And even if they did, state law protects the birth mother with the six month grace period."

"There must be something we can do!"

"Well, you could ask Nancy to present you with papers in order to release you from custody since you did assume that at the hospital. It's up to you, though. You wouldn't have to give the baby back until she presented them to you."

After Ron hung up the phone, he relayed the conversation.

"Even though we could ask Nancy for release papers," he said, "I'm afraid it will only prolong the inevitable. In fact, it might also only cement her decision to take him back. If there is even a remote chance of her changing her mind, I think we need to remain non-threatening."

"But I doubt she'll change her mind. She sounded very determined."

"So where does that leave us?"

"We can't give him up, honey," I sobbed. "He's our son. All we ever wanted was children. I would never give mine up. How could she force us to do this?"

"Well, it doesn't sound like there are any choices legally."

"What about illegally then?"

Ron's eyes widened as if unable to believe what I was saying.

"I know it sounds crazy," I continued, "but if we're not here, Nancy can't take him. At the very least, it might stall things long enough to figure out what's going on."

He pulled me close, hugging me. "I know what you're thinking and believe me, it's crossed my mind as well but we both know that's not possible. It's irresponsible and illogical."

"No more irresponsible or illogical than Nancy's decision," I said, spitting out my reply. "Besides, she's the one who put us in this position of feeling like we have to run away."

"I know. I guess the fact that it has even entered our minds shows how desperate we are. But we can't leave. We have our home, our family and our jobs. We have obligations—"

"Yes, those same obligations that make us stable to be Michael's parents! Instead, they're trapping us here, vulnerable to Nancy and her whims. I'd give it all up for Michael though."

"I would too honey but we can't spend the rest of our lives looking over our shoulders. We do not deserve that kind of life. Neither does Michael. Besides, what kind of parents would we be for him?"

"Better than Nancy," I offered bitterly. "She doesn't have a job or a home, not to mention a father for Michael. She didn't even plan to have a baby. At least we have always wanted him. Just because she's taking drugs in order to go on, she's the one who should have him? What does she think raising a child alone will be like? What kinds of things will she turn to when parenting becomes tough? Talk about irresponsible."

"I know," Ron said sadly. He was crying too.

We were both quiet for a moment, then Ron spoke up. "What do you think caused her to change her mind?"

"I've been trying to figure that out. I could understand if something had changed, like Jim marrying her, but nothing has changed. Three weeks ago, she gave Michael to us with God as her witness. Two weeks ago, she told us how happy she was in giving Michael to us. All her letters to us have confirmed that she believes she made the best decision. I've been concerned about her sadness recently on the phone, but I never had any indication that she was changing her mind. It just doesn't make sense."

"Do you suppose this so-called professional counselor had anything to do with it?"

"Who knows but I suspect this counselor is someone she met at St. John's. And since they haven't advocated adoption in the past, they couldn't possibly provide objective counseling."

"I have a sick feeling you're right."

"Besides, if this was such a great counselor, why hadn't she been seeing this person all along?"

"Well, I doubt Nancy could go back to Connie. After all, Connie has heard all the reasoning and plans for the past six months. It would be very tough for Nancy to give Connie this line about not thinking of herself. Connie would have seen right through it. Besides, Nancy probably didn't want to be reminded of the decision she made. In all reality, I doubt she was looking for someone to provide objective counseling. I think she wanted someone who would be sympathetic and treat her grief as a mistake rather than part of the process."

"You know what really irks me though? During our last few visits, when I've suggested that she see Connie, Nancy kept telling me she didn't have time. Now she tells me that she has been seeing a professional. When did she find time for that? Why didn't she just tell us she was reconsidering her decision—that she was seeing another counselor? It certainly would have been a small consideration under the circumstances."

"It's pretty unbelievable all right. We have spent the past six months of our lives openly planning and talking things out so there would be no surprises yet now, without even a hint, Nancy has changed her mind. If only she'd have told us, at least it might be easier to understand."

"Well, the only thing that makes any sense to me is that Nancy is grieving. Perhaps she just couldn't keep this huge secret from her family or admit what she had done. Either way, because she hurts so much, she thinks that taking Michael back will end her pain. But she is wrong. She already gave him up. Taking him back isn't going to change that nor will it erase her regret or grief."

"That's probably true. Regardless though, she has allowed it to be justification for backing out of what is probably the most important decision in her life. She's so wrapped up in herself and her grief that no one else matters, not even Michael."

Just then we could hear Michael stirring in the nursery. We walked into the nursery together, our arms around each other. As we looked down into the crib, I felt myself coming apart again. We loved this little boy so much. The thought of not having him tore me to pieces. Ron reached in to pick Michael up. We both kissed him on his head then I left to warm his bottle while Ron changed his diaper. We settled into the living room in a state of shock and numbness as Ron fed and talked to him.

"Michael, my little son, your birth mother is going through a hard time. She said she's going to take you away from us. We're going to do whatever we can to keep you but if we fail, please forgive us." Ron caught his breath as a sob escaped him. Then he continued, "We have so many dreams for you but you may have to live them without us. Just grow up and become a great man. You are so special. We love you son. If you ever need us, we'll always be here for you." It was as if Ron was trying to share everything a father would with his son in the little time he had left.

For hours, we talked and cried while holding Michael. We didn't want to put him down. Watching him, we wondered how we would ever go on without him. How could we say good-bye to him, to our dreams, and all that made life so complete? He had changed our lives. I wasn't sure what would be left of it without him.

Questions filled our minds. How could Nancy not recognize that by taking Michael she was taking a piece of us too? Didn't she realize she had no right to that part of us? How could she do it, after everything she had said to us? She promised she would never take him back. That was the one thing I was certain she would never do. How could she break her word to us? What about the oath she made to God and us at the adoption ceremony? Didn't any of that matter? It just seemed impossible that she could put us through this after everything we had already been through. What possible justification could she have come up with to do something so heartless and cruel?

"There must be some way we can get Nancy to see what a horrible thing she's doing," I blurted out in frustration. "After all, this is Nancy we're talking about, my dearest friend who I've known for over 10 years. Just weeks ago we were able to talk about anything. There has to be some way to get through to her. Somewhere buried beneath her grief there has to be a sense of responsibility to her and Michael. I just can't believe she's truly changed her mind!"

"I agree but how do we help her see that? How do we get through to her?"

"I think the only chance we have is to appeal to her based on the love and trust we once shared."

"Maybe we should ask someone to be here on Wednesday, like Mrs. Madsen or our attorney," Ron suggested.

"I don't know. Up until now, everything we've accomplished has been based on the relationship between the three of us. To call in outside forces might only appear threatening to Nancy. I think we'll just have to trust that the love between us still exists."

Despite my words though, deep inside I think we both knew it was over. After all, the very thing that made Michael's presence possible for us—the trust—was gone! Nancy had destroyed it with her call. It would take more than one conversation to rebuild that. Even if we talked her out of taking Michael now, she could still change her mind during the grace period and put us through this all over again. No, Nancy's word now meant nothing.

With the trust gone, I was sickened to realize that I could no longer keep my word to her either. Gone was the beauty of open adoption. Even if we somehow managed to keep Michael, what would keep her from showing up whenever she wanted? What if she demanded to be a daily part of his life? And if we didn't agree, what would keep her from snatching him? We would never be able to turn our backs without fearing that her actions or words might destroy our lives. Without the trust, we could no longer keep an open and honest dialog with Nancy as Michael grew up.

Then reality hit. As long as we had Michael, there would never be any peace in our lives. The once open and trusting relationship had dissolved into fear and distrust. It was unbelievable that just yesterday I trusted Nancy with my life. Today, however, I could not trust her with anything, least of all my child. It didn't look like that would be our choice though, for despite how much we loved and wanted Michael, it no longer seemed possible for us to keep him. Somehow, we would have to let him go. Otherwise his life, as well as ours, would never be whole. No one should have to live that way, especially not our beloved son.

Michael was awake again. It was time for his 10:00 p.m. bottle. Tears again erupted. Although grateful for this time with our son, each time we looked at him was a painful reminder that we would be losing him. We felt so much love for our son yet, within a day, we knew he'd no longer be ours.

As my tears fell, Michael's eyes widened, as if he were trying to understand.

"Oh, Michael," I whispered to him, "how can we ever tell you how much we love you and how we miss you already? And how can we possibly explain the tragedy that has come upon us?"

We knew that he would never remember us. We would forever be a part of his past. It hurt so much. I wondered if Nancy would ever tell him. I guess I wouldn't if I were her. I would be ashamed. How could you admit to your son that you once gave him up? How would you explain that after having done so you then took him back and thus caused so much pain and hurt so many people?

I couldn't even understand. How could a child ever be expected to understand? None of it made any sense.

Far into the morning, we held our son. Our arms ached yet we couldn't put him down. It was as if we were trying to pour all the love in our hearts upon him and having done so, we hoped it would be enough to last the rest of his life.

It was 4:00 a.m., Michael's usual mealtime. Despite having slept through the past two nights, he woke this morning. In the dark, I stumbled to the nursery. Suddenly Nancy's stinging comment filled my mind, *When you're a mother and have a child of your own, you'll understand.* Anger rose up inside me like a hot torch.

Well, if I'm not Michael's mother then why am I the one getting up so early in the morning to feed him? And if I'm not his mother, just where has she been all this time? Where has she been when he's cried for a bottle or needed comfort?

Bitterly I answered my own questions. Michael's "mother" was in California trying to figure out how to hide him from her parents. Meanwhile, we who never doubted our desire for him loved him as our own.

Entering Michael's nursery, disbelief crowded my mind. How could she take my son away? What kind of a person would do this?

Gently, I lifted Michael from his crib and he stopped crying. My heart softened. It didn't matter whether Nancy considered me Michael's mother. Michael did. He knew the touch of his mother and that is all that mattered.

Talking to him gently, I changed his diaper. As Ron warmed the bottle, I couldn't help but smile—thinking of how impatient Michael was when hungry. We had gotten to know our little son so well in the past three weeks. It had been so much fun. He had brought us such joy. It was not his fault or choosing that we should go through this sadness now.

As Michael dozed back to sleep, I could feel his soft breath on my neck. Long after he was asleep, I continued to rock him. In the quiet of the early morning, I prayed for a miracle. If I couldn't have that, then I prayed that our son would have a long and happy life. One thing was certain though; we would never forget the blessing of his life in ours.

Wednesday arrived, and with it a sickening sense of dread. The day was a blur as we continued to rehash the horror that would soon be upon us. In a state of numbness, I finished laundering Michael's clothes and packing his things. Two o'clock arrived. We waited in silence wondering if Nancy would truly come. At 2:10, the phone rang.

"We'll be there in a few minutes," Nancy said abruptly over the phone.

"Who is 'we' "? I asked.

"My parents and me." Instantly, I was perturbed. We too could have called in reinforcements but didn't out of respect for our relationship. What had we been thinking—what relationship? Without thinking, I blurted out, "Nancy, I think this is something you should do yourself. You're a big girl now."

Nancy stammered, "I'm not sure I can find your house. Besides, the van is all loaded and ready to go."

"Well, at this point, I think you owe us the courtesy of talking to us alone." The last thing we wanted was a house full of people who couldn't begin to understand what we'd been through in the past months. Certainly added support might have been easier for us too but this was between the three of us. If Nancy thought she could raise Michael alone then she would have to take him alone.

Hanging up the phone, I turned to Ron who was holding Michael. Our little one was looking sleepy. I wanted to put him in his crib before Nancy arrived. It would be easier to talk undisturbed. Before we laid him down though, I held him close. Putting his face close to mine, I talked to him as I covered him with kisses. I knew this would be my last opportunity to love him as his mother. Then unexpectedly, Michael smiled. Nothing could have meant more.

Tears erupted as I whispered, "Oh, thank you honey. Thank you for giving us your first smile. Thank you for being our son. How can we ever thank you little Michael?"

As we laid Michael in his crib, Ron and I watched, arm in arm, as our precious son drifted off to sleep one last time under our care.

A white van pulled up in front of our house. We watched Nancy timidly get out and walk across the lawn. Her family must have been in the van since Nancy glanced back over her shoulder as if to get some reassurance. She looked nervous. She was tidy and neat though, wearing the outfit that we helped her pick out for her trip home from the hospital; the one we purchased during our shopping trip last Christmas.

The doorbell rang. Opening the door, I told Nancy to come in and then firmly shut the door behind her. For a moment, I thought she was going to leave, uncertain what to do.

"Nancy, I think you owe us an explanation," I said, without even saying hello.

"Yes, that's the least you could do," Ron emphatically said in a near shout.

Nervously, she made her way upstairs. I pulled up a chair for her, accidentally hitting her ankle with the leg of the chair. She pulled back.

"I'm sorry. I didn't mean to do that," I said.

As she sat, she seemed to gather courage. "Well, I just couldn't live with my decision," she said flatly.

I sensed an attitude of arrogance and indifference. Watching her, I could not believe she was the same person. I tried to comprehend how she could be so cold to us after all we had been through together. Already it was apparent that Nancy had no intention of talking things out, let alone changing her mind. She was going to take Michael no matter what we said. Immediately, I was angry at myself for being naive enough to think we could reason or talk with her. I felt frantic as I tried to keep the conversation going, hoping to say something that would rattle her conscience.

"What about the letters you sent? What about God's plan?" My voice was trembling.

"I couldn't live with it," she retorted bluntly.

I caught my breath as a cold chill ran down my spine. Did she have any idea what she'd said? Her remark frightened me. It was as if the devil himself had walked into our house and demanded our son. I felt desperate. I knew she loved Michael but it was obvious she was not herself right now. She couldn't be the person I'd loved as my dearest friend. This was a stranger. I no longer knew what she was capable of.

"Can you provide Michael with anything more than we could?" I asked, motioning around the room.

Her eyes followed my hand. "No," she responded, "but I can love him more." Her answer seemed so vicious and unkind. How could she imply that we could not love Michael like she? Why was she being so cruel? What had we done to deserve her assault?

I proceeded on, trying not to be as hostile as I was now feeling. "So what are your plans from here?"

"That's none of your business," she said arrogantly.

"Oh, for goodness sake," I responded, filled with disgust. "What do you think we're going to do, kidnap Michael? If we were going to do that, we wouldn't be here right now. We'd have left."

"Besides," Ron added, "it certainly is our business. Michael is our son."

With a look of pure ice, Nancy looked directly at Ron and said, "He's not your son."

I felt as if Nancy had slapped me. Tears sprang to my eyes. "Nancy, how can you say that?"

Ron jumped in. "Michael is most certainly our son. You gave him to us."

Nancy seemed to lose some of her viciousness as she answered. "We're going to spend the summer with my sister in Colorado and then in August, Michael and I will be going back so I can finish school. I plan to take him with me to my overseas assignment next spring."

Ron and I looked at each other in disbelief. Although we said nothing, I knew we were thinking the same thing. Ron couldn't contain himself any longer as he angrily retorted, "Oh that makes sense. You are not only going to deny Michael two parents but are also planning to take him across the ocean, denying him any opportunity of a family. At least with us, Michael's whole family is right here in Montana."

"I don't have to listen to this," Nancy said angrily and began to stand.

Abruptly I also stood, unable to control the rage I felt. Blocking her, I firmly pushed her back into the chair. She sat down hard. Her eyes filled with terror.

"Denise!" she cried out.

Falling to my knees in front of her I shouted, "For a change Nancy, you will listen to what we have to say whether you want to or not."

She looked stunned as I continued, sobbing, "For the past months, everything has centered on you and what you want. Well, we have feelings too. You are not the only one who is hurting right now. Do you understand that? Do you have any idea what you're doing to us?"

Nancy was quiet, obviously shaken by my reaction. I could hear Ron calling out my name repeatedly as if miles away. I noticed my hands had tightened very hard around Nancy's wrists. I let go and eased back into my chair.

Shocked at my own behavior, I realized I had lost control. Immediately, I felt horrible. The one thing I didn't want to do was yell at or hurt Nancy, but I had managed to do both as emotion took over. Nancy's cool and calloused attitude had caught me completely off guard. I couldn't believe how insensitive she was to us.

Nancy's eyes were wide. Seeing the look on her face, I wondered what she had expected. Had she seriously thought she could simply waltz into our home and take Michael while we stood cheerfully waving good-bye? This was our son. We were about to lose him. Adding to the horror was the fact that a person I loved so much was forcing us to do this while showing no signs of remorse.

Ron had taken over the conversation. I didn't feel like I was even there. It was as if I were in a nightmare, waiting for someone to wake me.

"Don't you realize what hurt you're causing in taking Michael away from us?"

"Well, that's how I felt when you took Michael from me," Nancy said defensively.

"No, Nancy," Ron said. His voice was filled with sadness as he continued, "You gave Michael to us. There is a big difference between that and what you're doing now. We didn't take Michael from you."

She silently shook her head as if denying what he'd said. It appeared that somehow she'd convinced herself that we had actually stolen Michael from her. Treating us like thieves, she took on the role of a poor, innocent victim. She was the last person being victimized though. I wondered how she ever concluded that we had taken Michael against her will. It was almost as if she'd been brainwashed into believing a lie.

Thinking about the so-called professional adoption counselor, I asked, "Is this professional adoption counselor someone from St. John's?"

"Yes," she said. As if reading my mind, she continued attempting to justify herself, "But I've also been talking to other adoptive mothers and learned that I gave up Michael for all the wrong reasons. I hadn't thought about myself and what I wanted."

By now I beyond exasperation. It all seemed so pointless. With one final effort though, I said, "Nancy, I know you're feeling a lot of pain in giving up Michael, but taking him back isn't going to change that. Your grief will only be replaced with guilt for what you've done to Michael and us. Don't you realize that?"

Nancy looked at me as if I were crazy and then with all seriousness said, "I feel that Michael and I were in your lives to help you get pregnant. You'll have your own baby soon and then you'll understand."

"If we don't lose this baby after everything you've put us through," I retorted.

Nancy rolled her eyes. It was apparent she thought I was being quite dramatic. It enraged me however, that she would use our tender and joyous news as justification for taking Michael back. How dare she use it as ammunition for her lack of honor!

We were getting nowhere. I wanted Nancy out of our house, NOW! I just wanted it to be over. I stood up. "Well, it's apparent you're not going to change your mind so let me show you how to fix Michael's formula."

She stood and followed me toward the kitchen. Then, almost as an afterthought, she stopped and said, "Is there anything I can do for you?"

"Yes, you could leave Michael."

"You know I can't do that."

One last thought came to my mind. "Sure, there is one other thing. Ron and I have expended considerable time and money. I think the least you could do is compensate us for our expenses. Are you prepared to do that?" The money meant nothing to us compared to Michael, but I knew Nancy didn't have any.

I hoped my statement would make her realize that she couldn't pay us back, let alone provide for Michael.

It didn't seem to bother her though, as she confidently answered "yes."

"Fine," I said. "We'll put together a list and send it to you. There is also a final bill with the attorney. I think you should take care of that."

"I'll call him and settle the bill."

With that, we walked into the kitchen. I began telling her about Michael's schedule. It felt like I was giving instructions to a babysitter. I wondered how I could possibly tell her all about Michael's needs in these few short minutes. I wondered if she was even listening. I sensed she didn't think I had anything of value to say about Michael or his care. She already had it figured out. I proceeded on anyway. As I explained how to mix Michael's formula, Nancy said, "Oh, my milk came back in today. I'm planning to breast-feed."

How predictable, I thought sarcastically to myself. I had already considered that she would try to breast-feed again, having been so intent on doing it while we were there. Wasn't it amazing that her milk came in today, despite not having nursed for three weeks? Perhaps she had never stopped pumping.

I wanted to hurt her as much as she was hurting us. "Well, you won't have enough for him so you might as well take this formula." With that, I shoved the formula in the bag. I could feel my face reddening with shame for making such a mean comment.

"By the way," I added, "Michael is now sleeping through the night." Silently I hoped he wouldn't in the future. Perhaps that would eat at her conscience, knowing he had been doing better with us. Inside I felt horrible, taking such cheap shots at her. In desperation, I was trying to think of anything that would allow Michael to stay with us.

Ron began gathering Michael's things together. Nancy went to the van to get her mother, Marie. When Marie came in, tears filled her eyes. She reached to hug me, but I couldn't even force myself to respond. My arms hung limply at my sides.

"I'm so sorry," she said as tears rolled down her cheeks.

"You're not the enemy," I replied flatly.

Marie then turned to Ron and hugged him. I was grateful for her sincerity. At least she seemed to have some sorrow and compassion for what was happening to us.

When Nancy came back in the house, Ron lifted the box of her maternity clothes to take to the van. Nancy looked at me and with a surprised tone asked, "Denise, don't you want to use any of my maternity clothes?"

I wanted to spout back, *Oh please, leave me your clothes but take my son. Now that's quite a trade.* Refraining though, I looked away as Ron hauled the box to the van. I couldn't believe Nancy. Did she truly think our friendship would just go on as before, sharing clothes and long talks? Didn't she realize that, in betraying us so cruelly, she had thrown away our long and treasured friendship?

With the last box loaded, Marie again reached to hug me. This time I hugged her back. Then looking at Nancy, I asked, "Can we have a moment alone with Michael?"

She nodded. Ron and I went into the nursery and closed the door behind us. When Ron tenderly lifted Michael from his crib, he continued to sleep, unaware of the horror happening around him. We both kissed him and then opened the door to the nursery.

As much as I tried, I could think of nothing to say, nothing to make her change her mind. There was such a feeling of despair. I was going to lose my son and there was nothing I could do about it.

Carrying Michael into the living room, I noticed that Nancy was outside, for which I was grateful. Marie had laid out a beautiful quilt. Seeing the quilt, I started to object but then stopped. Although I knew the quilt would be too warm for Michael I also realized that he was no longer my responsibility. Quietly, I placed him in it. Then leaning to kiss him one last time, I whispered, "I love you son. I'm so sorry."

Marie let out a quiet sob and quickly covered her mouth, trying to keep from crying aloud.

I gathered Michael in my arms one last time and then gave him to Marie. It seemed such a sad irony that while she was seeing her grandson for the first time, we were losing our son and perhaps seeing him for the last time.

Just then, Nancy came back in the house. Taking Michael into her arms, she began making comments about how much he had grown. She continued to carry on as she stood on the stairs for what seemed an eternity. I couldn't take it anymore. "Nancy would you please leave? How much more do you have to put us through?"

Nancy looked at me with surprise but then quietly left with Michael in her arms as her mother guided her out. The house felt deadly quiet as Ron and I clung to each other. Sobbing, we watched the white van pull away with our little Michael inside. The suspense of the last few days was over. Michael was gone.

Glancing around the house, everything looked the same yet nothing felt right. Michael's swing was standing in the living room, a painful reminder of the child we no longer had. Ron moved it to the nursery and shut the door. The room we had decorated with such love now seemed like a tomb.

Chapter 10

WE WERE IN flight. The plane was heading to Hawaii and we were on it. Ron had somehow convinced me to go. "It's something we've always wanted to do," he'd said. "Now is the time, before our next baby arrives. Besides, we need to get away."

He was right. I was glad for an escape. The thought of staying home, facing life without Michael seemed impossible.

"How are you feeling?" Ron asked as the plane leveled out. He was going overboard taking care of me. I knew he was worried, wondering how losing Michael would affect our pregnancy. It worried me too. I had lost over five pounds and had felt some cramping in the few days since Nancy's call.

"Fine," I responded, smiling as I reached to squeeze his hand. We were both trying to be upbeat; acting thrilled to be going to Hawaii, but all we could think about was Michael. I remembered how Nancy wanted Jim to take her to Hawaii after the baby was born. She thought some time away would be good for her. Now it was us though, instead of her, trying to pull our lives together. I wondered how things could have gotten so turned around.

Settling back into my seat, I tried to relax. I was so tired. Never before had I felt so used. It was as if we had been emotionally raped and financially robbed. Gone were our dreams, our savings, and our trust in human kind, but most importantly, our child. I had never felt such intense pain. Even loss from death had not hurt this much.

Laying my head back in the seat, my thoughts went to Mom and her frantic attempt to see us. Since we had lost Michael just the day before, our family was still reeling with shock. Mom had wanted to come see us, but time wouldn't permit it since we had made last-minute plans to travel. Besides, Mom also had a trip planned and it would be impossible for her to travel to Billings and still make her flight.

As only God could have arranged though, it so happened that Mom's flight had a short layover in Salt Lake City at the exact time we were changing flights there. I could still see Mom rushing down the corridor trying to catch a moment with us before we boarded our next flight. We had cried together as she held me like mommies do when their children are hurting. How I loved my mom who was always there for me. I knew her heart was breaking too. She loved Michael so much, but I knew her heart hurt most for the pain she knew we were bearing. Thinking of Mom, I prayed that she had made her next flight despite taking time to find us. Somehow, I doubted that catching her flight was nearly as important to her as just seeing us. Mission accomplished.

Suddenly, my thoughts were interrupted by a familiar sound. It was the sound of a baby sucking on a bottle. Startled, I looked around. A young mother smiled at me, beaming with pride as she fed her new baby. I tried to smile back and then looked away.

"Oh God," I pleaded. "Please don't make me listen to this."

Tears were again streaming down my face. I missed our son so much. I should have been home with him, feeding and rocking him. It was hard to believe that just four weeks ago we had flown home with him. Now we were running away without him.

Closing my eyes, I tried to visualize him. Much to my horror, I couldn't remember what he looked like. Frantically I searched my mind but it was completely blank. How was it possible to forget how he looked? How would I recognize him again if I couldn't even remember how he looked now? It was as if he had never existed since even his image had disappeared.

Thinking back over the past few days, they seemed like a blur. I had managed to get a letter off to Nancy before we left, hoping she would take the time to think things over. Perhaps she'd change her mind.

I pulled a copy of it from my purse, reading it once again.

Dear Nancy:
We both feel such sadness in our hearts for what has occurred. It is just so unbelievable after all the months and hours we three spent sharing and trusting that it could come to such a tragic end. I'm just so sorry that you did not receive adequate counseling before so much hurt was inflicted on so many lives. We thank you for having enough faith in us to raise your child. We only wish we could have proven that your faith was in the right place.

Michael will always be our first born. We accepted him from you in the eyes of God with the promise to love him as such. Although we are soon to have another child, it is, and will always be, our second. How does one ever give up a child in their heart that they have loved so much?

We recognize that this is your decision and understand your desire to raise your child. Our hurt is that you didn't make that decision at the appropriate time. Please understand our hurt in losing our child. We are now the ones who grieve as do our family and friends. They are the ones who waited in anticipation for our child and loved him as one of our family.

I'm sorry that we couldn't seem to express our feelings when you were here without scaring you. However, I think if you put yourself in our shoes, you would have to admit that there is no way we could just sit there and let you walk out the door with our child. We had to try to remind you of what you'd planned for Michael before you felt so much pain. Maybe you won't see that now but someday I know you will.

You said you were prepared to compensate us for the financial losses that we incurred from our intended adoption. We have put together a detailed list of expenses and have attached it. Although it is not complete, we feel that resolving this is the first step in trying to pull our lives back together. After reviewing the list, should you have any questions or concerns please drop us a note. I hope you understand that what we have suffered financially is insignificant compared to the hurt and deception we now feel.

Michael will always be in our thoughts and prayers. Like us raising him for you, you are now raising him for us. Take care of him always. Please make sure he receives what he deserves in life, for he is truly one of God's greatest blessings.

May God bless and keep him. Ron & Denise

After carrying our luggage into our room, Ron and I flopped down on the bed. Exhaustion had overcome us. We'd left Montana over twelve hours ago, but it was still early afternoon in Maui. We took a short nap and then decided to go down to the ocean-side lounge and relax before dinner. Upon finding a table, we visited as the ocean breeze gently tugged at us. It was quiet and peaceful.

The frustrations and anger of the past days seemed to ebb away with the sound of the tide. Then glancing at the couple at the next table, I started to cry. The woman at the table looked just like Nancy's mother. I wondered if it was her sister. Although I had never met her, I had seen pictures and knew that she and her husband were fairly well off, taking occasional trips to places like Hawaii. I wanted to ask but didn't have the nerve. What if she was? What would I say then?

As I turned to look away, grief again welled up inside. Even here in paradise, it seemed we couldn't escape!

That night after a restless attempt at sleep, it finally came. Then suddenly I heard it. I sat straight up in bed and then paused to listen. I could hear Michael crying. I tried to sort out what was happening, confused by the strange environment. Then I remembered where I was and realized Michael was not here.

Glancing at my watch, still set on Montana time, I noticed that it was Michael's usual early morning feeding time. I tried to go back to sleep but couldn't. Instead, I thought of our son, wondering if he too was awake. Perhaps he really had cried thousands of miles away. If he had though, I could not be there to comfort him. Sobbing in the darkness, I prayed for our little son, asking for peace and comfort for him as well as for ourselves.

The days passed quickly, filled with trips around the island, window shopping, sunbathing, and relaxing. We got up when we wanted, slept when we wanted, did what we wanted. Despite such freedoms though, our minds were consumed with thoughts of Michael. We couldn't stop thinking of him, filled with wonder and worry.

Every morning before rising, we lay in bed talking about Michael. We wondered how he was doing. We wondered what he thought when he woke up from his nap that had begun in his crib and ended in the white van with Nancy. We wondered if Nancy was continuing his schedule or if he had to readjust. I knew he'd be flexible though. He was an easy baby. Although such issues filled us with wonder, we knew we would never know. Nancy would never humble herself to call, even if it was for Michael's benefit.

I was having another restless night. Dreams of Michael seemed to haunt me. It was the same dream, over and over. Michael was looking up at me. Nancy was there with her arms outstretched.

"Give me my son," she kept repeating in a demanding and arrogant tone. Then she stripped her breast and began nursing him. My own sobs always woke me. I tossed and turned for hours. I must have fallen back asleep because the next thing I remember was waking again in anger. Frantic with rage, I shook Ron awake.

"What's the matter?" he muttered.

"Tell me that you didn't have an affair," I demanded.

"Of course I didn't. What makes you think that?"

I told him about the latest dream I'd had. Ron had an affair. Colleen and Mom simply made excuses for him and then left us to be Nancy's family. It had seemed so real. Ron and I talked for a while as we lay in the darkness. He tried to reassure me, but even with his word I was crazy with distrust. For days, I drove him up the wall with my jealousy and paranoia. Paradise now seemed a threatening place as I angrily reprimanded him if his attentions weren't entirely on me.

I could tell he was upset with my distrust, but Nancy's betrayal had robbed me even of the security I felt in my marriage. Filled with questions, I wondered who could be trusted if she couldn't. Her betrayal was beyond my understanding. Now knowing such pain, I would have rather died than have someone betray me ever again.

A week later, we were back at home. The pain and emptiness without our son was unbearable. We wondered if Nancy had a clearer perspective of single parenting now. Perhaps she'd recognize that she couldn't give him the life that every child deserves, one with two loving parents.

Desperate for her to reconsider her actions, we decided to write one more letter. We had to try to get Michael back. We would never forgive ourselves if we didn't. We owed it to ourselves. We owed it to Michael. If nothing else, we needed closure. It felt as if we were stuck in a horrible rut. We couldn't seem to go on. We couldn't let go of the hope that there might still be a miracle in store for us. We desperately needed to hear from Nancy, even if the answer was the same.

Despite the sunshine outside, our moods were at their darkest. Today was Father's Day. This was the day we should have been celebrating Ron's new role as Michael's daddy.

Both of us were quiet as we went about the day, accomplishing meaningless chores while trying to ignore the obvious gap in our lives. We even avoided going to church, not wanting to hear the typical sermon about fathers. We just couldn't take another reminder of the emptiness that now enveloped us.

I was preparing lunch when I happened to glance at Ron. He was looking at me. His eyes were filled with sadness like I'd never seen. "When am I going to be a father?" he asked in a whisper. I could tell he was holding back tears.

I choked back a sob. "Next year honey, next year," I said, thinking of the baby inside me. I wanted to cry. I could have kicked myself for not doing something special. I guess I'd thought it would be easier to ignore the day but by doing so, I'd ignored the fact that Ron was already a father.

Anger quickly replaced my sadness. I was angry with myself for being so insensitive. I recalled how special Ron had made Mother's Day for me. Granted, we had Michael then and not now but that was no excuse for my lack of sensitivity.

My anger then turned to Nancy. She was the one who had denied Ron his rightful celebration as Michael's father. Ron had been Michael's only real father; the only father who truly loved him as a son. Ron had anticipated Michael's life, supported Nancy through her pregnancy, and been there when Michael was born, holding him moments afterwards. Ron had lovingly and willingly assumed the responsibility of raising the precious little boy we still loved as our son.

Angry and ashamed, I vowed that next year would be different. Next year our second would be born and there would be a child to help celebrate. Next year I would make sure that we had a special Father's Day to celebrate.

⋅→≡ ⊂≡⋅←⋅

Checking the mailbox, disappointment again overcame me. More than a month had passed since we'd written to Nancy. She had not responded. I was beginning to feel like a hostage to the mail. I was desperate for some closure to this agony.

With each passing day, my disgust for Nancy seemed to heighten. How could she not even respond? Why couldn't she give us the closure that we'd asked? It seemed such a small consideration. Perhaps she was rethinking her actions. Even though I knew deep down that wasn't likely, I couldn't help hoping.

Regardless though, I hated the control she seemed to have over us. I hated the pain she had caused. I even hated her. Everyone I knew and loved was hurting, even my two-and-a-half year old nephew, Anthony. He didn't understand.

"Aunt Denise can't find Michael William," he had said, sobbing in his mother's arms one night. His comment surprised Colleen. She'd been so careful—only telling him that Michael had gone with a friend. She didn't want him to think that people could come and take babies away. He had a baby brother too. Anthony had seen through it though and I hated Nancy for hurting even him.

Most painful of all though, was watching Ron in his sorrow. It was worse than dealing with my own. Gone was his usual jovial behavior and instead there seemed to be a cloud. I knew he was trying to hide his pain. For many who watched him, I'm sure they thought he was holding up well. However, I knew him, yet hardly recognized him. I hadn't heard him laugh in ages. I couldn't even remember how it sounded. I couldn't remember laughing either. It simply hurt too much.

Friends trying to offer comfort often said, "Well, at least you have each other."

I knew they meant well but I wanted to scream back, "Thankfully yes, but we also have each other's pain." They had no idea how horrible it was to watch the man who had always been so strong crumble in tears. There was nothing I could do to take his pain away. In fact, I felt responsible. After all, I had assured him and all our family that Nancy could be trusted; that she was a person of her word. They had placed their faith in my judgment and now, because of that, they were hurting like never before. No one blamed me, but I couldn't help blaming myself.

Life felt as if it were on ice. We had been frozen in time, unable to focus or go on. There seemed to be no past, no present, and no future. The tragic turn of events had affected our whole life, leaving nothing unscathed. All that remained was an incredible emptiness as we longed for our son.

Meanwhile, the world was going on without us. Children continued to play in the street, reminding us of the child we might never see again. Mothers pushed their babies in strollers, enjoying summer in Montana. Meanwhile, Michael's stroller was empty and locked in the nursery, as empty as our lives.

It all seemed so unjust. I was angry that life would go on without our son in our lives. How could time continue on as if nothing had happened? But then again, it seemed that even I had moved on, leaving the person I once was behind. I longed for that innocence, for the ability to trust humankind but it no longer seemed possible. Those qualities belonged to a person I doubted I could ever be again.

A dark cloud seemed to hang over us as we struggled to resume a "normal" life. Nothing felt normal though. Normal would have been having Michael with us. I wondered if life would ever feel whole again.

Physically, I was exhausted. My arms ached with loneliness for our son, and my heart felt like it was bleeding inside. I was often sick, my stomach in knots. The physical discomfort, however, was insignificant compared to the emotional pain.

Daily, I cried. I wondered if there would ever be a day I wouldn't. Replaying the events of the past months, I tried to determine what had gone wrong, what we could have done differently, what we should be doing now. There didn't seem to be any answers.

Distrust for others hung heavy. Ron and I began pulling away from the world, distancing ourselves from others and making excuses to avoid social events. We didn't know whom we could trust anymore. Ron even dropped out of his Exchange Club despite his upcoming presidency, telling the group he needed more time for his family. However, the truth was that withdrawing into ourselves seemed the only way to survive. We simply didn't have the energy to deal with people. We felt vulnerable as we wondered who would stab us in the back next.

We fought an urge to disappear and start over again. Perhaps that would erase the painful memories that life now held. That wasn't a luxury we had though. It seemed to have been one for Nancy, however. It was as if she had dropped off the face of the earth, along with our son.

We were at the grocery store. In our usual state of numbness, we stopped to gather a few essentials before heading to the solitude of our home. Making our way to the checkout stand, I caught a glimpse of a woman carrying a newborn baby. Immediately I burst into tears, sobbing out of control. I had to leave while Ron paid for our groceries.

Life now seemed to be a constant reminder of Michael and Nancy. The sight of a white van sent me into a state of panic, bringing to mind the horrifying scene of watching Michael disappear into one. In fact, I couldn't even go into a store if there was a white van parked in front. I was terrified I would run into Nancy's folks. I had no idea how I'd react.

While picking up a birthday card for a friend, I noticed a cute Jersey cow T-shirt. For a fleeting moment, I thought of buying it for Nancy, knowing how much she would enjoy it, but then I remembered.

Even my own pregnancy was a painful reminder of sharing Nancy's. I couldn't bring myself to look at maternity clothes or walk through a baby department. All the things a new expectant mother should have enjoyed only brought a flood of tears. Even the sight of another pregnant woman caused me to cry, despite the fact that I too was carrying a child inside.

I was so angry. We were finally pregnant but there was little joy in it now. The dreams seemed empty without Michael. We'd dreamed of the life we'd have with both children together. How could we have our second without our first? Compounding my grief and anger though was worry. I had continued losing weight after Nancy took Michael, despite conscience efforts to eat well and get some rest. I wondered what effect it was having on our baby. Then again, I felt guilty even anticipating another. It felt like we were betraying Michael.

My nephew Jacob was lying on the floor, smiling up at me. His giggle was contagious. He was only six weeks older than Michael was, so I figured Michael would be giggling by now too. Jacob had just started to scoot. I could almost see Michael trying too. Before long, he'd be crawling. In my mind, I saw him rocking back and forth on his hands and knees, trying to gather courage. I wished I could see that.

Filled with thoughts of our son, I continued to battle the unknown, unable to accept that we would never have him back. I wondered if this is what it felt like for families victimized by kidnappers; trapped in the memory of a loved one they could no longer be with, consumed with thoughts of them, hopeful that someday they would be reunited. At least I knew our son was safe, so I supposed

I could be grateful for that. I knew Nancy would care for him and love him. She would be a good mother in spite of how angry and hurt I was over her actions.

Still, I missed Michael so much. I missed being a part of his days and having him as a part of mine. Vividly now, I could see his little face when he smiled. I could see his inquiring eyes; his look that made me feel as if he was listening to every word. I longed to see him, to hold him, to smell him again.

I questioned who his example would be and who would teach him the values and beliefs that Ron and I held so dear. Angrily I thought, *Well, I doubt it will be Nancy. She can't even teach him the importance of honoring one's word.*

Such thoughts, however, only served to frustrate me more since I knew Nancy would be the one with the privilege of raising our son. We were, after all, just the adoptive parents, completely without rights or regard. Our values and beliefs were unimportant. All that mattered was Michael's birthright, not his upbringing. And all that remained for us were months and years filled with wonder about the little boy we loved as our own.

It had been another restless night. Stirring awake, I glanced at the clock. It was 4:00 a.m. Even though Michael had been gone for two months, I continued to wake during what had been his morning feeding. Life felt like a living nightmare. I could still hear his movements in the nursery even though the door remained closed. My maternal ear never seemed to rest as if waiting for him to wake so I could go get him. My only consolations were the sounds that seemed to linger. I thought I was going crazy. I'd never felt so alone or so vulnerable.

We knew that somehow we had to pull our lives back together. Inside me though, it seemed as if a war were going on. My heart literally felt like it was becoming stone. Anger and distrust seemed to be taking hold. I resented people who had children and despised those who didn't appreciate them. Now instead of constant tears, there were none. I couldn't cry about anything.

At the same time, I prayed like never before. I didn't want to become hardhearted or unfeeling. As I cried out to God, I felt Him pulling me close. I knew others were praying for us, and in an inexplicable way, I could feel it. A strength beyond my own kept me going. Some days simply getting out of bed and getting dressed took more energy than I had, and on those days, it seemed like God was carrying me.

It was during this time that we gained an understanding like never before, one that ultimately changed our lives. In our grief and despair, it occurred to us that if anyone understood us right now, it was God. After all, He too had given up His only son. The magnitude of His gift, the degree of His suffering, and the price He paid became very real to us. Although our experience couldn't compare to what Christ experienced, we had a new perspective of our Heavenly Father's immense love.

We loved our son and had there been any choice, any other way, we would not have given him up. Never would we have chosen to suffer like this. Yet, that is exactly what Christ did for us. He suffered and gave His life because there was **no other way** to save me. Such an amazing sacrifice just so that I could live forever in His grace. How could I ever have taken His gift for granted?

A sense of peace began to ebb away the pain in our lives. We knew we weren't alone. Even in this horrible valley of our lives, God was with us. He understood our pain. Wrapped in the comfort of our faith, we began to realize that there would be a time when the pain and sadness would not feel so intense. We knew life would go on. After all, we had another baby on the way. It would help to fill the emptiness. Such knowledge became a lifeline as we hung on, waiting for the storm to break.

Despite praying that we could at least talk with Nancy and better understand, there had been no word from her. Several months had passed since kissing our son goodbye. Somehow, it felt like if we could at least talk, we could find closure and move on. Now I questioned if we would ever hear from her. It appeared we'd have to find closure on our own. As God's peace slowly worked back into our lives, we began the painful process of convincing our hearts what our minds already knew. Our little Michael would not be coming home.

Chapter 11

I WAS IN my second trimester of our pregnancy when a package arrived from Colleen. Inside were dozens of wrapped packages, each with a note attached. On top lay a handwritten letter.

> Dear Denise,
> This is your official "advent calendar" for the weeks of your pregnancy. Enjoy—no peeking early. Open the gifts anytime during the specified week. Each time you open one; think of how excited we are for you and Ron. Ron really deserves a present too—next time maybe I'll get to spoil him.
> Denise, enjoy this time with Ron and your baby. It was such a special time for us. We are so happy for you. We love you more than you'll ever know.
> Love, Colleen and gang

Right under the letter laid the first package with instructions to open it immediately. It was so exciting. With all these presents, it felt like Christmas.

I opened a card titled, 'My Sister, My Friend!' Inside was a beautiful verse. Right below it, Colleen had written,

> Here's to many fun and exciting weeks waiting for your new little one. We've shared so much in the past, and I can't wait to share your ups and downs of pregnancy. The weeks will fly by, some more than others.

> Enjoy! Whenever I look back on those days, I smile, remembering those kicks, jabs, hemorrhoids, cramps, and excitement.
>
> I love you so much, Colleen

Inside the package was a pretty mug with the same title as the card. I felt overwhelmed with her thoughtfulness. It must have taken hours to find these gifts and then wrap them.

In the weeks that followed, I anticipated her weekly gifts with great pleasure. I couldn't wait to see what each package held. There were gift certificates to McDonald's for ice cream, a bag of M&M's, maternity nylons, and even a gift certificate for a nursing bra. In that card, she'd written,

> You won't believe what will happen to your breasts. I might suggest getting a size FFF.

Her usual wit and creativity always made me smile. With another gift, rainbow colored note pads, Colleen had written,

> Trust me, you'll need these. A unique biological process takes place during labor in which 90% of all remaining brain cells go. I believe it is nature's way of ensuring a continued population. Anyway, start now by writing notes to remind yourself of the basics—who you are and what you're doing.

I felt so close to Colleen each time I read her messages and opened the weekly gifts. With each one, my pregnancy seemed to be more real. I felt more focused as thoughts of our next baby began filtering into my mind. And with Colleen's continued excitement for the child I carried, I was reminded that, despite the horrendous grief we still felt over losing Michael, before long our days would again be filled with the blessings of a baby.

"Is this your first?" the woman in the restaurant asked as she noticed my pregnancy.

"No," I stammered.

"Oh, how old are your other children?"

I started to cry. The woman stood there watching, her mouth hanging open as she tried to determine what she'd said wrong.

It wasn't her fault though. She was only interested. I tried to reassure her but she obviously felt horrible.

The next time someone asked that question, I told her it was my first. Tears erupted then too. After all, this wasn't our first. I had lied by saying it was and betrayed Michael at the same time.

Every day I rehearsed a better answer to that question. It came up regularly with my pregnancy now being so obvious. I could never seem to get it right though. Each time I blundered, I left the inquiring party feeling bad. Once again, I was reminded of the joy, not the remorse, that should have been each time someone asked.

I decided it was time to clean out the nursery. We needed to prepare for our next baby. Colleen had come to help me, knowing it would be hard. I appreciated her being there.

Opening the door to the nursery for the first time since Nancy took Michael, I noticed a picture of Nancy lying on the floor. It must have fluttered out of something I'd packed to send with her. Picking it up, I burst into tears. The heartache felt raw and fresh once again.

We had been such special friends. I remembered the fun we'd had sharing her pregnancy as we'd anticipated Michael. She had been so excited about my pregnancy, promising to share it too. Well, now it was my turn, only she wasn't here. I felt cheated. I wondered where she and Michael were and why we hadn't heard from her. I wondered how she could have thrown our friendship away.

Suddenly, the void in my life seemed larger than ever. I missed Nancy so much. I missed our friendship. Gone were the closeness and the laughter we had often shared. It seemed such a horrible price to pay. I wondered if the person I had shared so many fond memories with still existed. It was as if she died the day we lost Michael.

"Oh, Ron," I said, "the baby is moving."

We were both starting to get so excited. My profile was definitely showing signs of the pregnancy, which added to our anticipation. Our joy was immense but still there lingered apprehension. This had been a very stressful time. I still hadn't gained the weight back after losing Michael.

Despite our best efforts to move forward, there remained a nagging hope that Michael would come home and that we could raise our children together. We tried not to think of it. We tried to stay focused on the child that would certainly be ours to keep.

Anxiously, I looked forward to my doctor appointments. It was such a thrill to hear our little one's heartbeat. I began visualizing what our baby would look like. I wondered if my hunch was correct—that it was a girl.

The baby was gaining strength. I could now feel its strong kicks daily. I was so anxious to see those little limbs that were generating such active pokes. With thoughts like this, ever so slowly, the promise of happier days began to creep into our lives and fill our hearts and minds with hope.

Once again, our home was busy in preparation for our baby. Often I would wander into the nursery simply to look into the crib. It gave me encouragement as I thought of how a precious new life would again occupy it. My nightmares of Michael being torn from our lives had finally stopped, and instead I dreamt of children playing. I could even look at other babies without crying although I still found it hard to hold them.

For the most part, the nursery décor was the same as it had been for Michael. I added a few decorations and bought diapers and other necessities. I considered redecorating in order to personalize it for this baby, but the décor seemed an insignificant detail. All I really cared about was having our baby. Besides, I just didn't have the energy. We would do something more personal once it was born.

Ron and I were again tossing around names. "Let's name it Amy Colleen if it's a girl," I suggested. "I still really like it. Besides, nothing would please me more than naming our daughter after Colleen."

"I agree. If it's a boy, what do you think about using William again since it's a family name?" Ron asked.

"I don't know—"

"Well, Michael is no longer Michael William since Nancy used a different middle name. Besides, just because she stole our child, why should we allow her to steal our name?"

However, the truth was Nancy had stolen our child and our name since I'd never be able to think of Michael as anyone other than Michael William. Sadly, I thought of how Ron had always wanted to name his first son Michael. Well, he'd gotten to do that, only Michael was no longer our son. Anger again welled inside as I thought of all that Nancy had taken from us. She would never know how her cruel actions had affected our lives.

I was now twenty-seven weeks along, two-thirds of the way there. Three months had passed since losing Michael. Colleen planned to have Jacob baptized in Helena. We were all looking forward to getting together. Colleen was most anxious to see my new and expanding figure.

Arriving at my grandparent's home, Colleen rushed out to greet us. "Well, it's good to see some progress," she said with her usual wit as she assessed my profile. We giggled and compared notes on pregnancy as she patted my stomach. It was such fun to be sharing a piece of motherhood with Colleen again.

"Please tell me when the baby moves," she said. "I'd love to feel the kicks."

"Oh, I will," I said. Her interest pleased me so much.

With that, we quickly changed clothes in order to attend our cousin's wedding that was also taking place over the weekend. Arriving at the church, we settled into the pews. Colleen made a point of sitting next to me. "Now if that baby moves, you tell me," she said.

I nodded that I would as the wedding march music began.

As luck would have it, right in the middle of the ceremony, I felt the baby move. "The baby moved," I whispered to Colleen.

"Oh, sure," she whispered back, "now when I can't poke it to keep it moving."

"I'll try to be more considerate of the timing in the future," I said, winking at her.

"Please do!"

Continuing to whisper, I added, "You may have to wait until morning though. That's generally when it does most of its wiggling."

Jokingly she pouted, disappointed to have missed this chance.

It was a busy weekend with the wedding and Jacob's baptism the following morning. Grandma planned to have a special brunch after the baptism.

Rev. Miles, who officiated the marriages of all three of us children, would be performing Jacob's baptism. As he began the service, he mentioned that he had done some research into our family in honor of Jacob's special day.

"I discovered that Jacob's birthday was also another special day for your family," he explained to our family as well as the congregation. "Some years back on April 19th, Colleen's father joined the church."

April 19th! I thought to myself. That was Michael's birthday, not Jacob's. Colleen noticed the mistake too and glanced nervously at me. Her eyes were sad as if apologizing. I tried to reassure her as I smiled back at her while inside, I once again felt torn and sad. It was an easy mistake though with our sons being born so close together.

Rev. Miles was unaware of his error though and proceeded with Jacob's baptism, emphasizing the coincidence of the day. For the duration of the service, I scarcely heard a word, as thoughts of Michael again crowded my mind.

After the service, Ron, Mom, and I were making our way to the car. "Can you believe what just happened?" I said.

"No, it's incredible; almost eerie," Mom said.

"Once again," I said, "it seems as if Michael and our family are linked together. This might sound crazy, but it's like there was a message in Rev. Miles' error."

"I know what you're saying," Ron said.

"It's just so odd," I added. "Here we're trying to move on without Michael yet reminders seem to keep resurfacing as if to make sure we don't."

"Maybe Michael is supposed to be a part of our family yet!" Ron said.

"But how?"

Silently, we drove to Grandma and Granddad's home, lost in our own thoughts. I wondered if it was a message from God. Was He telling us to continue trying to get Michael back?

Back at home, all was quiet. Even our baby seemed extra quiet. There had been no familiar kicks now for several mornings. The false contractions I'd been feeling since shortly after losing Michael were now growing more regular.

I called Dr. Fellow's office. When his nurse Holly answered, I explained my feelings and concerns. She told me to come right away. The urgency in her voice scared me.

Without the usual disrobing, Holly placed the monitor on my stomach. In silence, we both strained to listen for the familiar sounds of our baby. This time though, it was quiet. Where was the heart beat?

"Roll over on your left side," Holly instructed.

Obediently I shifted. Holly again placed the cold monitor on my stomach. I held my breath as I silently repeated over and over, *Come on baby, come on!*

An eternity seemed to pass. Holly removed the monitor. Her face was somber. "Denise, it doesn't look good." Tears were already falling as she continued. "Sometimes this happens. The baby becomes tangled in the cord. The placenta detaches and the baby dies. It's hard to say. I'll call Dr. Fellows. He'll do an ultrasound to make sure but, Denise, I'm not very encouraged."

I shook my head, not wanting to hear.

"This is such a nightmare," Holly said as she reached to hug me. I knew she was thinking what I was. How could this happen after already losing Michael? It just couldn't be.

"We've got to be optimistic," I said, trying to remain composed despite the flood of tears. "The ultrasound will show that everything is fine."

"I'll call Dr. Fellows. Just wait here," Holly said.

"Can I use a phone to call Ron?"

"Certainly, you can use this one," she said as she directed me to an adjoining room. Then giving me another hug, she departed.

I felt like I were in a trance as I tried to put some order to this horrifying prospect. I had never heard of anything like this happening. It was as if someone were playing a cruel joke on me. I always thought if you made it past the first trimester, you were home free. Sure, I had heard of those occasional tragedies that occur at birth, such as a cord problem, but I was twenty-eight weeks along. This had to be a mistake.

Suddenly, I was angry with Holly. *How dare she say such a thing! She is not a doctor. What could she possibly know about this?* I thought. No more had the thought crossed my mind though when I realized she wouldn't say it unless she was quite certain.

I picked up the phone and dialed Ron's office. It felt like I was reliving the day Nancy had called. Once again, I had to tell him horrible news. When Ron answered the phone, I began sobbing. He could hardly understand me as I choked out Holly's prognosis. "Dr. Fellows is on his way. Can you be here? I don't want to go through it alone."

I could hear his quiet struggle, just like that day three months ago. "I'll be right there."

Ending my call, I went in search of Holly. Approaching the nurses' station, I noticed them whispering among themselves. When they saw me, they stopped talking and lowered their eyes. Holly directed me back to an examining room. The two of us sat together.

"How did you say this could happen?" Questions filled my mind. I didn't understand. She explained it again, adding that sometimes we never know. I thought of the concerns we'd had during the pregnancy and asked, "Could stress have caused it?"

"Possibly but not likely. We can do some tests. We'll know more then."

Pausing to gather my nerve, I asked the question I was most afraid to ask. "If I had come in sooner, would it have made any difference?" Somehow, I felt like this was all my fault.

"No," Holly said tenderly. "Generally by the time you suspect anything is wrong, it's already too late."

Holly and I sat in a stunned silence as we waited for Ron and Dr. Fellows. My mind continued to race. This had to be a big mistake. It just wasn't possible. We couldn't lose this baby too. This child was going to fill the void in our lives. Certainly, God didn't think we could go through this twice. I had to believe there was a mistake.

Soon, Dr. Fellows rushed in looking flustered. He must have been at the hospital since he was wearing hospital garb. Anxiously, he directed me to another room where he could do an ultrasound. I glanced towards the waiting area but I didn't see Ron. I tried to loiter so he would have time to get there, but I hated to keep the doctor waiting.

Holly applied gel to my stomach. Dr. Fellows turned the monitor on and placed the instrument to my stomach. Right away, I saw our baby's form. It looked just like Michael's ultrasound that Ron had tenderly tucked in his wallet only months ago. I could see the head and chest. For an instant, I forgot why we were here as my heart soared proudly while admiring the image of our baby. Then I glanced at Dr. Fellows. He was sadly shaking his head.

"This is the baby's head," he pointed out. "And this is the chest. We should be seeing some movement of the heart. There is no movement. I am sorry. Your baby is dead."

Tears were streaming down my face. I didn't want to hear. Somehow, I had expected him to make this all right. I had so hoped he would have something, anything, different to say.

"Are you sure?" I asked, my voice pleading.

"Yes, I'm sure." He paused a moment to let it sink in. Then he continued, "The baby would eventually be born on its own, but I'd prefer to go ahead and induce labor."

"I agree. I can't imagine continuing the pregnancy knowing it's—" I couldn't say the word.

"Let's go back to the examining room," Dr. Fellows said. "I'd like to see if you've begun to dilate." With that, Dr. Fellows left as Holly helped me off the table. She had a box of Kleenex in her hand. She was crying too.

"I'm so sorry Denise," she said, hugging me again. She had been my nurse through all the years of infertility. She had met Michael during my first prenatal visit. She'd been praying for this baby. This was a horrifying end for her too. Now that the ultrasound had confirmed our fears, there no longer remained even the slightest doubt. Our baby had died.

On my way back to the examining room, I stopped to go to the bathroom. Everything about my pregnancy was continuing, including my weak bladder. When I reached the examining room, Ron was waiting. I could tell from the look on his face that Holly had told him.

I rushed into his arms. We held each other as we both cried. "I'm so sorry, honey," I said.

"It's not your fault," he said. "It's just one of those things that happen. There's no one to blame."

I was grateful for his response. I felt guilty and filled with so many what ifs. Ron already seemed aware of this. I wondered how he could have known what I most needed to hear. What a wonderful man God had given me.

Dr. Fellows then checked me and found that I had already begun dilating. He instructed us to go home, get a few things, and then check into the hospital. He would induce labor when we got there.

Back at home, I tried to gather some personal items to take to the hospital. "What am I supposed to take?" I asked Ron in frustration. "I haven't read that chapter in the book yet. I haven't even been through childbirth classes." I was so angry and confused. I wanted to scream at the injustice. The one thing I had dreaded most about being pregnant was having to go through the pain of childbirth. Now I would have to go through it, completely unprepared, and not even get to keep our baby. How could this happen?

In frustration, I finally threw some underwear and socks into a suitcase. Jerking my bathrobe from the hanger, I sank to the bed and cried, burying my face in the robe. Ron had bought it so I'd have something warm to wear at the hospital in November. I wasn't supposed to be delivering in August. I wasn't supposed to have a baby I couldn't bring home.

The reality came crashing down. I let myself cry. I wanted to run away, to take my pregnancy and my baby and somehow pretend everything was okay. I loved being pregnant. I loved knowing that I carried our child inside. This is what I had always wanted. I wasn't ready for it to be over, for my baby or me. How could I go on without our baby, this child who was a part of us? I didn't know how to let go. I shouldn't have to. I was so scared.

Finally, I gathered myself and closed my bag. Passing the mirror, I caught a glimpse of myself. I paused to look at my pregnant profile one last time. Running my hand over my stomach, I started to cry again. Would I ever have the privilege of being pregnant again? Would I ever again feel the joy as my child kicked and moved inside? It had been such a struggle to conceive this one. I didn't know if conception would happen again.

One thing was for sure though. This baby's life was over. It was time to get to the hospital. Delaying the delivery would not change that horrible fact. Our child was already in God's heaven and all that remained was delivering its little body.

Walking past the nursery in the maternity ward, I turned my head away. Normally I would have had my nose pressed against the glass. I couldn't look at the babies this time.

A nurse ushered us to a room. It looked so much like Nancy's birthing room, decorated in pink. Again, I was reminded—I resented the constant reminders of Nancy and Michael. This was horrible enough by itself.

A nurse entered our room. She introduced herself as Jennifer. "I understand why you are here. I'm so sorry about your loss." I appreciated her sincere compassion.

The unfairness of the past months came rushing forth. "This is the second baby we've lost this year," I blurted out. She glanced at my charts, searching for some information on a previous loss. I told her about Michael.

"You certainly have had your share of troubles. Was this a Clomid baby?"

"Yes, does that make a difference?"

"Not medically but it matters to me. A pregnancy loss is always difficult, but it is especially difficult when the baby is so desired. I am so sorry." Her eyes were moist. Clearing her voice, she began explaining what to expect with the inducement. I hardly heard a word. I felt as if I already knew the routine since I had been with Nancy during her labor. This time though, I was the participant rather than the observer.

"You'll have to decide on a method of burial," Jennifer said, her words bringing me back to the present.

I caught my breath. I hadn't thought about what would happen to our baby after it was born. Suddenly, it all seemed unbearable. This morning had started like any other day. We had dressed, eaten breakfast, and gone to work. Just hours ago, we had apprehensions and concerns, but now we would have to make decisions we never thought possible. The events of the day only seemed to get more horrifying as it progressed.

Jennifer continued, "You may want to have an autopsy and genetic studies done. If that is the case, you'll need to sign these forms. You don't have to decide immediately, but I wanted to give you time to talk things over." Jennifer paused and then asked, "Is there anyone I can call for you?"

"No, thanks," I said. "We've notified everyone who needs to know for now. My sister will be arriving in a few hours. Could someone show her in?"

"Certainly. Oh, and one more thing—I'd like to suggest you hold the baby after it is born. That may be difficult but it will help you in your grief."

"Yes, Dr. Fellows also mentioned that."

"Do you know when you last felt the baby move?"

Everything seemed a blur. Yesterday felt like years ago. I couldn't remember when I last felt it. She paused, waiting for me to answer. Then I remembered. It had been during the wedding when I had mentioned it to Colleen. Thinking back, I recalled being surprised with the intensity of that kick. It had been sharp and sudden, not smooth and fluttering like usual. Yes, that was the last time. That was when our baby had fought its last struggle for life, dying inside me without my even knowing it.

There was the sound of the blood pressure cuff expanding, periodically checking my blood pressure. It had been high when I checked into the hospital. Except for that though, the room was quiet; too quiet. I remembered the steady sound of Michael's heartbeat on the monitor while we waited for his birth. However, there were no sounds of our baby's heart beating. The silence seemed deafening.

Ron and I sat in a state of numbness, trying to sort through the decisions that lay ahead. I laid my head back on the pillow, trying to relax. I thought of our baby. I felt an odd sense of relief, knowing that nothing could hurt it during the delivery. At the same time, I felt vulnerable. What if something happened to me? I knew it wasn't likely but with the newly discovered death of our child, it seemed anything was possible. I needed to tell Ron how much I loved him, just in case.

"Honey?" I said, trying to get his attention. He'd been silently looking over the information Jennifer had left. He lifted his head to look at me. Tears were in his eyes. I began to cry again too. "Even if we never have other children, I'm just so thankful that we have each other. I am so glad I have spent my life with you. Thank you for being my husband."

He nodded, struggling with his words. "Yes, we've had a very good life together. We've been very blessed." He must have been thinking what I was as he added, "I just don't know what I'd do without you."

"We have our faith and we have each other. No matter what's ahead, I know we'll be all right."

We continued to talk, discussing our fears and apprehensions. Finally, we turned our attention to the decisions that we needed to make. It didn't take us long to decide. There weren't many options.

Labor was definitely underway. The medications were making me sick to my stomach. I couldn't stop shivering. Waves of nausea left me feeling weak. Each time I felt sick, Ron helped me out of bed, to the bathroom, then back into the bed. He was concerned, but Jennifer assured him it was a normal side effect. He wasn't convinced though. Nancy hadn't reacted like this. Jennifer gave me a shot to ease the discomfort. Almost immediately, I became drowsy. I struggled to stay awake though. I didn't want Ron to be alone.

Just then, Colleen arrived. She rushed to my bed, crying. She was trying to be strong but it was no use. Our news had devastated her too. We talked briefly, but I couldn't seem to stay awake. I was glad she was here. Now I could sleep knowing Ron would have someone to talk with.

Dozing off, I could hear everything they said but was unable to participate. It was like I was in a state of semi-consciousness. I felt so helpless, but it was nice to be able to relax as the contractions steadily continued. A Christian radio channel was on, and they were interviewing Sandi Patty. She told how she had lost a baby but then was doubly blessed with twins her next pregnancy. A spark of hope filled my mind. Perhaps there would be more children for us too.

An hour passed. My head began to clear. As I opened my eyes, Mom entered the room. She looked exhausted and frantic. She must have driven like a maniac to get here so quickly. Although we hadn't expected her, she was a welcome sight.

Dr. Fellows came in moments later to check on the progress, followed by Holly. Holly sat on the edge of the bed and talked. I was so grateful for her compassion and concern. Dr. Fellows checked me over and then they left.

It was nearing dinnertime. Mom suggested that Ron get something to eat. He reluctantly agreed. He had barely left the room though when I began to feel anxious. Contractions were coming much faster and stronger. I didn't want to have the baby without him. I asked Mom to go get him. Mom tried to reassure me that we had time, but I insisted. Once she left, I started to cry. I felt so out of control. Colleen took my hand and tried to help me with my contractions.

Pointing to a floral picture on the wall, she instructed, "Focus on that flower and breathe with me."

I was so glad she was there. At least she had some experience.

Finally, I got a break in the contractions. "Colleen," I said, "I hope you understand that I don't want you or Mom here when the baby is born. I just don't know what to expect myself."

"Of course, I understand. I knew you would want to be alone with Ron. Having a baby is a very private moment. I will make sure we are both gone."

"Thank you," I said, squeezing her hand. "Now if only Ron would get back."

As I worked through my next contraction with Colleen, I was so grateful for my special sister who recognized the importance of our private and special delivery, treating it as if there was nothing unusual about it.

It seemed an eternity before Ron and Mom were back. Colleen immediately ushered Mom out, explaining they needed to check on her boys who were at our house with their daddy. With Ron back, I felt more relaxed as I continued trying to work through the contractions.

Jennifer gave me another shot and suggested I use the bathroom again. I was so weak I could hardly walk. I just wanted to lie there and die, but Ron helped me get up. I was so grateful for his strength. As soon as I reached the bathroom, I realized the baby's head had crowned. Delivery was imminent. I panicked.

"We need to get back to the bed," I ordered Ron. All I could think of was Jennifer's insistence that we deliver the baby in bed. That way they could see if there were any cord or placenta problems.

I literally ran back to the bed holding the baby's head in as Ron followed, trying to keep up with me as he pushed the stand with the IV attached. As I leaped on the bed, I pushed the nurse's button. Everything seemed to be happening so quickly.

Then I saw her. She was lying at the end of the bed. Seeing her little form, I felt relieved. Even though our baby was deceased, I didn't want to hurt her by dropping her on the floor. The panic that filled the room just moments ago dissolved. Time seemed to have stopped. There was a sense of peace as Ron and I looked in awe at our newborn baby. She was beautiful. Instantly we felt overwhelmed at the sight of our child, created from our love. It didn't seem to matter that she was gone, only that she was ours.

She made no sound and laid perfectly still. Once again, memories of Michael crowded my mind as I recalled his first cries. Our baby wasn't going to cry though. The reality of her death came crashing down.

Jennifer arrived in the room and looked over the umbilical cord. "I don't see any problems," she said, as she cut it. Turning to the clock, she noted the time of birth, 7:00 p.m. August 23rd. My 30th birthday was only two days away. I always wanted to be a mother by the time I was thirty. This was not as I had planned.

Jennifer picked up our daughter and laid her on my stomach. Ron and I couldn't take our eyes off her. She was perfect in every manner. The sight of her tiny body, completely formed, was overpowering. I noticed her little hands and tiny fingernails. She had such long fingers. For a fleeting moment, I thought how she might be a wonderful piano player just like her Aunt Colleen. Then reality hit. Our little girl would never be a pianist, at least not here on earth.

Then I looked at her legs, so small and frail, bent slightly at the knees. She was so pretty, so perfect. There were ten perfect little fingers and ten perfect little toes. I thought of all the parents who excitedly proclaimed that their child had ten fingers and toes. *So does mine*, I thought, *only that wasn't enough for her to live*.

Jennifer wrapped our daughter in a blanket and then put her in my arms. I looked up to Ron with tears in my eyes as he lifted her and began gently carrying her around the room, rocking back and forth on his feet as if comforting her. Instantly, I noticed the tender look on his face. It was so full of love, just like when he first held Michael only four short months ago. It was apparent that this father's love extended not only beyond bloodlines but also beyond life itself. He loved both our children as much as any child could be loved.

Turning to me, Ron whispered, "Isn't she beautiful?"

I nodded.

"I want to somehow memorize everything about her. I don't ever want to forget what she looks like," he said.

I began to cry, angry at the injustice of it all.

A short time later, Colleen and Mom poked their heads in the door. "Can we come in?" Colleen asked.

"Oh, yes. Come see our little girl. Isn't she beautiful?" I stated with excitement and sadness mixed together.

Mom looked at her in Ron's arms. Colleen rushed over to me. Somehow, I think she had expected that this was a big mistake. She had so hoped that our baby would be alive. She started to cry. The last possibility of hope was gone.

"We'd like to name her Amy Colleen. Would that be all right with you?"

Colleen hugged me. She nodded yes but could not find the words to go with her nod.

"I'm just so sorry she won't get to know you," I added. Then we both cried.

"I'll take your baby and get her measurements," Jennifer said.

I did not want to be away from our daughter. Moments ago, she had been a part of my body. I didn't want her to go. It felt like my heart was being ripped from my chest. I must have cried out.

"I'll bring her back later if you'd like," Jennifer said, and then left the room. Minutes passed, then Jennifer came back. I expected to see her with our baby, but instead she had a certificate, indicating Amy Colleen weighed one pound and was twelve inches long. Her tiny ink footprints were next to her name.

"Dr. Fellows said you could go home tonight," Jennifer said, having conferred with him after he had checked the baby and me over.

"I'd like to," I responded. I could hear other babies as they cried with their first sounds of life in nearby rooms. It hurt so much that mine hadn't. I didn't want to stay here where all this sadness had occurred.

Before I could go, they insisted I eat even though I wasn't hungry. Then, slowly I dressed and gathered my things together. Jennifer brought a wheelchair. Ron was holding the certificate with Amy's footprints as well as a Polaroid picture of her.

It was time to go. I was tired and my head felt like it was in a fog. I hesitated to go though. I wanted to see our baby girl one more time, but I didn't know how to ask. Therefore, without the courage or strength to do so, we departed, carrying only the few physical reminders of our little girl. As we drove away from the hospital, all I could think of was how I wished I could have kissed our precious Amy good-bye.

Chapter 12

STIRRING AWAKE THE next morning, I felt the familiar fluttering of movement inside. My hopes lifted. Touching my stomach though, I realized that our baby was gone. I was angry that my body would play such tricks. Like a heavy wool blanket, horrendous sadness and disappointment fell over me. I felt like I was suffocating as I struggled to breathe.

I forced myself out of bed and into the shower as I tried to clear my head. My family would be waiting for us upstairs. I was anxious to see them. They would help to distract me from reality. Besides, my nephews would help to cheer me. They were so dear to me.

As I pulled open the closet in search of something to wear, reality again slapped me. The maternity clothes now seemed to mock me. I thought of how there wouldn't be a baby to show for all those billowing clothes. Resignedly, however, I put them on since there was nothing else in my closet.

I kissed Ron, who was still lying in bed, and then headed upstairs. Anthony, unaware of the previous day's tragedy, immediately greeted me with a cheery hello. Seeing his happy little face, I was so grateful that at least this time he wouldn't have to face the disappointment. He had not seen Amy like he had Michael.

Turning to the rest of our family, despite my efforts to stay composed, with the first hug I dissolved into tears. Thus went the rest of the day as I struggled in a sort of shocked daze while battling tears that were near the surface.

Colleen and her family had already planned to come for the weekend in order to celebrate my birthday. Our tragedy had caused them to come a day earlier. However, since Anthony had helped bake a cake, a birthday needed to be celebrated despite the turn of events. His sneaky mother had told him several weeks ago that his third birthday was right after Aunt Denise's birthday. He was most anxious to get mine over with so that they could get on with his.

Although it was a somber day, once again we saw God's hand at work in the support and love of our family. As Ron led us in prayer at dinner that evening, his words included thanksgiving for all we had been given, including a beautiful daughter that we loved so much. There were tears with our thanks, but we truly did feel blessed as we ate dinner surrounded by our family.

When Mom and Colleen's family went home the following day, once again it was just the two of us. Once again, there was an incredible emptiness. For years, it had just been Ron and me. Why did it feel like such an adjustment for it to be just the two of us again?

"That must have been it," I told Ron. "It was the diet pop I drank that weekend."

Ron shook his head.

I didn't let him respond though. "Or maybe it was the day I got too hot and didn't come in like I should. Or do you remember when we danced at that wedding reception? I might have overdone it."

"Stop doing that to yourself," Ron said. "You didn't cause Amy's death."

"I'm the only one who could care for her, so it had to be something I did."

"Honey, many women don't take care of themselves nearly as well as you did and they have perfectly healthy babies. It was not anything you did. You were so careful. You've got to stop blaming yourself."

But I wasn't done yet. I knew it had to be my fault. If it wasn't something I'd done physically then it had to be something emotional. After all, I had been a complete wreck after losing Michael. Continuing to assault myself, I began crying. "I should have handled Michael's loss better. I should have gone to counseling even if Nancy wouldn't go with us. If only I'd talked things out, Amy might still be alive."

"You handled it the best you knew. We lost our son. How were you supposed to handle that?"

"I don't know, but I should have known better. When Dad died, I lost weight then too only I wasn't pregnant. I didn't have a baby counting on me to keep it alive."

"Denise, you didn't cause this!" Ron said with finality.

"Well if I didn't, who did?" I sobbed. Anger filled me as my thoughts turned to Nancy. "Maybe Nancy is responsible since she's the one who caused this stress in the first place. She was so eager to take credit for our baby's conception; perhaps she'd like credit for its death too."

Ron tried to reason with me. "Even if we knew for sure what caused Amy's death, it's not going to bring her back to life."

He was right, yet I did not want to believe him. Sobbing into his shoulder, I choked out my frustrations. "But how could our baby, any baby, die? And for no apparent reason? How could death come before birth? Why couldn't she be a part of our life? How could her purpose be complete when her life never extended beyond the womb? I just cannot accept that Amy's life was in vain. There has to be a reason for all of this." I continued sobbing as Ron quietly held me. There were no answers to the endless questions.

Without answers though, I couldn't seem to accept what had happened. In a state of denial, I continued to wear my maternity clothes as if to somehow hang onto my pregnancy. I had resigned my body to the growth of our baby. I did not want it back. I wanted to be pregnant. I was embarrassed that I wasn't. Filled with shame and guilt, I tried to hide the truth, mostly from myself.

Five days had passed since Amy's death. Ron and I were working on a project in the basement when the doorbell rang. When I answered the door, the UPS driver had me sign for a small box. It was from the crematory. Trembling, I took the box. Once again, our daughter was in my hands. All that remained of her was inside this box.

Carefully, as if to not disturb the contents, I carried it to Ron. Tears were again streaming down my face. Ron swallowed hard. His hands were shaking too. "Should we open it?" he asked.

"I don't know if I can. This seems so final. I've never seen anyone's ashes before. How could this be our baby?"

Ron's arms were around me. He began to cry too. "Let's just leave it for now," he said.

I felt relieved. I wasn't ready yet.

All day I kept thinking of our baby—how impossible everything seemed. That night though, there was a strange sense of peace knowing that Amy was at home with us again. In an odd sort of way, it felt as if we were together again.

"Mommy, Mommy!"

I woke with a start. I had been dreaming about Michael. The nightmares of losing Michael had started all over again. In this dream, Nancy was taking him from me again. I had no choice but to give him up. Just as I handed him to her though, he looked at me over her shoulder. Holding his arms out to me, he had cried out. For the remainder of the night I tossed and turned, unable to put Michael's terrified face out of my mind.

Amy's death shattered any healing that had occurred since losing Michael. Our grief was magnified as thoughts of both our children consumed each minute of the day. I longed for just one moment when my mind was free from such painful memories. I could not believe that our dreams of becoming a family had been denied once again. All I could feel was the void, the emptiness.

Although the nursery door was again shut, sounds of Michael moving in his crib once again seemed to echo in the house. Compounding the emotional suffering was physical pain. Nature had continued, preparing for a baby to nurse despite none to feed. I was swollen and miserable with pain. Each movement reminded me of what should have been. It all seemed so unfair. How were we supposed to go on? This time, there wasn't even another baby to look forward to in November—only a looming sense of despair.

One week after Amy's death, we received a most unexpected call. It was Lynn. For a moment, I wondered if she had heard about Amy but I could not imagine how.

"It's so great to hear from you," I responded warmly. Despite the tragic results of our adoption, Ron and I felt a fondness for Lynn. She had been such a dear friend to us during our long months awaiting Michael. She'd taken such good care of Nancy and thus Michael. We loved her for all she had done for us too.

"How are you?" she asked.

I began to cry. "Not too good. We lost our daughter Friday."

She gasped and started to cry. "What happened?"

"We don't know. The autopsy and chromosomal studies didn't show any irregularities. The only disparity was her size. She was very small, as if only 24 weeks gestation. I know our dates were right though."

"So you don't have any answers?"

"No, which really makes it hard. I cannot accept that she died for no reason. I guess deep down, I blame the stress after losing Michael. I really haven't done too well since then. I'll probably always wonder if things would have been different had we not lost him."

"Oh Denise, this is horrible. I had so hoped your baby would help to fill your lives. I am so sorry."

"Thank you Lynn. It has been devastating. I can't believe that you called. It's almost as if you knew we needed to talk. How are you?" I asked.

"Fine, although I'm still shocked over what occurred with Michael. I just don't understand what happened. Do you have any idea why Nancy changed her mind?"

"Not really. However, I do believe she acted out of grief. I just don't think she was prepared for the sadness."

"That makes sense," Lynn said.

"Hasn't Nancy talked to you about it?" I asked.

"No, in fact, she hasn't talked to me much at all."

"Why?"

"I don't know."

"Isn't it ironic that we were the only ones included in her pregnancy, yet now all three of us have been cut off?"

"I think she'll come around again. She probably has some things to work through yet," Lynn added.

"You're probably right. Have you seen Michael?" I asked tentatively.

"Yes, he and Nancy were at the family reunion in July. He was darling."

I began to cry. "I miss him so much."

"I'm sure you do. Would you rather not hear?" Lynn asked.

"It's okay. I want to yet it really hurts, especially now that Amy is gone too. It's just so hard not having them in our lives."

Lynn continued sharing the details of Michael. "I got to hold him," she said. I quietly cried as I thought of how much I would love to hold him.

As our conversation ended, I thanked her for calling. It was so good to discuss all that had happened. She was one of the few people to whom I didn't have to try to explain it. She knew what had happened. It helped to be able to talk about it and pour my heart out.

The following day, Ron came in from the mailbox carrying a package. I figured it was a belated birthday gift, but then I noticed the look on Ron's face as he brought it to the table. I could not imagine what caused such concern. Anxiously, I glanced at the package and recognized Nancy's handwriting.

Ron and I stared at the package for a moment. We weren't sure we wanted to open it, especially right now. Three and a half months had passed since Nancy had taken Michael from us. Now, in the midst of our fresh grief, we were finally hearing from her. Were we ready to handle whatever she had to say?

Unable to stand the suspense, we finally opened it. On top lay a letter from Nancy along with pictures of Michael. I glanced at them but instantly felt tears erupting. I set the pictures aside. It hurt too much to see them right now.

The necklace we had given Nancy was in the box, as well as the friendship plaque and the maternity dresses I had made for her. She probably thought I could use the dresses.

Finally, I opened the letter and read it aloud to Ron.

Nancy's letter conveyed her difficulty in being able to write to us sooner, her sorrow for hurting us, and a plea for us to understand and recognize the good that had come out of the ordeal. Her first paragraph horrified and angered me. How selfish of her to delay a response to us just because it had been difficult for her. Did she have any idea how difficult it had been for us waiting to hear from her?

Her apology for the hurt she caused felt like a stinging slap. She had taken our son, betrayed our friendship, and destroyed the trust between us. The hurt she'd caused was a side effect. Certainly, she owed us an apology for hurting us, but where was the apology for taking Michael, for betraying our trust and friendship? Furthermore, how dare she ask us to understand when she had shown so little understanding for us! What good had come out of this ordeal? She had caused devastation in our lives, as well as in the lives of our loved ones, and now she was proclaiming the goodness of it all. How dare she!

From there, Nancy bounced from one source of blame to the other, never accepting the responsibility for the outcome. She claimed it was God's plan for her to have a baby. She credited our pregnancy to hers—claiming God's only purpose for our involvement in the adoption was so we could get pregnant. She claimed to go through with the adoption in order to fulfill our lives without any thought of her own desires. Furthermore, our pregnancy was simply a sign from God indicating that she should back out of the adoption. From Nancy's perspective, it was clear she assumed no responsibility for what had occurred. In her opinion, it was all simply a result of poor counseling, misunderstanding God's plan, and good intentions gone bad.

As I read her endless rationalizations, my anger mixed with sadness. I wondered if she had any idea what really had happened. Instead of accepting the truth and thus some responsibility, it appeared she'd built herself the perfect alibi in order to declare herself innocent. Yet, how was she going to find any peace in her life if she didn't face and accept the truth? I felt sorry for her. Perhaps it was the only way she could live with what she had done. What a sad existence.

Nancy's letter continued with an update on Michael. Although I was grateful to hear how he was doing so well, it hurt so much, particularly combined with Amy's death. I was also shocked to read that she was taking him to the same pediatrician I had chosen. Nancy knew I had painstakingly selected this pediatrician for Michael and presumably Amy. Once again, I felt violated. It was as if she had taken every advantage of me by allowing me to do all the research and legwork only to then take over.

Even more upsetting though was the realization that if she had been taking Michael to the same pediatrician, then Nancy must have been in Billings this whole time, not out of town as she had told us. All this time, waiting for word from her, she and Michael had probably only been blocks away. It tore my heart to shreds. We could have gone to counseling together or attempted to repair our friendship. We could have seen Michael. We could have—.

Nancy continued her letter by telling us she did not feel obligated to pay any of the $13,000 of expenses we had incurred because of the adoption. We had already realized that was her conclusion since we had received the attorney's final bill despite Nancy's promise to pay it. Nancy further asked that we return Michael's baby picture taken at the hospital. She included her new out-of-state address where she would be moving in order to finish her master's degree. It appeared from the date on the letter that she had written it just prior to moving. Nancy's letter concluded with words of her love for us and her assurance of happier times as she reminded us that our pregnancy and the child were our "dream come true."

As I finished reading her six-page, handwritten letter, tears were streaming down my face. Her words had only multiplied our pain since there would be no dream come true for us. I hated her shallow assurances and overconfidence combined with her complete lack of responsibility. However, in spite of the pain her words caused, there was also a sense of relief. After all these months of waiting, we had finally received a response. Her message was clear. There would be no opportunity to talk. Michael would not be coming back. Nancy's letter had provided the long-awaited closure that we had so desperately sought.

In one short week, we'd held our daughter long enough to say good-bye. Now in that same week the final flicker of hope of ever having Michael back had also been extinguished. Just as we had anticipated Michael's and Amy's lives together, we would now have to accept their losses together. Michael and Nancy were going on in their new life and so must we.

Chapter 13

EVERYTHING SEEMED JUMBLED up and impossible to fathom. I put up a shield as if trying to protect myself from further hurt. I felt as if I were a robot, methodically going through the day, completely drained of all zest for life. I couldn't seem to concentrate. All I thought about was our children. It seemed that everyone around us was watching, waiting for us to crack. We kept going though, putting on a tough front as if in a play, acting out roles that had nothing to do with our true selves. It was like watching our own lives from a distance.

There was emptiness too about our lives. The challenges of work that I had once loved now felt petty and unimportant. Simple tasks seemed to take more energy than I had. My tolerance was short. My patience was even shorter. In spite of our faith, life seemed meaningless.

I began questioning my own mortality having survived our child. Although I wasn't ready to die, somehow death felt near. Anxiously, I worked to get my life in order so Ron could go on without me. I got the bookwork done, the files organized, and the safety deposit box inventoried. I even wrote my obituary. All he would have to do was bury me.

I was desperate for answers. Frantically I searched my faith, pleading with God to give me some understanding. I began dissecting everything I'd been taught, analyzing its relevance in light of our tragedies. I knew that God would never give us more than we could handle, yet did He know we had hit the wall? Did God truly intend for us to suffer such heartache? Was this really His will and, if so, what was the purpose?

I remembered reading in my Bible in I Peter 4:13 that I should consider myself fortunate to suffer for Christ, but how was this suffering for Christ? It wasn't as if I was a martyr in some foreign country persecuted for my faith. I was just a mother who mourned her children. It felt like such a senseless and useless suffering. It felt so unnecessary.

Filled with confusion, I spent hours reading my Bible as well as other books on spiritual matters. I didn't want to become bitter. I didn't want to blame God, nor did I want others to blame Him. I just wanted to understand. I needed to find some peace and, more than anything, I just needed the strength to get through it all.

Many friends were supportive and caring, for which we were so grateful. They were the ones who listened to our sorrow more than once and allowed us to cry without expectations. However, there also seemed to be a barrage of comments that were meant to be comforting but were instead hurtful.

"It was meant to be," a friend said, trying to offer comfort upon hearing of Amy's death.

"Your next one will be perfect," another said.

I smiled politely with each comment, but inside I wanted to scream. They had no idea how insensitive such comments sounded to us. How could they say we were meant to go through such pain, that our child was meant to die while they had children to tuck into bed each night? Besides, what made them so certain?

To assume that our daughter hadn't been perfect was a far cry from the truth. The doctors had not found anything wrong with her. It wouldn't have made any difference though. She was our daughter. Our love for her, even in her death, exceeded any physical or mental perfection. Given the choice, we would have chosen her life over perfection.

"You can have another," others were quick to say. We didn't want just any baby though. We wanted Michael and Amy. Certainly, another child might lessen our sadness, but it wouldn't change the longing for the children we'd been denied. It seemed incredible that others were so willing to dismiss one life for another, as if children could easily be replaced. It made about as much sense as telling a widower that he could have another wife, or a grieving child that their surviving father could remarry and they could have another mother. No child, not even a perfect, living child could ever replace the two we had lost.

I tried to be tolerant, knowing that others couldn't know what we felt. I resented that we did. I wished that we too could be so ignorant. Such naiveté, however, had died along with our dreams for Michael and Amy.

Just when I thought I had heard every insensitive comment, there seemed to be a new one. "I knew someone who lost their baby in the eighth month of her pregnancy!" one woman proclaimed. I wondered if she thought this was a contest. Did she honestly think our grief was any less just because our daughter died a month earlier?

"It's good it happened before you could get attached," others said. What an absurd comment, as if we weren't already attached to our children. We had loved them both from the moment we knew of their existence. And even though Michael came home with us while Amy never did, our attachment to both of them was intense.

Certainly, time would have granted us more memories, but isn't it the memories that make living without a loved one bearable? I felt cheated, only allowed the subtle kicks of Amy as she moved inside me. What I would have given to see her smile or open her eyes. I wished I could have kissed her just once while she lived. What a treasure it would have been to have a picture of her to hang on my wall. Those simple things would have meant so much.

There never seemed to be an end to the reasons people gave us for the tragedies we had been forced to face. The comments only made me angry though. I felt like our losses were belittled since our children had only been babies. Some seemed to have found a way to put our tragedies into a nice and simple little package and then, content with their own profound explanation, quickly tuck our tragedies away. For us though, it would never be so easy to understand. Besides, we were entitled to our grief. However, the more we heard these comments, the more isolated Ron and I felt in our private grief.

I could hear the ice cream cart in the distance, its carnival music playing. It was heading our way. Suddenly I couldn't breathe. My chest was pounding. My hands were clammy. I started sobbing uncontrollably.

Mom's words spoken only months ago as she held Michael echoed in my head—*We're going to have so much fun eating ice cream on the steps when you get a little bigger.* Having ice cream with Michael or Amy however would never be our privilege.

I was envious of Nancy. I felt robbed of so many special days. She would be the one delighted this Christmas with the look of wonder in Michael's eyes as he watched the Christmas lights. She would be the one to cheer him on as he mastered his tricycle and went to school. She would be the one to play catch with him. Even waiting on the steps for the ice cream man would be her pleasure. It seemed so unfair. We had been the ones who had anticipated such days with him.

The ice cream truck though was only one of the many everyday things that sent me into total chaos. We were bombarded with telephone sales calls congratulating us on our new baby as they tried to sell encyclopedias and children's books. They must have gotten our name from the magazine we had subscribed to, another painful reminder. A diaper company continued to send sample diapers through the various stages of Michael's growth. Every television program seemed to have a baby in it. If that weren't enough though, there were the bizarre events, like the day a customer walked into my office and introduced himself as Michael Williams. It seemed I was constantly bumping into our tragedies, being reminded of what we had lost and the plans and dreams that would never be fulfilled.

My anger grew with each reminder. I was angry at the price we had paid. I still could not believe that the friendship, once filled with such love, enough to make us parents had instead cost us that very privilege. I questioned whether it had been worth it. I wished I had never met Nancy. In fact, in my wounded anger, I wished just about every ill of her possible. Although I knew God wanted me to forgive her, I wondered how I would ever be able.

Colleen had come for the weekend. When she arrived, she handed me an envelope.

I opened it, and a small silver object fell out. Picking it up in my hand, I realized it was a bookmarker. Engraved on it was:

Amy Colleen
August 23
Our Little Angel

"I wanted you to have something you could keep as a special tribute to your first daughter," Colleen said. I was so grateful. We had so few things for Amy. Turning to the card, I read:

Dear Denise and Ron,

I just wanted to let you know how honored I am that your little Amy and I share our name. Thank you so much. Amy is the closest piece of Heaven I have ever seen—so small, yet so perfect. She will always be special in my heart; for the excitement she brought and the promise of tomorrow during such difficult times. May this be a special reminder of your daughter. I will always love her. Thank you for the special tie between us.

I love you, Colleen

As I read Colleen's words, it was as if a new realization came over me. Although our little girl had never lived outside of my body, her life had not been in vain. She truly had been our hope for brighter days after losing Michael. She had given us a reason to go on without our son. She had made a difference even in her short life. What would we have done without that hope in those dark days?

I was so grateful to Colleen for her wisdom and sensitivity. Although I still didn't understand, perhaps her words could help me find some peace.

Since Colleen was here, I decided it was time to do something with the advent calendar package that Colleen had made for my pregnancy. Dragging the box from the closet, I sadly looked at its contents. There were still a number of unopened packages that were meant for my final trimester.

"Do you want to save these?" I asked Colleen.

"No, they were for your pregnancy with Amy. I'll want to do something different when you have another baby. Besides, most of the items are things you can use anyway. If it doesn't bother you, let's open them."

I was glad, curious to see what else she had bought. Besides, it might help to cheer me. Trying to be jovial, I opened the first card. Immediately though, tears were brimming in my eyes. Her note was filled with the usual excitement for our baby, the baby we would never be bringing home. I decided to save the remaining notes for another time and simply open the packages for now.

Soon the two of us were laughing, enjoying the twelve remaining gifts. There was a certificate for a haircut, hard candy for labor, potato chips for whenever the munchies hit, and items only a sister would buy. Naturally, we sampled any of the food items. It was like having a party.

The final gift contained a CD.

"I found it particularly soothing during labor," Colleen explained. "I still like to listen to it when I'm relaxing."

I put it in the CD player. Soft music filled the room. Suddenly, the grief of the past months came crashing down. Clutching each other, Colleen and I sobbed. It felt like our hearts had been ripped wide open. I didn't think we'd ever stop crying.

The months that followed continued to be a lonely time. People had quit asking how we were doing. They expected us to go on and leave our pain behind. I didn't know how.

I learned of a support group for people who had suffered the death of an infant. As a Christian, I thought I should be able to handle this solely with God's help. I kept thinking about the group though, wondering if it would help. Finally I went, desperate for some solace. It was the best thing I ever did. Every month, I took my hurts, worries, anger, and confusion. No one treated me as if I was crazy. No one expected me to get over it. No one judged me for talking about it even though time had passed. Most comforting of all though was just being with others who understood. They had been there. They knew what it felt like. I no longer felt so alone.

I realized that sometimes God helps us through other people. I didn't have to be the rock. He was. He knew my needs better than I did and as a result, led me to the support group. I just had to be willing to accept the help. As month after month passed, I began to find healing. I learned that going on in life didn't mean leaving Michael and Amy behind but rather learning how to live life without them.

"Read this," a friend said. I was at the office muddling through the endless papers.

"I found this in a closet upstairs," she continued. "I've seen it a million times but have never paid any attention to it. For some reason though, today I stopped to read it. I have no idea why it was even there, but I think it was meant for you."

Turning to the yellowed paper, I read,

THE LOAN
"I'll lend you for a little time, a child of mine," God said,
"For you to love the while he lives, and mourn for when he's dead.
It may be six or seven years, or twenty-two or three
But will you, 'til I call him back, take care of him for me?
He'll bring his charms to gladden you, and shall his stay be brief
You'll have his lovely memories, as solace for your grief.
I cannot promise he will stay, since all from earth return
But there are lessons taught down there, I want this child to learn.
I've looked in the wide world over, in my search for teachers true,
And from the throngs that crowd life's lanes, I have selected you.
Now will you give him all your love, not think the labor vain,
Nor hate me when I come to take him back again?

I fancied that I heard them say, "Dear Lord, Thy will be done!
For all the joy Thy child shall bring, the risk of grief we'll run.
We'll shelter him with tenderness; we'll love him while we may,
And for the happiness we've known, forever grateful stay.
But shall the angels call him much sooner than we've planned
We'll brave the bitter grief that comes, and surely understand."

Author Unknown

Tears again flooded my eyes but this time they felt so good. A sense of warmth and peace rushed over me. It was as if God had given us a miracle in this yellowed paper, long forgotten in a lonely closet only to be found now.

In the days that followed, I read the poem over and over. I began to realize that though I was confused and filled with questions, God was not surprised or lacking understanding. He could see the bigger picture. Once again, I leaned further into Him as I considered the mysteries of this life. Perhaps someday, I too would understand God's design and plan but for now, I found comfort as I pressed closer to Him. He knew my pain and hurt with me. Despite the turmoil of the tragedies we had endured, God was still in control.

Although thoughts of our children continued to plague my mind, they weren't always sad like they'd been in the past. Thinking of Amy, I wondered what she would have looked like. I wondered if her hair would have been wavy like her daddy's or straight like mine. I could almost see her dressed in pink ruffles and bows, dancing in heaven as her little dress swirled around. She was so beautiful in my mind.

I thought of all the things she would miss. She would never be a bride. She would never have children. I felt sad for her, denied such joys. At the same time though, I knew she would never know the pain in losing a child or the betrayal of a friend. She would never be concerned with the injustices and hurts of the world.

It also warmed my heart to think of Amy being in heaven with my dad. It seemed appropriate that he should get to spoil her first after waiting all these years for grandchildren. Heaven seemed more real and personal. I even felt thankful that she was there, waiting for us.

Yes, Amy had gone ahead, living her next life and experiencing something we had yet to experience. After all, our God is her God. She just was privileged to see him first. As such, He would be her only teacher. I began to feel at peace with her life and death, knowing that someday we would be together again.

If only I could find that same peace with Michael.

"Aunt Denise, what happened to your baby?" my niece Maria asked. She was four. Ron's sister Krista and her family had come from Helena to spend some time with us.

The room suddenly got quiet. Glancing up, I noticed that Maria's father had a stern look on his face. Perhaps they had discussed this. Perhaps Maria had been instructed not to ask. She couldn't help herself though. She was curious. Besides, she knew I'd been pregnant. Having recently observed her mother's pregnancy with her little sister Britney, she knew what a pregnancy meant.

I tried to reassure her father with a smile, but I sensed that everyone was nervous. I didn't mind her question though. In fact, it was a relief that someone had finally brought it up. The past days and weeks of polite condolences were driving me crazy. Everyone had been so careful as if tiptoeing around the subject. I wanted to talk about it though. I took a deep breath.

"Our baby died," I answered. I did not want to cry. It might only make Maria feel bad.

"But didn't you have a baby and then another baby in your tummy?"

"Yes, I did Maria."

"Well, what happened to your babies?"

My mind was whirling as her question echoed. How could I possibly explain what happened without scaring her? She was too young to understand the horrible truth, yet I didn't want to lie. Perhaps when she was older, I could explain the whole story but for now, I had to come up with an acceptable answer, despite how unacceptable it all seemed.

Finally, I took a deep breath. "You remember Michael, don't you?"

She nodded yes.

"Well, Michael was only staying with us a short time—like you stay with your baby-sitter. His mother wasn't able to take care of him at first but now she can so he is living with her." As soon as the words left my mouth, I wanted to scream. It was so far from the truth. I hated myself for having to deny Michael's role as our son but didn't know how else to explain it.

Despite my valiant attempt though, Maria knew better. She had seen us with Michael. She had even helped to open baby gifts at his shower in Helena. My explanation did not make sense. "Aunt Denise, why did you give Michael away?"

My bravery was shattered as I crumbled into tears. Maria's eyes widened, but she remained silent as she watched me. I reached to hug her. Finally, I gathered myself enough to respond. "Maria, it's all right to ask me these questions even though it makes me cry. I'm just very sad right now."

Inside though, my rage and bitterness towards Nancy grew. I was angry that once again I had been put in a position of lying for Nancy's benefit. Perhaps if she had to explain this to my nieces and nephews, she would have been more careful about her actions. She wasn't the one, however, who had to explain or even live with it. All I could do was somehow protect our little ones from the truth.

Thoughts of our little Michael continued to fill me with concern. I wanted him to have a good life, a good upbringing. It seemed even more important now that Amy was gone. It was as if I needed him to live for both of them. I wondered how he was doing, adjusting to another new home with Nancy. I wondered if Nancy had him with a babysitter while she was at school or if she had made other arrangements.

I wondered if we would ever see Michael again. Perhaps he'd be a teenager or young adult before we were given the opportunity. Would I still recognize him? How would I feel?

I allowed myself to fantasize. Thinking of seeing him made me feel excited yet nervous. I hoped he wouldn't mind me hugging him. There was so much I'd want to tell him. I'd want him to know what joy he'd brought to our lives. Perhaps we could even look through his baby book together and share the pictures of his first month of life. Such times were ones that only Ron and I could share with him. After all, although I was Michael's second mother, he was our first son. We would always love him. I prayed that someday we would be able to tell him.

I wondered if our life would always be filled with such suspense, wondering about him, hoping to see him again. I knew we would never stop waiting though. There was a void in our lives left by Michael. Perhaps seeing him again could fill that void.

It was October 23rd, two months after Amy's death. Like so many other nights, Ron and I were talking about our children. Michael, however, was most on our minds because on this day a year ago, Nancy had called asking us to adopt him. It seemed unreal that so much had happened in one short year. Michael was six months old now. The waiting period for the adoption would have been over. He would have legally been ours.

As Ron and I finished dinner, the phone rang. It was Colleen.

"Denise," she said. Her voice was shaky. I knew something was wrong.

"What's the matter?" I asked.

She started sobbing as she choked out, "Oh, Denise, Michael died!"

With Colleen's words, it was as if a pillow had been shoved into my face as my throat and chest tightened. I couldn't catch my breath. I felt like every inch of my body was going to shake apart as I trembled. This couldn't be true. Michael could not be gone. This conversation had to be a nightmare!

Colleen continued, choking back tears, "Nancy's mother just called. Two days ago, Michael was at the babysitter's home. He went down for a nap around 2:30. At 3:00, the baby-sitter felt a strange urge to check on him. When she did, she found him dead. She attempted CPR but she could not revive him. It appears he died from Sudden Infant Death Syndrome. I talked to Nancy too. She told me to tell you that it's over."

Ron had been watching me with obvious concern. As I hung up the phone, I blurted out Colleen's news. He said nothing as he sadly shook his head. Tears were in his eyes.

We both sat in a numb state of shock. Finally Ron spoke. "Nancy's right. It's over."

Although I cried, it felt as if there was nothing left in me to cry.

"Nancy is planning to bury Michael in Montana," I said. "Do you think we should go to the funeral?"

Ron was quiet before he spoke. "I don't think I can. I have already said good-bye once. I don't think I can do it again. Besides, funerals are for the living—a place for them to draw strength and comfort from their loved ones. I'm not sure Nancy considers us one of her loved ones anymore."

In a way I was relieved he didn't want to go. Although I could certainly understand what it felt like to lose Michael, I had no strength left to give in order to comfort Nancy. I was spent. I felt like a shell, completely empty.

"It might only cause Nancy further pain if we were there," I said. "It would be hard on us too. I can't imagine having to act like a friend when Michael was our son too." I could almost visualize people gathering around Nancy, hugging and comforting her while we were left standing alone. It made me feel cold inside. It almost seemed like we needed to have a gathering where our friends and loved ones could say their goodbyes.

This time though, Nancy had to say good-bye. She needed to be with those she felt closest to. While she found comfort among her loved ones, we too would have to find a way to grieve for our precious Michael, one more time.

That night I could not sleep. Tears were again flowing as I thought of our children. One year ago tonight I couldn't sleep either, but it was because we were so excited about Nancy's phone call asking us to adopt her unborn child. Tonight was a completely different story.

The picture that Lynn had bought of the children in the garden came to mind. I thought of Michael and Amy. Instead of entering the world together as we had planned, the picture now seemed to symbolize them leaving the darkness of the world, entering heaven hand in hand. Ever so slowly, the turmoil of the past months eased away. Our children were finally together just as it always seemed they should be. Life had gone full circle.

Although we had prayed that Michael would have a long and full life, oddly his death was what had finally brought closure and peace. Gone were the worries, the wondering, and the apprehensions. Instead, there was certainty. Michael's future was clear. He was now enjoying a life far richer than either Nancy or we could have given him. Yes, Nancy was right. It truly was over.

When we shared the latest sad news with our family and co-workers, many were as stunned as we. Once again, there were comments that brought more pain.

"It's good you didn't have to go through that!" one said upon hearing of Michael's death.

I was angry. Why was she so insensitive? She acted as if we were lucky. Granted, we didn't have to make Michael's funeral arrangements, but we were certainly going through his death. In fact, we had already lost him once. How was it possible to lose him twice? This was our grief too. Besides, what made her think that saying good-bye to a living child was any easier than saying good-bye in death? We had done both in the last six months. We would not have wished either on anyone.

People were not sure what to do. One friend sent flowers. Many sent cards. We were so appreciative. Meanwhile, Ron and I labored over what to write to Nancy in a sympathy card. It was like having to extend our sympathies to someone else for the loss of our own child.

A week later, an envelope arrived. I knew what was in it. A friend had promised to send a copy of Michael's obituary. I unfolded the article and a darling picture of Michael looked back at me. Although he was a bit older, it was definitely the same little boy we had held as our own only months ago. He had a terrific smile. His eyes sparkled.

I glanced through the article as tears threatened to fall. Then I handed it to Ron. Disappointment engulfed me. I knew I shouldn't have expected it, but I had hoped that we would be mentioned, not necessarily as adoptive parents but at least as special friends.

As Ron finished reading, he expressed what I had been thinking. "I can't believe it," he said in a whisper. "She never even mentioned us."

I started to cry. It hurt so much to not be included. It would have been such a small act of kindness. If nothing else, it would have shown some appreciation for the love and care we had given during Nancy's pregnancy and Michael's first month of life.

I read the article more carefully. "Michael and his mother spent the summer in Montana, visiting his grandparents, aunts, and uncles," it said. Jim was mentioned as Michael's father. Disbelief came over me. How could Nancy acknowledge him but not us? This father was the one who wanted to end Michael's life before he was even born—a man who offered no support to Nancy or Michael.

Then her entire family was listed. I cried even harder. Michael had been our son—not a grandson, nephew, or cousin. We had awaited him, loved and prayed for him long before they even knew of his existence. Yet, despite our love for Michael as our son, there was no evidence of him ever being in our lives. There wasn't a birth certificate or death certificate. It was as if our relationship had never existed. It hurt so much.

Although everything in the article was factual, none of it seemed real. There was no hint of the confusion or the turmoil—only a perfect life for a little boy. Perhaps Nancy believed that. Perhaps it was good that Michael would never know the truth.

With tears still in my eyes, I folded the article and slipped it in Michael's baby book. Then pulling out our family Bible, I wrote:

Michael William Johnson
Our beloved son
Born April 19
Died October 21
Forever in our hearts

Several weeks later, another friend mailed us a copy of Michael's funeral bulletin. Opening it, I was stunned. On the inside cover of the bulletin was the poem, "The Loan"—the same poem my friend had found in the abandoned closet that had given me comfort after Amy died. Again, there seemed to be such a connection between Michael and Amy—the two babies who were now spending eternity together.

Chapter 14

Dr. Fellows had encouraged us to wait six months before trying to get pregnant again. I thought I would die if it didn't happen. As the weeks ticked by, I counted them like a prisoner waiting to be released. That's how I felt. It was like living out a sentence so I could begin life again.

I pondered whether I would go back to Dr. Fellows if I got pregnant again. I respected him as a physician yet there were so many painful memories. He had been the one who told us that Amy had died. The examining room was a memory of great sadness. Even the waiting room was a painful place. It was always full of pregnant women who talked of their children and pregnancies. I wouldn't be able to participate. Anything I might say would only horrify them. Dr. Fellows knew our history though, and his nurse Holly was very dear to me. I knew they would be sensitive and cautious if we were fortunate enough to get pregnant again.

I was scared though. What if we couldn't conceive again? What if our only chances to have children were gone? Equally terrifying though was the thought of having another child. There were no guarantees. We could lose another too, just like Michael and Amy. I wasn't sure we could risk losing another. I wasn't sure I'd survive.

However, life would never be complete without children. We knew what it was like with them. The void was horrendous without them. Our options seemed narrower than a year ago though. Adoption was out of the question. We just wouldn't put ourselves through that again. If Michael's adoption hadn't worked, I couldn't imagine that any would.

Getting pregnant seemed our only choice. I wondered how I would ever be able to relax and enjoy the pregnancy. What if another child died inside of me? My body felt like more like a death trap than a safe place for a baby to grow.

Amy's due date came and went. The holidays were upon us and with them, a deep sense of dread. This was the Christmas we had planned to have not only one, but two children. They would have been wide-eyed as they watched the lights on the tree. We would have been buying special toys for own children. The new year would have been full of joy and promise.

Instead, we couldn't muster up any enthusiasm for the holidays. We didn't even have the energy to put up a Christmas tree or decorate. I tried to focus on the real meaning of Christmas, but everything seemed shrouded in a dark cloud of despair. We felt raw and vulnerable. My arms and back ached. Simple tasks like vacuuming or mopping left me exhausted. My chest hurt too. I could not seem to get enough air. I was so tired, but sleep evaded me. I felt like a walking zombie. I was told these were normal symptoms of grief. Whatever it was, I was exhausted both physically and emotionally. Death was so final. I felt cheated. I missed both our children so much.

Several months later, a letter arrived in the mail from Nancy's mother. It was sad and tender. She wanted Ron and me to get together with Nancy and talk. I wondered if Nancy wanted the same or if it was only her mother's wish.

The letter also said, we need to know what happened during the first three weeks that you had Michael. And I'm sure you'd like to know about his last five months.

There seemed to be a tone of comparison—they had him for five months compared to our insignificant three weeks. Perhaps they were searching for a reason for his death. I couldn't blame them. I had wanted something to blame when Amy died. However, I knew we had nothing to offer that would answer their questions.

What an irony though! What we would have given to be able to talk before Nancy took Michael. And in the months afterwards, we had pleaded with her to talk with us but again our pleas had gone unanswered. What was the point in talking now? What could possibly be gained?

In the past months, we had been through more loss than we thought we could ever endure. Now we were working very hard to move forward while still grieving for our children. I remembered all too well the grief in those early months. I just didn't have the energy to go back to that pain and relive it. I could not sacrifice what little energy I had, especially at this time in our lives.

My doctor had given us the okay to start trying to conceive. I had to stay focused on that goal. I had to get pregnant!

Once again, I began taking Clomid to try to pregnant. Two months passed before we got the news—we were going to have another baby. The cloud of darkness lifted instantly. Ron and I were thrilled beyond words. Our lives were full of hope.

When we made our announcement this time though, there wasn't the big fanfare like when we announced Michael and Amy's pending arrivals. We didn't take cupcakes with booties on them to work. We didn't pass out chocolates. We didn't even wait to tell our family in person. Instead, we shared our news immediately and called our family on the phone. We were determined to make this child's life a celebration. It might only last the pregnancy, or it might last a hundred years but either way, we planned to treasure each day.

My due date was November 5th. Amy's due date had been November 17th the previous year. I was a bit fearful of going through another pregnancy during the same seasons.

Almost immediately, my pregnancy became apparent. I looked like a normal pregnant woman this time. I was glad to get back into maternity clothes.

Anxiously, we waited for the time when we could hear a heartbeat. It came through loud and clear at ten weeks. Dr. Fellows ordered an ultrasound just to make sure things were okay. Everything looked great. All the other tests came out normal too. Soon the familiar flutters of movement started. Before long, Ron could feel our baby too. We felt so blessed.

Our days were a mix of joy and grief as we continued to work through our losses of Michael and Amy while anticipating our new baby. People told us we shouldn't think about those sad days of the past. It was time to move on and put them behind us. We couldn't forget though. We didn't want to forget. They were our children. They were our next child's brother and sister. They all had a place in our lives that couldn't be denied.

Despite our joy as we awaited our baby though, we made no efforts to prepare for it. Although the crib still stood in the nursery just as it had when Michael was there, there were no other signs that a baby was arriving. Those details seemed insignificant and unimportant. All that mattered was bringing our baby home.

April arrived. Easter fell on what would have been Michael's first birthday. We thought of the fun Easter we'd had the year before with Nancy as we waited for Michael together. Adding to that were memories of his birth that seemed burned in my mind. I could visualize Michael looking up at Ron, his eyes so full of curiosity. I remembered the pride in Ron's face as he talked to his new son. Even the smells of that moment seemed fresh.

Each day thereafter was another anniversary—the day of the adoption ceremony, bringing Michael home, the baby shower in Helena, Mother's Day, the day Nancy called, the day she took him from us. There was still such a void in our hearts. I wondered if we would ever feel whole again.

On Memorial Day weekend, we attended Ron's college fraternity reunion at Chico Hot Springs. Everyone there had children. As they gathered their little ones together for a group picture, I had to leave the room as I burst into tears. It was so unfair. Our two children should have been in that picture. It seemed the pain would never end. It exhausted me.

"How do you feel?" a friend asked, referring to my pregnancy.

"Well, excited and scared," I answered.

"Oh, just have faith and trust."

I stared at her blankly, unable to believe her comment. Did she honestly think that faith and trust were all there was to having children? Didn't she realize that even the faithful have tragedies?

I resented her flippant assurance. We'd had more faith and trust than most people had in awaiting Michael and Amy's births. In fact, at times I think we were only ones who did have faith, particularly in regard to Michael's adoption. There had been so many times we had been confronted with fear and could have backed out. However, we had trusted Nancy and the process. We had trusted God's ability to bring it all together. Lack of faith and trust had not been what destroyed Michael's adoption nor had it been the reason for Amy's death.

In fact, our faith had grown. We wouldn't have made it through and been able to pick up the pieces if it hadn't been for our faith. We certainly wouldn't have tried to have another baby. I was so sick and tired of hearing judgmental statements and thoughtless reasoning.

Suddenly, I felt it. I waited, wanting to be sure. Then it happened again. It was a contraction—but it could not be. I was only four months along.

I called Holly. I tried to sound calm although I felt panicked. "It feels just like the week Amy died," I explained.

"Come right down," Holly said. I could hear concern in her voice.

Arriving at the clinic, Holly immediately escorted me to a room and put the monitor to my stomach. Relief washed over me as I heard the sound of our baby's heartbeat. I crumbled into tears, thankful that our baby was still alive. My urine test was also normal. All looked good. I was feeling a bit foolish, as if I had cried wolf.

"Just to be sure though," Holly said, "let's check the cervix." As she checked, her face became clouded.

"What is it?" I asked.

"Well, it feels much softer than it should be at this point. You have dilated a little. I can also feel some pressure that I don't like."

"What does that mean?"

Holly hesitated as if deciding whether to answer, but then she did. "It looks like you're in pre-term labor."

I sat in stunned silence. Holly excused herself in order to confer with Dr. Fellows' partner since Dr. Fellows was gone for the day. Moments later, she was back.

"We'd like you to go home and get your feet up. It is too early to stop this with medication, so we will have to try bed rest. Drink lots of fluids and try to relax."

I quietly nodded my head as I struggled to hold in the tears.

"Dr. Fellows will be in next week," Holly said. "He'll want to see you then."

I promptly went home as instructed and called Ron. That night we called our family. Somehow, we felt we should prepare them. Besides, we needed their prayers. We might lose this baby too.

A week passed. I had an appointment to see Dr. Fellows. I hadn't slept much, so I was feeling worn out. I was so scared. I didn't want to hear how bad it might be. Ron went with me. We wanted to hear the news together. We tried to prepare for the worst.

Dr. Fellows was examining me. I scarcely breathed, waiting for the prognosis. He had a puzzled look. Finally he spoke, "Everything feels normal."

I couldn't even find any words to respond. It was as if we'd been put through a bad dream.

"It's very unusual for things to reverse themselves," he continued. "I have only seen it happen on one other occasion. Everything looks fine though. As far as I'm concerned, you can resume your normal life."

Ron and I both had tears in our eyes as we left. The nightmare was over. Our baby was safe. It seemed we had received a miracle. Now if we could just get through week twenty-eight of the pregnancy—the week Amy had died.

The following day was a busy one at work as I tried to catch up after my week at home. By evening, I was tired. I had a rough night filled with pain and discomfort. I debated whether to go to work the next day but decided to go ahead.

All morning long, I had cramps. There was so much pressure. It felt like my insides would fall out. At noon, I went home. I knew what was happening. The best thing I could do was get in bed. There was nothing more Dr. Fellows could do.

Alone at home, I sobbed. I should have listened to my body and stayed home rather than pushing it. Now our baby's life was again in jeopardy. I was so angry with myself.

"Please God," I begged, "Give me another chance. I will not overdo it again. I'll do whatever it takes to keep our baby."

The next day, Dr. Fellows confirmed my fears. Labor had progressed. He wasn't very optimistic as he ordered another ultrasound, hoping to determine the cause of labor.

We could see the baby much more clearly this time. Again, all looked good. There was no indication of any problem. Upon further testing though, he found bacteria in my uterus.

"I suspect that is the cause. I will prescribe medication to clear this up but even after the bacteria is gone, labor will likely continue since it is already underway. Bed rest is the one thing that we know can prolong a pregnancy. It's your decision but it's the best shot we have for now."

I made the decision. Calling my boss, I told him I would not be back to work until after the baby was born. Thus began the loneliest vigil of my life.

I felt like I had stepped off the world. Everyone was going about their life as usual, except for me. It was like reliving the same day over and over. I got out of bed. I showered. I put on comfortable clothes and then, after filling a pitcher of water, lay down on the couch, generally on my left side. If I lay on my back, labor would start again.

Day after day, time ticked by. The hours were lonely. With nothing else to think about or be concerned with, I thought of our baby. Talking to it, I tried to cheer it on, "You've just got to make it," I said, rubbing my stomach as if to comfort our child. "You keep on fighting. Your daddy and I need you so much."

I knew my chances of carrying our baby full term were slim but I refused to surrender. We had been so fortunate to conceive this child. I was going to do everything in my power to keep it. Pouring all the love in my heart into it, I determined that somehow our baby would know how much it we loved it, even if this was my only chance to tell it.

I was in bed reading a novel set in the early 1900s. About halfway through, I read:

> "Dad carried the baby from their bedroom. He said it was dead. I wanted this baby so much. I was going to be a big sister."

The words were like a trigger, as if a bomb went off inside. I threw the book across the room. Never before had I felt such anger. I felt like my body would explode with the rage inside. My mind was whirling as questions consumed me. How could my pregnancy be in jeopardy? Why couldn't I just have a normal pregnancy? When was it enough? Why couldn't we just have a baby like everyone else in the world seemed to be doing? I was so tired. I just wanted to enjoy life again.

I worried about Ron too. He looked tired, yet seemed to have an unending supply of strength as he held me together, setting aside his own hurts and concerns. I felt selfish, leaning on him so much. I wondered how much more he could take. I wondered when he would cry; really cry as I had been doing. I knew the events of the past year were eating him alive, yet I felt unable to give him the support he was giving me. All my energies were consumed in trying to pay attention to my body. I did not want to miss any of the signs. I was the only one who could recognize them. Our baby was depending on me. I knew that God was in control but even so, somehow it seemed as if it were up to me to keep our baby alive.

Two weeks passed. We were still hanging in there. Dr. Fellows could now prescribe the medication to stop labor. I started taking Terbutaline. He warned me that generally a resistance was built up to the drug when taken over a long period. At some point, I would probably need to take a stronger medication or perhaps be hospitalized. For now though, the hard contractions stopped. I soon discovered however, that if I missed a dose by even a half hour, the contractions started again. Day and night, I set my alarm at four-hour intervals to remind myself to take the medicine.

It had disturbing side effects though. My heart raced as if I were running a marathon. I was constantly out of breath and couldn't make it up the stairs without getting winded. My hands trembled, making it difficult to write letters or do cross-stitch.

Ron shouldered all the responsibilities between work and home. Mom and Colleen came over occasionally to help with the cleaning and cooking. It was so nice to have the company, and it also gave Ron a chance to get away and not feel bad about leaving me alone.

Ron came home every day for lunch. It helped to fill my loneliness. But he was lonely too. We used to do everything together, but now he did it all alone. I would have loved to go to a movie or even go grocery shopping with him. Even our intimacy was gone, for that would also threaten labor. Nevertheless, weeks were passing and we still had our baby. With each passing day, we were getting closer to when our baby could survive outside the womb.

It was Father's Day. Last year we were anticipating Amy, certain she would be a part of this year's celebration. Once again, however, we were simply waiting, hopeful that we would get to share life with a child. This year I was determined to make this a special day for Ron.

Colleen had been here the previous weekend and helped me with the purchase of a remote controlled car. Ron was always kidding me about getting one. Whenever we would pass through a toy department, he would steer me in their direction. "Oh, look at that one," he would say. "Kids are so lucky these days. There weren't all these neat toys when I was growing up!"

When morning arrived and Ron was showering, I retrieved his wrapped gift from the closet and had it waiting on the bed. When he saw it, he sheepishly grinned.

"What's this?" he asked.

"Well, you'll have to open it and see," I prompted. I could hardly wait to see the look on his face when he opened it.

He pulled off the paper and opened the cards. The first one was from me. The second said—Give this a spin for us Daddy. Love, Michael and Amy. Then written underneath, But don't wear it out! Love, Johnson Junior.

When he saw the car, he laughed with disbelief. He never would have guessed I would splurge on such an impractical gift. It wasn't my style. He enjoyed it and for several hours afterwards, he drove it around the yard like a little kid.

I was an hourglass, slowly ridding itself of time. We were almost to week twenty-six—that is when the baby would be considered viable. That week came and went. Then I counted the days to week twenty-eight—the week Amy had died. If only we could make it through.

With many lonely hours and too much time to think, my mind seemed to be in a battle as it drifted from fear to quiet resignation. I knew God loved me, yet could I truly trust Him with the outcome of my pregnancy?

Refusing to waste any time with television, I used my time journaling my thoughts and feelings, and writing down whatever I could remember about Michael and Amy. I wrote letters to the baby I carried and, in the midst of it all, I kept praying.

As time continued to tick by, I began to appreciate my solitude. It became a time of reflection. All of my life, I had a sense of pride in doing for myself. I had put myself through college. I worked very hard in my career to gain a reputation of honesty and diligence. As a couple, Ron and I were self-sufficient, financially independent, and stable. Bottom line—things were under control. The past year though had taught us just how little we truly did control. We had been brought to our knees and felt very humbled.

Now in bed rest, I was primarily dependent on Ron and my family to care for me and our baby. This certainly hadn't been how I envisioned spending a pregnancy. I was supposed to be out showing off my blossoming figure and shopping for our baby. Instead, I was forced to rest.

However, God was showing me something. Stuck in bed, I suddenly had a very dramatic perspective of what God means when He asks us to rest in Him. Isolated from society, I had to slow down and step away from life. God was my constant companion and, with my focus finally on Him, the long process of healing finally began to take place.

Slowly, the pain and anger of the past year began to ebb away. My energies were rebuilding. I began to understand that God didn't want our independence but rather our dependence on Him. He wanted us to rest in the knowledge that He could be trusted to make something good of even this period in our lives.

It was during this time that it occurred to me that life isn't about our efforts, our skills, our intelligence, or even our ability to have babies. It is about God's faithfulness. With this realization came an understanding that unless I placed Him first in my life, I would never find true peace.

God already knew the outcome of this pregnancy. I had done all I could to prolong the pregnancy by going on bed rest. Now it was time to put aside the millions of worries and trust in God's purpose. It was time to simply REST in Him.

Amy's birthday was a particularly difficult day. I missed her so much. I spent the day rereading all the sympathy cards we had received when she died. I also could not help but be concerned about the baby I carried. I prayed that God would help our little one continue to fight for its life. Even with my new resolve to rest in God, old habits and nagging feelings kept resurfacing, threatening to pull me back under with worry.

By now, the pressure was intense and very painful. It hurt to walk or sit. It felt like the baby would fall out if I stood, so I continued to spend the days on the couch or in bed.

Occasionally, I would go for a short ride with Ron, lying on my side with the passenger seat fully reclined. That is how we went to Lamaze classes. Once we arrived, Ron would stretch out a blanket where I would spend the time lying on my side. I felt self-conscious as other expectant parents shot inquisitive looks my way. Although we explained, I still felt like an odd ball. Even in this group, I felt isolated. I had no energy for the socializing I heard often occurred in Lamaze classes. Nevertheless, I was grateful that at least with this pregnancy we would learn what we needed to know for the labor and delivery. Granted, we'd been through it all with Amy's delivery but it had happened so fast. I hoped that this time we would be better prepared.

The intensity of the physical pain combined with the emotional battle, however, caused panic to rise again. I wanted the baby to come out—now! I just did not trust my body. The baby was still alive. Why risk it, especially if it could survive outside now? I was so scared that some freak thing might happen again. I just wanted to be able to hold our baby and know everything was all right.

I confided in Dr. Fellows.

"I know it must be hard, Denise, but there is no reason to think the baby is in danger. All looks normal. The longer it stays in the womb, the better. It is just too early. The lungs aren't developed enough for it to breathe on its own. Besides, we know the risks of premature birth. They are far greater than carrying the baby. It has a better chance of surviving inside of you than outside in an incubator."

I wanted to believe him, yet I was scared. I had trusted that assumption before and Amy had died. I didn't want to risk that again. Dr. Fellows wouldn't budge.

Checking me again, he noted that I had dilated further. The baby had also dropped. "I don't think you'll go much longer but it's still too early," he again warned me. "You need to be in strict bed rest. Don't get up for anything except to go to the bathroom."

Three more weeks passed. Much to everyone's surprise, I was still pregnant. Ron had finished labor and delivery classes without me. I was grateful that he continued to go, bringing home the information and sharing it with me. I loved him so much, especially for everything he was doing to help us keep our baby.

The baby was moving a lot. It got the hiccups often. I was glad. They assured me it was still alive. I felt like I had been pregnant forever.

When week thirty-five arrived, Ron took me to the clinic for an exam. Dr. Fellows kept shaking his head, unable to believe that I was still carrying the baby.

"This baby is so low!" he said shaking his head. "It can't get much lower without being born."

I could have told him that. There was so much pain, so much pressure. When I walked, I stooped like an old woman as I carried my lower stomach as if to take the pressure off. Everything hurt. I had hoped my doctor would say I could stop the medication and allow the baby to come but he didn't. Instead, he asked me to continue for another two weeks. I wanted to cry. It felt like he had given me a life sentence. I just wanted to have the baby.

When week thirty-seven arrived, Dr. Fellows finally took me off the medication and gave me the okay to resume moderate activities. Anxious to be out in the world again, and determined to bring on labor, I took a short trip down to the office to say hello to my co-workers. Although each step was painful and slow, I was so excited to show off my pregnancy to my friends whom I hadn't seen in over four months.

Not long into my outing though, I started feeling sick. My face and legs started to get puffy. I felt like a marshmallow. I decided to head home but, as an afterthought, stopped by the clinic just to make sure things were okay. Holly checked me over. She told me I was retaining fluids and that my blood pressure was up. She ordered me back to bed rest.

Another week passed in bed rest. I finally started having some regular contractions. I wanted to have the baby so badly, but today was October 21st, the one-year anniversary of Michael's death. I couldn't have the baby today. That would almost be creepy. The timing made me feel nervous and upset as I thought of Michael and the sadness of today.

However, the timing of this birth was out of our control, so Ron and I tried to focus on the issue at hand. As we were timing contractions into the evening, the electricity in the house went out. None of the flashlights had working batteries so, by candlelight, we attempted to time the contractions with our watches.

"Can you believe it, Ron?" I said between contractions. "We're the only couple in town who both work for the electric company and the night we're in labor, the lights go out!" At least we found something funny in the midst of the moment.

Late into the night the contractions stopped. I was relieved to have made it through the day without having the baby, yet now that the day was over, I was more anxious than ever to deliver.

Two days passed without further incident. I was back at the doctor's office having my blood pressure checked. While I was there, the doctor put a fetal monitor on my stomach in order to check the baby's heart rate. It was erratic, at times dropping below 40 beats per minute compared to the usual 150.

"We need to induce labor today," Dr. Fellows said. There was an edge to his voice that made me nervous. "The baby may be on the umbilical cord which could account for the irregular heart rate. Regardless, we need to go ahead with the delivery. We are risking disaster if we wait. I'd like you to go to the hospital and get checked in."

"Do I have time to go home and get my overnight bag?"

"No, I want you to go directly to the hospital."

I felt like I would be sick. His obvious concern was frightening.

I called Ron and then drove the four blocks to the hospital. Once there, I put on a gown, and the nurse started the IV with medication that would start labor. A fetal monitor was also attached and watched closely.

Ron arrived soon after. I could tell he was as nervous as I. Labor was progressing quickly—almost too quickly as I fought to catch a breath between contractions. Everything seemed to be going smoothly when suddenly an alarm on the monitor went off. Almost immediately, a nurse rushed in the door looking worried. She abruptly instructed me to roll to my left side.

I tried to move but it was difficult. Five months of bed rest had left my body stiff.

"Quickly," she ordered.

Ron grabbed my hand and pulled me forcefully to my side. Our fears escalated once again. Although I know Ron did not intend for me to hear, I heard him whisper, "Please God, don't let us have another dead baby."

Time seemed to stop. I kept waiting for the nurse to say something, but she was quiet as she searched the monitor. Another nurse rushed in and began observing. Ron and I remained in a stunned silence. Finally, the nurses seemed to relax as a sigh came from both of them.

Turning her attention to us, our nurse asked, "Do you know what just happened?"

"No," we said, shaking our heads.

"Well, it's hard to say, but perhaps the baby rolled onto its cord. Its heart rate plummeted but it appears to be all right now."

The nurse stayed in our room and kept a constant watch on the monitor as labor continued with contractions coming rapidly. Within a half hour, it was time and the doctor arrived.

"Okay, push when you're ready," the doctor instructed, trying to sound calm. Once again, I could sense concern as he was watched the monitor.

Anxiously, he waited as time after time I gave it all I had. Finally, I could feel the baby emerge. Then I heard a newborn cry. As tears rushed to the surface, my only thought was, *Our baby is alive!*

"It's a boy," the doctor announced.

It was 4:01 p.m., October 23rd. They put our son on my stomach. He was screaming his lungs out. It was the best sound in the whole world. Ron was smiling as he reached to take our son's hand. Tenderly, he talked as he tried to calm our little one.

Tucker William had thick dark hair with tiny curls. He looked just like Ron. Already he was chewing on his hands, looking for something to eat. The nurse wanted to measure and clean him up first though. When she weighed him, she announced, "He weighs 7 pounds, 5 ounces."

I caught my breath. "That's what Michael weighed," I said to Ron with surprise.

"Who's Michael?" the nurse asked.

We told her about our son. "One year ago today, we received word he had died."

No one spoke. There seemed to be a sense of reverence in the room. Finally, one of them broke the silence. "You certainly have been given a miracle with Tucker!"

We certainly had. Word of Tucker's arrival quickly spread. The staff began calling him the miracle baby. How appropriate, for God's hand had truly been on our son.

Like Michael and Amy, Tucker was born on a Friday. Ironically, for all three children, the twenty-third of the month was significant. It was Tucker & Amy's birthday as well as the day Nancy officially gave Michael to us at the adoption ceremony. Perhaps these similarities were coincidental, but I believed it was God's doing. Reaching down from the heavens, He had given our children something in common, something to tie them together. I believe He gave us a message, recognizing us as a family despite the veils that separate us.

Tucker quickly became our life's biggest joy. Little did I know when the doctor announced his gender how fitting his proclamation would be! He certainly fit the stereotypical role of a boy!

As a two-year-old, he loved to put dirt in his hair, play with grasshoppers, and drink water from the dog's dish. He also loved to jump in mud puddles and spill juice on the floor just to have the fun of spreading it around. His greatest fun was being outside. After all, that's where the dirt was. Even in the cold of winter, his little hands would be like ice, but still he'd cling to the door jam, trying to keep from coming inside. His laughter seemed to come from his toes and his happy smile was contagious. His tender heart allowed for lots of hugs, kisses, and cuddles, much to our delight.

Watching him grow was been nothing short of a miracle. His gentle wisdom was often beyond his years and often left me wondering, *Why didn't I think of that?* As we reflect back, it is hard to believe how close we came to losing him—at least in our minds, even though God knew the outcome all along.

Tucker has been such a blessing to us. We have experienced so much joy, but at times it was hard to separate the pain. In his baby years, I remember battling the fear that his life might end prematurely. Tucker tended to spit up a lot as a baby like Michael did. Such similarities often brought fear, and I had to fight such thoughts with prayer as I clamored at the doors of heaven for God's peace.

There were also some terrifying times. Since my employer had been so supportive of me through all the months of bed rest and both my maternity leaves, I decided to return to work. Meticulously, I selected a daycare provider. One week before returning to work, the provider called. She sobbed as she explained that there had been a SIDS death in her home the previous day. I feel completely apart. How could this happen at the daycare I had selected—just before I was going back to work? Life seemed to be validating all my worst fears as I again wondered if we would be allowed to keep Tucker. Again, I pressed forward and begged God to help me learn to trust Him more.

Tucker's six-month birthday fell on the two-year anniversary of the day we had brought Michael home. Again, I felt such fear, thinking of how Michael had died at six months of age. Ron and I took the day off. We just had to be home with Tucker as if to somehow make sure he lived through the day. It turned out to be a day of celebration though. We were so grateful that God allowed us to have Tucker for even that amount of time. It seemed like a lifetime compared to how long we'd had with Michael and Amy.

When Tucker's first birthday finally arrived, there was such relief in knowing that he wouldn't die of SIDS. However, as promptly as that thought evaporated, I pondered the million other things that could happen to him. There could be a car accident or a disease. It was hard to imagine my child living beyond infancy. In fact, when other friends talked of enrolling their children in school, I found it difficult to imagine having a child live long enough to go to school. Every thought and effort seemed to go towards the moment, not the future as, once again, I struggled with resting in God and trusting His purpose.

God is a good teacher though, and I have come to recognize more than ever that He is in control of everything, even the length of Tucker's life. It is not up to me to worry or attempt to control things, in spite of my nature. Now I try to focus on the treasured time we do have and the pleasure we have in raising such a special boy.

Tucker truly is a unique and special child. God gave him a gift of insight and even as a young boy, I was amazed by how deep his questions were and how obvious God was to him. He would share with me conversations he had with Jesus and give me jewels of advice or information beyond his years. There were even times when he spoke to Jesus, telling me that he could see him in his bedroom. At other times, he would tell me about the angels that were around him. I admit feeling a pang of jealousy that I couldn't see them too, but I knew he wasn't making them up.

As Tucker has grown, he has shown a deep sense of responsibility and an intense concern for others. He is a true friend with a strong sense of loyalty. I am anxious to see how God's plan for Tucker's life unfolds. Truly, God has special purpose for Tucker's life, for it is only by His saving grace that Tucker survived the womb. Not a day goes by that I don't thank God for blessing us with our son. It is a privilege to be his mom.

Chapter 15

WHEN TUCKER WAS about two years old, the question we heard most often was, "So when are you going to have another baby?" I had lost track of how many times I'd been asked that. Everyone seemed eager for there to be a sibling for Tucker. It was unthinkable for many that we would have an only child. Each time the question was asked, I grew more and more indignant.

Certainly, we wanted more children but things were not as black and white as they were in years past. After all, we had had three children and yet, only one remained. There was such a deep feeling of injustice with it all. It was almost as if there was a feeling of betrayal to Michael and Amy—like they would be forgotten if we had more children. Deep down though, we knew that even if we had 20 children, they would not be Michael or Amy any more than Tucker was. All three were unique, set apart and loved as individual treasures in our life.

However, we had never intended to raise an only child. Once again, we thought of how differently we had planned things. If only Michael or Amy had lived, we wouldn't be dealing with this. But then again, had they lived, perhaps we wouldn't have had Tucker. With two children only seven months apart, our thoughts about having more children could have been different.

Many fitful nights were spent thinking and praying about the issue of more children. In all reality, we felt like we had been given the greatest miracle in the world to have one healthy, happy, living child. It almost seemed selfish to expect more. Nevertheless, the issue of more children could not be easily dismissed. It nagged at us. I felt unfulfilled as if there was unfinished business.

For a few months, Ron and I again tried to conceive. With each unsuccessful month, disappointment was again fresh as we remembered the frustrations of infertility. Finally, we stopped trying. I wasn't willing to go through all the fertility issues again. It just took so much time and energy, and I did not want to waste either. Our time with Tucker was just too precious to give up for something that left us feeling so frustrated and desperate. Besides, I wasn't sure I even wanted to be pregnant again since another pregnancy would be high-risk. Perhaps I would never feel ready.

Meanwhile, I was plagued with feelings of emptiness. I felt like an adoptive mother, yet there was the obvious void. Whenever I would see articles about adoption in a magazine or paper, I would cut them out, read, and then file them in my growing adoption file. I felt like there was a role in my life that I wasn't fulfilling. Yet, how could we possibly even consider adoption again?

We continued to pray about our desire for another child, but from my perspective, God was not being very clear about what direction we should take. I struggled with my lack of patience as we tried to wait on God.

I thought of my life-long desire to be a foster parent and decided to enroll in classes to check it out. At the end of the ten-week session, I still didn't feel any clear direction. What should we do?

Although God continued to remain quiet in this area of our life, I felt Him nudging me to become a stay-at-home mom. Ron and I talked at length as questions plagued our minds. Could we afford to live without both incomes? Were we willing to make the sacrifices? Would I even enjoy being home full time? Would I regret it later if I didn't take this time to be home with Tucker?

The more we hashed it out though, the less important the answers seemed. Deep in my heart, I sensed that God wanted us to trust Him on this. Finally, we took that step of faith and I resigned, ending my twelve-year career. I remember it feeling a bit like stepping off a cliff. We had no idea where the decision would lead, what to expect, or if it was even feasible. All we knew is that it was something we had to do.

As I look back on that now, I can't believe how much we struggled with the decision. In hindsight, it was such an obvious choice. There were days when I missed the work environment, but I would never have traded it for the treasured time at home with my son. I loved being a mom all the time, not just at the end of a long day. Although every day had its share of exhausting moments, time with Tucker was a joy as I grew to know my son better.

Immersing myself into motherhood, sometimes I wondered what happened to Denise the person, the professional, or even the wife. There were days when my role as Mom was all that seemed to exist, as I would pour myself into bed, drained of energy. However, I never forgot how at one time, we thought we would never be parents. This would be a short season in life, and I wanted to savor it as much as possible.

With all my heart, I know that it was God's will for me to be at home at that time. I am so grateful that He pointed it out to us in such a way that we could not ignore it. I am also grateful that He gave us the faith to follow through. Although we had to make sacrifices, God repeatedly amazed us with His provisions. Yet, in spite of all I witnessed of God's grace and provision, I was not prepared for His greater plan that unfolded because I chose to be a stay-at-home mom. Little did we know He was laying out the groundwork for our next miracle!

When I answered the phone, I was surprised to hear Dr. Fellows' voice. I had been in for my annual physical the previous week. This was the first time, however, he had ever called to give me a report.

"Denise," he said, "There were some abnormal cells in your pap exam that concern me. These cells called psammoma bodies often surround a benign tumor. However, since they can also be around a cancerous tumor, I would like to do some follow-up testing."

My head was swimming with questions, and I bounced them off Dr. Fellows as fast as they entered my head. However, most could not be answered without further testing so Dr. Fellows said he would schedule some blood tests, an ultrasound, and a hysteroscopy to view the inside of the uterus.

The following week I completed the follow-up tests. The ultrasound looked clear but since Dr. Fellows wasn't able get an adequate look, he scheduled a laparoscopy along with another hysteroscopy for the following Monday. These procedures would allow him to get a thorough look at the inside and outside of my reproductive organs to see if a tumor was present. Both would be done during surgery on an outpatient basis.

Attempting to put the surgery out of my mind, I headed to Helena to spend the weekend with our family. Mom was celebrating her 60th birthday and my brother Dave, my sister Colleen, and I had planned a surprise party. We were beside ourselves with excitement, hopeful that somehow it had remained a surprise for her.

Adding to the fun though was a surprise visit from Uncle Don, Mom's brother. Colleen and I picked him up at the airport and then hustled around Helena picking up party supplies. As we scurried around getting the party organized, we drove the side streets so we wouldn't inadvertently cross paths with Mom. We felt like we were on a secret mission as we lurked around making the final arrangements. Finally, we made our last stop to pick up the cake.

As we pulled into the parking lot, my cell phone rang. When I answered it, Dr. Fellows identified himself. I hadn't expected to hear from him. He went straight to the point, "Denise, I just got your blood work back. The levels are elevated, indicating there may be a problem, possibly ovarian cancer. I need to you come into the office a little earlier on Monday in order to get some pre-op work done."

"Yes, doctor," I said. My voice was quivering. My stomach felt like it had hit the floor.

Colleen's face clouded with concern as she realized who was on the phone. She signaled to Uncle Don and the two of them went into the store to collect the cake, leaving me alone to finish my conversation.

Dr. Fellows answered my questions and finalized the details for Monday. When I hung up the phone, a panicky feeling came over me. Did he just say ovarian cancer? What a bombshell. I took in a deep breath. I needed to compose myself. I certainly didn't want to let on, at least not right now with the party only hours away.

Moments later, Colleen and Uncle Don returned, carrying the cake. After placing it in the back of the car, they both got in. Colleen was wearing one of those, "Okay, what's going on?" looks.

So much for bravery, I thought silently, as I started to tear up. Quickly, I repeated my conversation as Colleen and Uncle Don sat stunned.

"But hey," I said, gathering myself, "We have a party to attend. Let's forget this. We can talk about it tomorrow."

Thankfully, they both agreed but we all felt a heaviness. Ovarian cancer? This couldn't be. I had so much to live for. I had a three-year-old son to raise. I had so much I wanted to do in my life. In a state of shock, I silently prayed that God would give me the time to do it all. I prayed I didn't have cancer.

Later that evening, we genuinely surprised Mom at her party. It was a wonderful evening full of laughter. Many family friends arrived and we shared stories of the past and caught one another up on family happenings.

It was Uncle Don though who really pulled off the big surprise. He had been hiding in the kitchen and when we gathered to cut the cake, out he walked with a wine glass raised. "I'd like to propose a toast," he stated. Without hearing the toast, Mom broke into tears of joy. She so appreciated and enjoyed her special birthday celebration.

Back home after the party, Monday arrived. I was early to my appointment, wanting to allow time to ask questions. When Dr. Fellows arrived, he went over the test results again.

"Denise, if I see any cancer, we'll need to do a hysterectomy. Ovarian cancer is not something you want to mess with. We don't want to give it any time to grow."

"I understand."

"I'll have an authorization form for you to sign at the hospital."

"What if you don't see any cancer?" I asked.

"Well, then I'll take a biopsy to analyze if there are any cancer cells that are undetectable to the eye. If that comes out clear then we can forgo the hysterectomy but we need to stay on top of this. Ovarian cancer is difficult to detect in the early stages. Often by the time it's visible, it's too far gone."

As I left the clinic, I began crying. I did not want to have a hysterectomy. We weren't sure we were done having children yet. And that thought of cancer. I was having trouble getting my mind to stay calm. There was so much to fear.

I made a call to Ron and told him about the possibilities of the hysterectomy.

"You won't have to go through with that. They aren't going to find cancer," he said.

I didn't know if he was just in denial or simply trying to keep me calm, but his confidence did not sit well with me. Somehow, I felt I needed to be prepared for the worst. I could have cancer. I could have to spend time with follow-up treatments. Even more unnerving though was the possibility that my childbearing years could be over. My choices were again becoming more limited. The unfairness of it all seemed to slap me in the face as I bitterly cried.

Several hours later, Ron met me at home and we drove to the hospital together. Neither of us said much. At the hospital, I gowned and the nurses prepared me for surgery. A half hour later, a nurse returned only to discover that the IV wasn't working. She proceeded to start it over again in a second location.

Ron was angry. When she had left the room he spouted, "It's bad enough that you have to go through this without them messing up the IV."

That was my first clue that he was struggling even though he had tried to be so confident. I was touched by his defense of me as if trying to protect me.

Alone with Ron again, I thought of the things I wanted to talk out—just in case. "If they do find cancer," I said, "we may have some decisions to make."

"Let's not think of that now," he answered.

"Okay, but let me ask you—if we only had a few more years together, would there be anything you'd want to do? Is there anything you'd regret not doing together?"

He was quiet for a moment and then he said, "No, how about you?"

I hesitated before answering. This might not be the right time but there had been something on my mind. Finally, I said, "Actually there is one thing I would regret not doing—being a foster parent. For as long as I can remember, it's something I've wanted to do—like God has called me to do."

"Well, when this is over then, let's check into it. Perhaps we could get into the next training class."

"I'd like that," I answered. "You know, since leaving work, I've really felt as if I'm being nudged in this direction. Have you noticed that every time we turn on the television, there seems to be an ad requesting that people become foster parents? Or whenever I read the paper, there seems to be an article about abuse in the system? I just feel it's time to do something. Perhaps this is how God intends to complete our family."

"Who knows," Ron concluded, "but I'm open to checking it out."

Just then, the nurse arrived to take me to surgery. Ron walked with me as I was wheeled down the hall. At the door, he kissed me good-bye. I tried to remain brave, but as soon as Ron was out of sight, tears erupted. What would the doctor find? Our lives could be so different in just a few hours. I was scared. I didn't have long to think about it though before the anesthesia took over—

Disorientated and in a fog, I came to. Quickly, I realized the surgery was over and reached to touch my stomach. Was there a large abdominal incision indicating a hysterectomy? Sluggishly, I groped. There was no incision. He must not have seen cancer. The sense of relief was indescribable as tears again spilled out.

Soon after, Dr. Fellows met me in the recovery room. Ron was there too.

"I didn't see any signs of cancer," Dr. Fellows said, confirming my conclusion. "However, I took several biopsies and we should have the results back in a week. If they come back abnormal, we will need to go back in and perform the hysterectomy. If they are normal, I'll want to continue monitoring your blood levels on a quarterly basis. We need to stay on top of this."

The following week, the biopsies came back normal. Dr. Fellows ordered a CT scan to rule out tumors in other areas. All was normal. I was so relieved but still felt unsettled. Why would two separate and unrelated tests indicate a potential problem, yet none could be found? Obviously, we were grateful but I couldn't help but wonder if they had missed something. I was glad Dr. Fellows would continue monitoring things. If a problem existed, perhaps it would show up while still in the early stages. For now though, we could push this to the back of our minds. I was anxious to move on to our next goal—becoming foster parents.

So without hesitation, the next morning I contacted social services. When I asked about the classes, the social worker told me that the next one started the following Monday. My heart lifted. I was grateful we wouldn't have to wait long. Before I could settle on that thought though, she continued, "I'm sorry, the class is already full."

"Could we come anyway?" I asked, my voice pleading. I felt such a sense of urgency. It seemed too coincidental to have called just in time but not be able to attend.

She hesitated but then said, "Sure, perhaps everyone who registered won't come."

I was so relieved.

When we arrived at class the following Monday, the room was packed. Ron and I leaned against the wall since there were no seats left. When the social worker, Julie, got everyone's attention, she asked if anyone was willing to wait until the next session. Ron and I pressed ourselves against the wall as if to disappear. We did not want to be asked to leave. Finally, several people volunteered. When all was said and done, Ron and I were in the class. Oh, praise God! We were ecstatic.

Classes were three hours every Monday for ten weeks. As we learned more about the process, it was exciting yet scary. A rather dismal picture was often painted of children with emotional problems or physical disabilities, little ones who had never bonded, children with destructive behaviors, and ones who may hurt other children due to their own abuses.

One day Julie described how even though these children might be in difficult, unhealthy, and even dangerous home situations, often they would rather stay there than go to a healthy, safe home simply because it wasn't "home" to them. The descriptions and scenarios of abuse and emotional brokenness were disturbing, and I found myself fighting tears. Still, I wanted to proceed. With each passing week, my desire to become a foster parent seemed to burn stronger. I could not stop thinking about it. I couldn't ignore it. It almost felt like I wouldn't be able to breathe if we didn't follow through with this.

One afternoon I said to Ron, "You know, I feel as if God has already picked out a child for us. We need to be ready."

Ron shook his head. "Now don't go getting your hopes up." I knew he didn't want me to be disappointed all over again.

I ignored his comment and continued, "If only we could figure out a way for there to be three bedrooms on one level of the house. I just want all of us to sleep on the same level, especially if there were an emergency."

"Well," Ron responded, "the only way to have three bedrooms on one level is to make the family room into a bedroom."

I about jumped for joy. I had been struggling with that detail for weeks. Why hadn't I thought of that? What a perfect solution. That day I called a contractor and arranged to have a closet built into the family room. Without any guarantee of a child, we forged ahead on our remodeling project as we converted the family room into a cozy bedroom. I felt driven to keep moving, to get ready. I had no idea what lie ahead, but I just knew there was a child waiting for us. I trusted that God had a special plan.

The goal of the foster care program is to provide a safe place for children until they can be reunited with their birth family. We understood that. We also knew it would be hard to let a child go once we had it in our home. Deep down, we wanted to foster parent a baby we could keep but there would be no guarantees. We hoped that we wouldn't have to give up another child, but we knew if we had to, we could do it. After all, we had done it before and survived. We wanted to be parents again, and the risk was worth it.

We decided to request children that would be younger than Tucker in order to preserve his position in the family. It seemed like it would be an easier transition for him. We also learned that infants would only be placed in homes where one of the parents was home full time. I wondered if this was why I'd felt such a nudge to become a stay-at-home mom.

As the weeks passed, we continued to pray that God would have a baby for us to care for. Wouldn't it be fun to have a baby in our home again? Perhaps it would be a newborn. Even more perfect would be a baby girl. Maybe the void in our lives would not seem so large if we could parent a daughter as well. We tried not to get our hopes up though. The likelihood of getting a newborn was very small. Furthermore, the likelihood of adopting a newborn was even smaller.

As I thought of the prospect of adopting, I couldn't believe how natural it felt. The disaster of Michael's adoption no longer seemed to hold us back. God had healed us, quietly along the journey, and prepared our hearts to fulfill this special calling in our lives. My heart felt full as we anticipated what might lie ahead. I could feel it with everything in me that soon there would be another child in our home.

With each passing week, my excitement mounted. One day Ron said to me, "Just promise me that once classes are over, we'll talk about this before making any definite decisions." I promised him I would. In the meantime, we began to share our hopes and plans with friends. Most were very excited for us. Others, however, were guarded.

"I don't think I could do that," one friend said. "I mean, what if the child had problems as a result of their parents' drug or alcohol abuse?"

Perhaps I was being naïve, but that really wasn't something that concerned me. It was not the child's fault if its parents were addicts. Every child deserved a stable and loving home even if its own parents couldn't provide it. Besides, how was that any different from my own family? For all we knew, a relative in our lineage had alcohol or other addictions.

All I could think about was how each child was one of God's. It didn't have to come with a pedigree or clean bill of health. It just needed to be loved and cared for. Besides, I had a need to love and care for another child. Somewhere out there, I knew there would be a little one who needed us too. Maybe it would just be a temporary placement, or perhaps we could adopt. It didn't matter. I just wanted another child.

In the weeks that followed, I tried not to think of the end result. Instead, I tried to focus on one thing. As foster parents, we would be allowed the opportunity to influence a child's life. We would have a sweet little face to pray for every night even if it didn't remain with us. Perhaps for the first time in a child's life, they would experience the love in a family and more importantly, God's love. We knew that through the experience we would come out as better people no matter what it cost us. God was with us. We just had to rest in his purpose and plan—once again.

Chapter 16

MOM AND I were visiting over the phone during our usual weekend chat when she casually said, "Oh, by the way, I heard that Nancy had a baby girl."

I felt a pang of sadness as I thought of our lost friendship. News of Nancy's life occasionally came through mutual friends since we no longer communicated. For years, she had been a part of my daily thoughts, but when Mom mentioned Nancy, I realized that I had not thought about her in quite some time. Our lives had become busy with Tucker. We were moving on.

Several years before I had heard she was getting married to a guy we knew from college. I felt sad then too—not because she was getting married but because we wouldn't be sharing it together. Our wedding days were something we had talked about in college with such anticipation. We certainly wouldn't miss sharing that day with each other. She was there for mine and it was such a happy memory.

When her wedding day approached, I had agonized over it. I wished I could have been there to celebrate with her, but I hadn't been invited. Since God had helped me to forgive Nancy, I no longer held anger toward her. However, our friendship hadn't been restored. I only wished we could put this all behind us and be friends again. I considered just showing up but doing so might cause her pain at her joyous time. Still, I wanted to express our congratulations, so we sent a gift. I hoped she would feel our sincere best wishes for her.

Now as Mom shared news of Nancy's daughter, I was again thrilled for her while also saddened. How wonderful that Nancy would have another opportunity to parent. I knew this baby would help her to heal. I was happy that she could share this joy with her husband. At the same time, I felt sad for what we could have been sharing as friends.

That night I tossed and turned in bed, rehashing and reliving all that had happened during our friendship. I cried a bit for Nancy, thinking of how difficult it might be for her raising a baby after losing Michael. Once again, this was something we could have shared.

As I lay in bed trying to sleep, I was also surprised at the intense sense of anger and jealousy I felt toward Nancy—anger I thought I had dealt with a long time ago. Regardless though, I was angry. Nancy had her baby girl but I didn't have mine. I was ashamed of myself for feeling like that but I couldn't shake it.

Certainly, we had Tucker and I was so grateful for him. He had filled our lives, and the voids of our hearts, in so many ways. We were blessed with raising a little boy and yet, there were still all the little girl things we missed being able to do, things we should have been able to do with Amy. Easter Sundays were always difficult as we observed the darling little girls in their frilly dresses. What fun we would have had picking out something for Amy to wear on Easter.

News of Nancy's daughter seemed to refresh the void. Grief for our little Amy welled up inside. It had been a long time since I had cried myself to sleep, but that night I did. I missed our baby girl so much.

With nine of the ten foster parenting classes behind us, I was feeling like a wound-up toy, ready to spring with excitement. Our now completed remodeling project was a bedroom, ready for a child. I could not wait to see what God would do next.

Fortunately, we didn't have to wait long. A call came in just days before our final class. "Denise, a baby is due any day," the social worker Kathy explained over the phone. "We don't know if it's a boy or girl or even the nature of its health due to the mother's history. However, there is a good chance this baby will come up for adoption since it already has siblings in foster care. We can't make any promises though. With that in mind though, would you be willing to take the baby?"

"Oh, yes, yes," I immediately said. Then I remembered my promise to Ron. "Let me talk to Ron though first and then I'll call you back," I concluded.

"Great, just let me know right away. We'll need to find another family if you're not willing at this time."

I was beyond excited. Quickly, I dialed Ron's cell phone number and heard, "I'm sorry but the cellular customer you are trying to reach is out of range or has left the area."

"No," I said aloud. "This can't be happening. I have talk to him." Then I remembered that he was out of town for the day. I began calling everywhere that I thought Ron would be, leaving messages for him to call me immediately.

For two hours, I continued trying to get through on his phone. I was going nuts wondering if the state had found someone else since I had not called back right away. I pondered just making the decision without Ron's input but knew that wouldn't be fair.

Finally, the phone rang. I grabbed it off the wall.

"Is everything okay?" Ron asked. He sounded worried.

I could hardly contain myself. "Yes, but do you remember that talk we were going to have once the classes were over? Well, it's time."

He was quiet as I rattled off what little information I had.

"Let's take the baby, Ron," I said.

I could tell he was nervous. He didn't respond right away. There was so much uncertainty—so much possibility of a broken heart all over again. Finally, he agreed. Although we had talked about the risks and heartache of giving up a child, it was real now, and it was scary. Could we really do it? Then again, how could we not? If we didn't, we would always wonder what might have happened if we'd have taken this child. We just had to trust in whatever plan God had laid out.

The next few days were a blur. Now that we knew that our new bedroom was going to be a nursery, we frantically shuffled furniture out of the room as we moved baby furniture in. Yes, this room would be a nursery! We could hardly contain ourselves as we set up the crib. It was wonderful seeing it again. We were both so excited and yet in a way, we were in a state of disbelief as we wondered what was next.

Meanwhile, three-and-a-half year old Tucker watched with great interest and was full of questions. Something inside me kept me from just blurting out that we would have a baby. After all, it hadn't been born yet. We knew all too well that things didn't always go as planned. This baby might not make it, or might have serious health problems that would prevent it from leaving the hospital. Yet, we had to prepare Tucker somehow that we could soon have a baby. We couldn't just bring it home unannounced.

"So what would you think about having a baby in the house?" I asked him.

"What do they do?" he asked.

"Well, they mostly sleep and cry but they are really fun to hold."

"Would it play with me?"

"Not right now but after it gets bigger I'm sure it would."

He was thoughtful before he answered but finally said, "That would be all right."

"I don't know how long we'll get to keep the baby," I tried to explain. "Its mommy and daddy just can't take care of it right now. Someday, the baby might go live with them."

I shuddered as I recalled how I had given a similar explanation to our nieces and nephews years ago when Nancy had reclaimed Michael. I wondered how Tucker would handle having to say good-bye after becoming attached. That is what worried me most about foster parenting. We were adults. We were making this decision and yet, it would affect Tucker too. I wondered if this would damage our own son's sense of security. I wondered—

Tucker interrupted my thoughts. "Am I going to go live with someone else?" he asked.

"Oh no, honey, you live with us. We are your mommy and daddy."

"Did someone else take care of me when I was a baby?"

"No, we've always taken care of you. You are our special little man."

"Will I always live with you?"

"Yes, you will always live with us," I tried to reassure him.

"Okay, then the baby can live with us," he said. Although he seemed to have reached an agreement regarding this new concept, he still had questions as we continued preparing for the baby.

Days passed with no word. Anxiously, we waited by the phone. Every time it rang, I about jumped through my skin with excitement. As we waited though, we added the new baby to our prayers, praying that it would arrive healthy and safe. We were so excited as we anticipated having another baby in our home.

The following Monday we finished our final class. We didn't say anything to our classmates since we knew others might be resentful that we were getting a placement so quickly. However, we couldn't seem to stop smiling. We felt as if we had a big, exciting secret. It was so much fun.

Although we would love having either a boy or a girl, deep down I kept hoping for a girl. How I would treasure parenting a daughter even for a short time. Either way though, we would love it.

Days later the call finally came.

"It's a girl," Kathy said.

I was in tears. This was unbelievable. It had only been a little over a week since I'd cried myself to sleep thinking of Amy, Nancy, and her new daughter but now, God had given us a baby girl too.

Kathy continued, "She's as healthy as a horse. I am hoping they will release her today but if not, sometime tomorrow. Do you have an infant car seat?"

"Yes, we're ready. Just let us know what you need us to do."

"I'll give you a call once I know when she'll be released and we'll go from there."

Immediately, I called Ron. He took the rest of the day off so we could go shopping. We needed formula and diapers but most exciting was purchasing the pink blankets and pink layettes. What a thrill to be able to finally buy pink.

It was the following morning before Kathy called to say our foster daughter could leave the hospital. She would bring her to the house around noon.

I felt as if I was bouncing off the walls as we waited for them to arrive. With loads of nervous energy, I cleaned the house, wanting it to be spotless for her homecoming. In all our excitement, I had forgotten to ask what the baby's name was. It seemed like such an insignificant detail though. I wondered if we'd like her name or if we'd choose one. I knew I was getting ahead of myself though. Obviously, we would choose a name only if we were able to keep her, and we had no idea what the long-term picture would be yet.

As noon approached, Tucker watched out the front window. "Someone's here," he announced.

Anxiously, I opened the door. I had never met Kathy. I was nervous about making a good impression. Kathy introduced herself as I directed her to the kitchen where she set the infant seat on the table. A blanket covered the baby, and I couldn't wait to see what she looked like. Eagerly, I pulled away the receiving blanket to get a peek. Instantly I felt intense love for this tiny little girl, asleep in the carrier. What amazed me most though was how much she resembled Tucker when he was a baby. I could not believe my eyes.

"I wish I could tell you that you can keep her," Kathy said.

Silently I thought, *I wish you could too.* I remained quiet though. This was all so new to me and I didn't know what was appropriate to say. Besides, a lump was forming in my throat and I was afraid I might cry.

"Her name is Kassi," Kathy continued. "The birth mom didn't bring any clothes for her to wear home so we'll need to get these back to the hospital."

"No problem," I said, almost in a daze. I couldn't take my eyes off this darling. She was so tiny and frail. I had forgotten the helplessness of an infant.

As Kathy gave me instructions on the feeding schedule, I began to lift Kassi from the infant seat. Suddenly, I thought of Tucker. I had been so taken in with the baby that I hadn't been paying attention to him. Looking around, I smiled as I noticed him hiding behind the couch. All this activity had evidently scared him. Who could blame him? Five days certainly was not much time to prepare for new competition in the family.

"Tucker," I said, "Come and see the baby."

Hesitantly, he crept from behind the sofa but kept his distance. As soon as Kathy left though, Tucker was right beside me, helping me check out Kassi's fingers and toes.

"Can I hold her?" he asked timidly. As I placed Kassi in Tucker's lap, his face lit up with a broad grin. He was so pleased to hold this new baby all by himself.

Once again, Ron and I felt in complete awe. God had filled our hearts with so much love as we nurtured our new daughter. It didn't take long to settle into a routine. Kassi was such a good baby. She seemed so content and seldom cried. I wondered if she was bonding with us. The sounds in our house must be so different from what she had heard in the womb. I thought of how experts say a baby hears their parents' voices while in the womb. Did she miss that or wonder where they were?

Although we knew she wasn't ours, already we loved her as if she was. It seemed she had always been in our lives.

Kassi was two days old when I prepared her for her first outing. That afternoon, she was scheduled to have a visit with her birth mother. I wanted her to look fresh and clean so had given her a bath and put a cute ribbon in her wisps of hair. As I was holding her, I felt such a huge surge of love for her. Suddenly, I burst into tears.

"Oh, how did we ever think we could give up another baby?" I said aloud. "What a horrible mistake we've made in deciding to be foster parents. I love you so much Kassi. I cannot bear the thought of letting you go. What have we done?"

Although not audible, I immediately heard these words very clearly in my head, *I never said my work would be easy*!

It caught my breath. I knew God had just spoken to me. I can't say that I'd ever experienced something like that before, but I knew without a doubt that those were God's words. As great as my regret had been only seconds ago, so was the intensity of peace that quickly enveloped me.

That's true, I thought silently. *You never did. And since this is your work, it's not up to me to worry about it.*

I realized that I needed to let go of the need to control. It was time to let God handle it. I knew that no matter what happened or how often I had to kiss our precious Kassi good-bye so she could visit her birthparents, it was my job and privilege to simply love and care for her for however long we were allowed.

As the days and weeks passed, I was grateful God had laid this calling of foster parenting upon our hearts. Because of that, Kassi was a part of our lives. It was such an incredible privilege to be able to parent this beautiful baby girl.

Tucker too seemed to be adjusting to our new addition. He was thrilled to hold her and feed her the bottle. His fondness for her continued to grow, as did ours, and soon he began to refer to her as his baby sister.

Visits with her birthparents were difficult. I fussed about what to dress her in so they would see how much she was loved. When Kathy would arrive to pick Kassi up, I would put on a cheery face and kiss our baby girl good-bye. Tucker would stand at the door and watch Kathy. Every time she left, he would ask her, "Will you bring Kassi back?" Every time she said she would. Each time I felt like my heart would break. What would happen if sometime her answer was no?

When Kassi was gone, I would pray and play with Tucker as we both tried to pass the time. Then when she returned, we'd both turn our attention to her. Kassi generally smelled of cigarette smoke since her birthparents smoked so, after loving on her, I would give her a bath so she would smell like our little girl again. I loved her as our own even though I knew that I was just the foster mom. The birthparent visits were a constant reminder to keep things in perspective.

Months passed. Kassi's first teeth appeared. She was rolling everywhere and beginning to crawl. She continued to grow and delight us as she said her first words, "Mama, Dada and Guck" (for Tucker). Tucker was delighted by her every move. Sometimes he tired of her but for the most part, he adored her. It was clear she adored him too as she followed him everywhere as fast as she could in whatever means possible. Occasionally, I reminded him that we might not get to keep her. He needed to be prepared too, but each night as he said his prayers, he asked God to let him keep his little sister.

Our lives were busy with activities for Tucker as well as appointments for Kassi in order to comply with state foster care requirements. I always dreaded doctor appointments since I had to identify her as my foster daughter. She didn't feel like a foster daughter. Sometimes I felt like others didn't validate our relationship since "foster" was a part of it. Often I found myself explaining that although she was our foster daughter, we'd had her since birth and therefore, she was like our own.

Then there were the hundreds of times I heard, "Oh, I could never be a foster parent. I just couldn't give up a child."

My response was always the same. "There are no guarantees even with a birth child."

They almost seemed stunned. "I guess that's true," they would often say.

The comments bothered me though. Did they honestly think it would be easy for me to give up a child? Did I appear so hard-hearted that giving up a child would be a like a walk in the park? If it was, then I was not the right person to foster parent either. These children needed someone to love them. They deserved to have heartstrings attached to them, ready to break should they return to their homes. This was not a job for someone who could easily give away children.

I guess we had the advantage, if you could call it that. Before Michael and Amy, my response might have been the same. However, we had learned something about ourselves—that sometimes you have to do things that you never thought you could. Some things you think you will never survive, but you do.

We prayed that we would never have to give up Kassi, but we couldn't allow that to be our focus. We had to think of Kassi. I was grateful for whatever time we had. It was more than we'd been allowed with Michael and Amy. Besides, God was in control. For whatever reason, I knew that Kassi was supposed to be in our home at this time. We treasured and cared for her. Had we not taken this risk to love this beautiful little girl, she might not be in a safe home. I couldn't imagine...

One year had passed since my cancer scare. My doctor had continued testing my blood every three months and to date, things were actually improving. When I went in for my annual exam, I had my blood taken again. This time though, the levels were once again above the normal range.

When Dr. Fellows called me with the news he stated, "If you're done having children, I highly recommend we proceed with a hysterectomy."

I didn't know if we were done. Nothing was firm with Kassi yet. Although she was now eight months old, we still had no idea if we would get to keep her. What were we supposed to do? I was lost in my thoughts of uncertainty as Dr. Fellows continued. "Denise, I have conferred with two gynecological oncologists. From their experience, with this many red flags, if you don't already have early stages of undetectable ovarian cancer now, it is likely to develop. They've never seen a case where it didn't."

"I'll get back to you," I told him. I needed to stall. If only we knew for sure that we could keep Kassi. I could not fathom making such a drastic decision with so much uncertainty. However, it could be months before we would have any definite answers regarding the possibility of adopting her.

Ron and I talked and prayed about what to do. I continued to put off the decision, but a week later Dr. Fellows called me again. I told him our frustration. We still wanted more children, especially if we didn't get to keep Kassi. Dr. Fellows pressed me though to make a decision, again pointing out the risks if we delayed.

"Okay," I finally said. "Let's go ahead and schedule the surgery."

As I hung up the phone, I could hear the relief in my doctor's voice, but my head was reeling. Was that the right decision? Would I regret it if we couldn't keep Kassi? There seemed to be no end to the questions and worries that had again become a part of my days. I knew I needed to trust God. I knew I shouldn't worry, but I just couldn't seem to help it. So much was at risk.

Filled with all these thoughts, I laid Kassi and Tucker down for their naps. Perhaps I could think more clearly as they slept. I went back up to my desk and put my head in my hands as I tried to pray. I felt a barrage of frustrations as I realized the finality. This would be the end of our ability to have more children. I felt a fresh wave of grief—grief for the children we would never have. It just seemed so unfair. Certainly, we could continue being foster parents or even adopt, but this was definitely the end of childbearing. In spite of the regrets though, I felt grateful that I'd had a year to come to terms with this. I felt better prepared than I had a year ago.

As I continued to mull over the strange and sad feelings, the phone abruptly interrupted my thoughts. Quickly, I answered it before the ringing woke my napping children.

"Sounds like you were right by the phone," Kathy, our social worker said.

"Yes, I was," I answered.

As Kathy spoke, my thoughts quickly shifted from the pending surgery to Kassi. Her call reminded me that today was the day Kassi's birthparents were to appear in court regarding custody. Although I had no experience with this sort of thing, I figured this proceeding was the beginning of a long process since they claimed a desire to keep Kassi, despite dismal efforts to see her.

Kathy continued, "Well, are you sitting?"

My mind started racing. What was this about? Was this the call I had dreaded—the one informing me that Kassi would be returning to her birthparents?

"Yes," I said, holding my breath with tears near the surface.

"Kassi's birthparents relinquished custody this morning. Both of them!" her voice was breathless with excitement. Then she added, "You get to keep her."

Tears began pouring down my cheeks. I couldn't speak for a moment. I was so stunned and surprised. I had no idea this was even a possibility today.

Kathy and I laughed and cried together for a while longer. As we ended our call, I kept thanking her repeatedly. Then I called Ron and together we called our family. We were so excited and stunned as we again pondered the power of God. No one but God could have planned the timing the way it happened. It was as if He had given us that last assurance. Kassi would be ours. It was okay to proceed with the surgery. Our family would grow even if we could no longer conceive.

Sixteen months later, Kassi's adoption was finalized. She was two years old. As our family joined us that day in the office of the judge, Kassi twirled around in her pink dress, completely unaware of the significance of the moment. When the judge spoke gently to her, she stopped only long enough to eye the stack of papers on his desk as if planning to rearrange them for him.

The judge then asked Tucker if he would take care of his little sister, to which he emphatically agreed. After a series of questions directed to Ron and me, the judge signed his name, legally making Kassi our daughter, confirming what God had put into place from the moment of her conception.

Kassi grew into a beautiful little girl with the energy of three little girls. I could hardly believe how she could exhaust me in so little time. She was daring, independent, and adventurous and as a result, always giving me a scare. Shortly after her second birthday, she scaled the six-foot cedar fence only to fall off the top landing on the other side. Filled with dread, I ran around the end of the fence expecting to see a crying little girl. Instead, I found her picking herself up and brushing off the dirt. The moment she saw me her face lit up in a big smile and she shouted, "FUN!" I knew from that moment on there would never be a dull moment in our lives.

As we've watched Kassi grow, we know without question how great our God is. She certainly couldn't have come through all her antics unscathed without Him. In fact, I have often thought God must have placed an entire army of angels around her just to keep her safe. Her constant motion, her laughter that sounds like a rippling brook, and her tenderness, particularly to her big brother are all signs of God's constant love.

Kassi has a heart for serving others. As a little girl, whenever I gave her a snack, she would continue to stand at my feet looking up as she said, "Gucker too." She refused to leave without getting a treat for her brother as well. She loved to get out the pretty china to serve her snacks even if it is just our family. She is always eager to help and has served in the church ministry since she was old enough to do so. I am so anxious to see how God uses Kassi's gifts of service, generosity, and hospitality for His kingdom. God has a perfect and awesome plan for Kassi, and I am so grateful that part of that plan included us being her parents.

Chapter 17

THE HOLIDAYS WERE approaching. This year Kassi was officially ours. We felt so blessed with our two beautiful children. In light of everything we had been through, it was more than I ever could have hoped. At times, I almost felt as if I needed to pinch myself as I thought of those days just a few years back when we wondered if there would ever be children in our lives. Now there was no doubt about it. The quiet order of our home was long gone. Instead, there were fingerprints on every window, a swing set in the backyard, and toys that never seemed to be in their proper place. However, life was no longer about simple orderly things. It was about raising children and enjoying the process. God had been so generous. My heart was full of thanksgiving.

Thinking of Christmas, I pondered how to make the meaning of Christmas more real to the children. My mind was mulling this over as I finished the Christmas cookies we had started earlier that day. Tucker and Kassi had grown tired of the project and were playing outside. It was unseasonably warm that day for winter in Montana and, through the open kitchen window, I could hear them giggling. Again, my heart swelled with gratitude. I was finally a mommy just as I had longed for all my life.

As I put the last of the cookies in the cookie jar, the phone rang. It was Kathy, our social worker. We'd had little contact since finalizing Kassi's adoption, but she held such a special place in our heart. She had helped to build our family, and I would forever be grateful to her.

After a short greeting, Kathy went right to the point. "Are you and Ron interested in doing more foster parenting?"

Love To Give

We hadn't really given it any thought, but I felt a sense of dread with Kathy's question. Ron had just received notice that his department would be laid off right after the new year. The uncertainty of the future seemed to loom. Adding to that were my father-in-law's recent health problems, not to mention all the Christmas shopping and preparation yet to do. In all reality, I was feeling a bit overwhelmed. The timing was just bad. I could not imagine adding one more thing, most especially another child.

I apologized as I explained our circumstances and she graciously accepted my excuses. I felt guilty though as I asked, "I suppose you have a little one in need?"

"Yes, we have a three month old that needs care for a few weeks, but it sounds like your plate is pretty full. Just let me know when you're ready again."

As I hung up the phone, I felt a tugging at my heart. I wanted that baby. After all, it would just be for a few weeks. A baby for Christmas—that would be fun. What a special way of making Christmas meaningful for the children. Besides, perhaps it was time to give back to the system that had blessed us so much with Kassi.

By the time Ron got home from work, I could no longer think of a single reason for refusing the baby. Ron agreed as did Tucker, who added with excitement, "It would be just like having baby Jesus for Christmas."

That was all I needed to hear as I headed for the phone. As soon as Kathy answered I said, "I talked to Ron and we'd be willing to take that baby."

"Oh, I just placed it with another family," she said.

Horrendous disappointment enveloped me. Adding to the letdown was the sight of Tucker standing eagerly by the phone. As I told him the news, he dropped his head and sadly went to sit on the sofa.

Later that night as I tucked Tucker into bed, he said, "Mommy, maybe someone else will want us to take care of their baby this Christmas."

I thought I would cry. "Yes son, maybe so," I choked out. I felt bad for getting him excited about something that was not likely to happen now.

The next morning as I sat down for my devotional time, I could not shake the sadness I felt about missing out on this baby. My eyes fell on what I had written in my journal the previous day. From the Bible I had copied: Do not ignore it, after reading Deuteronomy 22:1-4. Then below I had written: How easy it is to ignore the needs of this world. Lord, I know I am here to serve you. Give me a new opportunity to serve you by helping another—do not let me ignore the needs of this world.

As I read the words, I felt horrendous shame. Just yesterday, this had been my prayer but hours later, wrapped up in the busyness of the day I had forgotten it. Tears filled my eyes as I wrote a new entry in my journal: How quickly I forget. I am grievous and disappointed in myself. Lord, please forgive me for not recognizing your call. Please allow me to serve you in this way again if you so desire. Then I called Kathy back and told her we would be interested should another baby come up.

The next day, I was surprised to hear from Kathy's supervisor. Much to my surprise another baby was in need of a temporary home. I didn't even hesitate and, within minutes, we had worked out a plan for the baby to be brought to our home. I felt as if I were walking on clouds as I shared the news with Ron and the kids.

Baby Matthew arrived several hours later. He was a prince of a baby. Tucker was thrilled to have a baby brother even if it was just for a short time. Kassi loved having a real baby to mother, and Ron and I were delighted to have a baby for Christmas. God had certainly given our family a most unusual Christmas gift.

On Christmas Eve, Tucker suggested we hold a Christmas pageant. He was Joseph, Kassi was Mary, and Matthew was baby Jesus. Ron and I were asked to be the wise men. How could we refuse? It could be the last time our children would consider us wise!

Christmas Day was special. We had purchased gifts for Matthew and the children loved giving them to him. They fussed over and played with him all day. It was a wonderful Christmas.

A week later, Matthew went home to his own family, and we all cried. We had so enjoyed having him in our lives. Ironically, we'd had him for twelve days during Christmas. He had been our Christmas gift in so many ways.

After Matthew left, we talked about him every day and prayed for him every night. Ron and I felt a sense of emptiness. We realized we had room in our lives for more children. We decided we wanted to do more foster parenting. This time though, we wouldn't expect to adopt a baby. We were content with the size of our family and felt blessed beyond what we deserved. We couldn't ask for or expect more. However, we could help another child. We could foster parent on a temporary basis as we had with Matthew. We could give back to the system. We could give to God and honor Him by loving and caring for another one of his children.

It was six weeks later before we received another call. "We have another newborn, a baby boy. I just wanted you guys to have the first chance at him," Kathy said. We did not hesitate to say yes.

The next day, Joshua arrived at our home. He was so tiny, less than six pounds. He was so small that he fit under a washcloth while sleeping on Ron's chest. We were all in awe of him and yes, we fell instantly in love. Before long, it became clear that Joshua would need a permanent home. We already loved him as our own so, without hesitation, we began the adoption process. Joshua was sixteen months old when he became a permanent member of our family. His adoption was finalized on Kassi's fourth birthday; what a special birthday present—not every little girl gets a baby brother for her birthday!

Joshua has given us joy and surprises beyond imagination. When he was four months old, he lost his breath while crying. Ron observed the problem and immediately picked him up. As he did, Joshua went limp and turned blue. Moments later, I was dialing 911. Just then, Joshua took a breath. All I could think of was SIDS. It frightened us both, but the doctor checked Joshua out and assured us that he was fine. He told us that Joshua may be a breath holder and would likely do it again. Fortunately, it has never happened again. To this day, we are not sure what really happened, but I thank God He allowed Ron to be right there in order to notice Joshua's distress.

Another memorable time was when an older man who served in the church nursery pulled me aside when I picked Joshua up after Bible study. In a whisper the man said, "Your son is very special. There is something about him. I think God is going to use him in an amazing way." I was a bit surprised as I thanked him. He persisted though, "If your son doesn't have a Bible, I'd like to buy him one." I assured him that Joshua had one and again thanked him, but as I left, I tucked his comments in my heart.

As Joshua has grown, I have so appreciated his precious personality. He tends to see everything at its best while wearing a happy smile. He is the first one up in the morning, full of giggles and tall tales of his adventurous dreams. While the rest of us are dragging around getting going, he's coming down the stairs, flinging his socks in the air and singing, "Life is Good; Eternal Life is Better."

He is like a ray of sunshine and has a belly laugh that makes everyone else laugh. We have more fun observing him watch a funny movie than if we actually watch the movie. He has a gracious spirit and is always ready with a thank you. I remember when he told Kathy, our social worker how happy he is that God gave him our family—to which we all agree.

I have often been astounded at the depth of Josh's questions, particularly concerning spiritual issues. He has a wonderful perspective of God and heaven. It is common for him to tell me as we are saying goodnight how anxious he is for Jesus to come and get us. "I can't wait till I get to heaven," he will say.

"I can't either," I'll agree, "but until then God has work for us here too."

I cannot help but agree with that older man at the nursery and am eager to see what God has in store for our little guy. We are so grateful that we have been allowed to have Josh in our lives and thank God for His gift. It is such a privilege to be Josh's parents.

As I look back on all that occurred, I am filled with awe at how God works. Remember the baby we missed out on—the one I said no to? We later learned that the baby was Matthew. Oddly, his first placement had not worked out. Obviously, God wanted Matthew in our home that Christmas. Why else would we have been given the unlikely second chance? It was the unexpected Christmas baby that had made us realize there was a hole in our lives, and without him, our hearts might not have been prepared for Joshua. Clearly, God had a plan beyond our own. He was not done with our family yet. His Christmas gift of Matthew was instrumental in working His plan. That experience also taught me that we can't give more than God. In our attempt to give back to God for the gift of Kassi, He gave us another child. It is His nature because we are His children, and just as we enjoy pleasing our little ones and bringing them joy, He does the same for us.

I am humbled by God's work in our lives and grateful beyond words for how He created our family. With all my heart, I believe that from the beginning of time, God intended for Kassi and Joshua to be our children just as much as He intended Tucker to be ours. However, in His omnipotent power, He knew having children would be a struggle, so He provided another way. He found families who could not care for their children, and they became the conduits through which our children were passed to us.

I thank God for Kassi and Josh's birthparents. We are so grateful to them for allowing our children to be born and not choosing abortion even in the midst of difficult times. They may never know what treasures and blessings they brought into our lives and the world. Perhaps someday we will have the chance to thank them.

I am in awe of the journey that God allowed us to walk in order to become parents. God built our family in the most perfect way. I am now an adoptive and a biological mother yet there is no difference. I am simply the very fortunate mother of five beautiful children. Through Kassi and Joshua's adoptions, God gave us peace and fulfillment about Michael's adoption.

Kassi and Joshua have always known they are adopted and as such, are special gifts from the Lord to us. When they have asked why their parents didn't keep them, we told them that they wanted to but just couldn't take care of them. We keep in contact with some members of their biological family. When Kassi and Joshua are older, if they would like to meet their biological parents or siblings, we will help and encourage them.

We have learned so much and grown in so many ways because of our experiences. We treasure time and human life more and have learned not to take things for granted. Although I would never wish for anyone to survive their children, for a moment, I wish all parents could know how it feels. Perhaps all children would then be appreciated and loved for the gift they are.

Although I am far from a perfect parent, I understand the privilege of being a parent more than ever. With parenting comes a surrendering to some degree of one's own personal time and pleasures. What a small sacrifice compared to the joy of being a parent. It is the most difficult yet enjoyable task in life. Certainly there are times of frustration when I feel at my wits end and long for simpler days when there wasn't so much to care for, but never have I felt more fulfilled than when I'm being mom—the quiet talks, the opportunities to pray, the snowmen to build, the cookies to bake, the bedtime backrubs and storybooks. I feel so lucky to be able to comfort my children, play with them, and help them grow. Not everyone is as fortunate. Some never get to have children. Others lose theirs and would give anything to be with them again, even in the most trying of times.

Tucker, Kassi, and Joshua fill our lives with so much joy and challenge. I am very proud of them. Being their mother is truly one of the greatest privileges God has given me.

God also allowed our experience to enrich our marriage as we learned to draw on each other's strengths. Although we still have so much to learn in this life, our commitment, love, and respect for one another have grown. Through it all, a fabric was woven that is strong enough to survive even the most difficult of times. However, the fabric is strong only because Christ is woven through it like a steel chain.

Our faith in God is also deeper. It is more alive and fresh. We were forced to look our faith in the eye and to draw on the Lord. It was through His grace that we finally were able to forgive Nancy. It was one of the hardest things I have ever done. However, it would not have happened without God. He softened my heart and drew out my anger. It was a long and painful process of grieving and praying. Not until after I forgave Nancy though, did I find true peace in the circumstances of Michael's life and death.

Nancy and I had an opportunity to see each other eight years after she took Michael. It was at our college roommate's wedding. I knew we would see each other, so I called Nancy prior to the wedding. It was the first time we had spoken in all that time. Although it was awkward, it broke the ice.

Several months later at the wedding, when Nancy arrived, I gave her a hug and told her we loved and forgave her. She didn't respond, and I sensed that she was still deeply hurt, perhaps having never found peace or forgiveness herself. I continue to miss our friendship but have turned that over to God. I trust that if it is meant to be reestablished, God will provide a way. In the meantime, Nancy and her family hold a very tender place in our hearts. I will always love her for allowing us the brief privilege of being Michael's parents.

Our experience taught us some very important things about our God and His desire for us. I never understood how personal He wants to be with us. Our children though, helped me to realize that His desire is for a personal relationship with us just as we desire with our children. We are, after all, His children. Being a Christian is more than going to church and partaking in religious rituals. It is about having a relationship with the one and only God.

I have come to trust and love God very deeply, and my spiritual journey has moved from a sense of religious obligation to true fellowship and love for my Father and Savior Jesus Christ. If enduring the trials of becoming a mother is what it took to understand relationship with God, then it was well worth the price. Nothing is more important to me now than my relationship with Jesus Christ.

I also have a better appreciation for just how deeply God loves me; how deeply He loves all of us. Perhaps that is why He blessed us with children: so that we might get a glimpse of how deep His love is for us. To think He loves us even more than we love our children! It's hard to fathom. Our children are like God's grace. We don't deserve them and did nothing to earn them. They are simply a gift.

Although Ron and I have continued to have many challenges in life, we know that God is always there with us. We have our children's story as a point of reference. If God can give an infertile couple five precious children and heal the tragedy of a failed adoption with two more adoptions, then nothing is beyond His power or control. He has shown me that no matter what we go through, in the end, it will be for His glory and my good. God is faithful and can be trusted in all circumstances.

God also showed us how His timing is perfect. Sometimes I will admit I don't want to wait on His timing and have been tempted to move ahead with my own plan. However, I know His plan and timing are always better than mine.

I am not sure I will ever understand the whys of what happened but, to my surprise, they no longer seem important. God has given me my own personal experience of His peace—peace that is above any reason or understanding as referenced in Philippians 4:7: "And the peace of God, which transcends all understanding, will guard your hearts and your minds in Christ Jesus."

We will always miss Michael and Amy. There are still difficult days when our hearts ache for them, but we feel very fortunate and blessed. At least we were able to hold our children, know their gender, and have the chance to name them. We have a few treasured pictures. The joy in having them was worth the pain in saying good-bye.

All five of our children will always be our greatest blessing. Tucker, Kassi, and Joshua know about Michael and Amy. Every Christmas we hang 3 silver rocking horses on the tree for Michael and 3 angels on the tree for Amy. When Tucker, Kassi, and Josh have their own homes, they will each have an ornament for Michael and Amy to hang on their trees. Although we wish we would have gotten to know them, we also recognize that we'll be together in heaven someday. Heaven seems closer with our children awaiting us.

I know that God has a special purpose and plan for every life. Since death came so early in Michael and Amy's lives, one can only imagine what God's purpose and plan was for them. Perhaps by sharing our story, it has helped to fulfill it. Or perhaps Michael and Amy's purpose was to help keep our eyes straining for the next life. Jesus said in John 14:2, "I am going to prepare a place for you and I will come back to take you with me." Michael and Amy may be part of God's way of preparing heaven for us. But whatever their purpose was, I know that it was accomplished because our God is so faithful.

He gave us these five beautiful children, a loan from Him. Someday I will be called to account to God as to how I raised His children. However, I cannot be a good parent without Him and so, at the end of the day, I thank God for bestowing upon me the exhausting and yet satisfying honor of motherhood. Then I ask Him to give me the strength to do it all over again tomorrow.

As we await our day to be with Jesus and our loved ones who await us in heaven, it is my desire to help Tucker, Kassi, and Joshua to grow in their knowledge and love of God. I pray that as they live out their lives they will choose to use their time, energy, and hearts to bring honor and glory to our wonderful God. What greater purpose or privilege could there be in life?

Chapter 18

ALTHOUGH I ORIGINALLY published our story in 2007, as is the case with a living God, He wasn't finished writing it. When our children were in their teens, our journey to become parents took a whole new dimension.

Kassi was 12 when, quite out of the blue, she said, "Mom, I want to go to Africa and tell children about God." Her interest caught me completely by surprise, but the moment she said it, my long-forgotten dream of someday serving in an orphanage flickered back to life. In the years of raising children, such dreams had slipped to the back of my mind. Occasionally, I would ponder what it would mean to serve in an orphanage but deep down, I knew that since America doesn't have orphanages, it would mean leaving the United States. I couldn't imagine doing that while I had little ones of my own to raise. But with Kassi's comment, my mind began to consider the possibility. *Why not Africa?* Then again I thought, *But seriously, who really goes to Africa? I mean, could that really happen?*

But the spark had been ignited, so a few months later while doing our New Year's goals in our yearly resolution book, right next to Tucker's 15-year-old goal of getting a girlfriend and Josh's 10-year-old goal of learning to play tennis, Kassi wrote: Go to Africa someday! Looking at the entry I remember thinking, *Well, it's a bit of a reach but who knows. It could happen.*

Nine months later I noticed a post in our church bulletin. It read: "Looking for short-term missionaries to serve in an orphanage in Ethiopia." I felt a chill go down my spine. I nudged Kassi, who was sitting next to me, and pointed to the notice. As soon as she read it her eyes widened and, without a word, we both knew that we were GOING TO AFRICA!

We immediately applied to be on the mission team and about a month later, received word that we had been accepted to be part of the team. Kassi and I were so excited we could hardly contain ourselves. The trip was initially planned for the coming spring but it was delayed which was actually a blessing since it allowed us more time to raise money as well as get our passports and shots. Since Kassi hated needles, I expected a bit of a challenge, but she didn't even complain or flinch. The opportunity to go to Africa was worth it.

We wrote letters asking for financial support and many partnered with us in raising the $2,800 each. We were grateful for every dollar contributed as well as every prayer said. Our final funds came as a result of Ron's father's estate. We decided that using his inheritance would be a perfect tribute to Grandpa Johnson, who loved children, especially his grandchildren.

As the trip drew closer, our excitement grew but so did my worry. By now Kassi was 14. What if I really was crazy to take her to a third world country, like many had said? Was she ready for this? And what if I lost our passports or, worse yet, lost Kassi? It seemed there was plenty to be worried about, but I could see God's hand in it all. After all, what were the odds of even going to Africa and, still, it had all come together!

The day finally arrived. In the early morning hours we checked our luggage and waited for our team of about 15 people to arrive. Then the team and our loved ones, who had come to send us off, gathered into a large circle and prayed for our trip and for those we were leaving at home.

Saying good-bye to Ron, Tucker, and Josh was really hard. Although it would only be a two-week trip, it would take us to the other side of the world. I couldn't help but wonder if I'd ever see my guys again. It might sound odd but, in the weeks prior to our trip, I had made preparations in case I didn't return. I'd gone over details of the finances with Ron so he'd know how to handle the issues I generally dealt with. I left love notes for Tucker and Josh so they'd have something special from me. I even updated my own obituary and included thoughts and special songs should a funeral need to be planned. Perhaps it sounds morbid but there was something different about this trip, so I had made different preparations.

Waving good-bye from inside security, serious, sobbing tears escaped me. I already missed the boys. I would miss Tucker's 18th birthday and it broke my heart to think of not being with him. I couldn't help but wonder if there would be other important events I would miss as we left our world of comfort for something completely unknown.

Once the plane left the terminal though, sadness turned into excitement. We were going to Africa! In our wildest dreams, who would have ever thought we'd be doing this? Perhaps that was the greatest lesson of the trip. It made me realize that our dreams are gifts from God that He fully intends we fulfill, if only we're willing to make ourselves available. It's not about convenience or ability, but rather being open to what He has purposed for our lives.

Our flight took us to Denver, then onto London where we had an eight hour layover. With time on our hands we left the terminal, loaded onto the train, and made our way to Big Ben, Buckingham Palace, and many other famous sights. We jogged from site to site since time was short and we wanted to take in as much as possible. It was a thrill to see the architecture in the buildings that had been built years before America ever became a country. I kept feeling like I had to pinch myself. Never in my life had I thought I'd ever go to London. Time passed quickly and soon we were back on the train, going through security, and waiting for our final flight to Africa.

Landing in Addis Ababa, often referred to simply as Addis, one thing became immediately obvious: We were in a third world country. The airport appeared to be the nicest building around yet even there, toilets didn't have seats or toilet paper. Clearly these were scarce commodities in this culture. Getting through security was a bit unnerving as we tried to explain why we had garden hoses and other items that could be confiscated if the security people didn't understand the purpose. We also had to avoid being charged exorbitant custom fees, thus needed to communicate what was staying versus coming back with us.

Once through customs, we were greeted by Suleiman and Dawit who welcomed us as if we were long-lost family. They oversaw the operations of the orphanage and took care of every detail of our stay now that we were in Africa. My love for these men grew with each step of the trip, feeling as if our very safety and welfare rested on them. After exchanging our U.S. dollars for birr we then reloaded onto the bus and began the trek through the city and ultimately toward Ambo.

As we drove through the city of Addis, I was astonished at the sights: men lying in the gutters of busy streets, infrastructure that was disintegrating, farm animals wandering the streets, women and children wearing rags begging for money...poverty beyond words. The smells were nauseating as the combination of garbage and human and animal waste mixed with diesel fuel filled my nostrils. My stomach lurched and churned as the bus driver braked abruptly and beeped his horn at people, often just barely missing them or other vehicles on the road. I got to the point where I couldn't watch where we were going as I reminded myself that I was exactly where I was when home in America...in the hands of God.

I was relieved when we made it out of the city of Addis and began to see rolling hills. The landscape reminded me of Montana in the springtime. I was thinking that those who live in the country must be way better off than those who live in the city. At least they have space and fresh air. But as we drove farther from the city, it was like stepping back into a previous century, years before technology. The countryside was dotted with tiny thatched huts, men driving carts with donkeys or using oxen to plow fields, cattle being herded down the road, and women carrying heavy bundles of grass or colorful tanks of water on their backs. Even the children were carrying loads of grass or other children. Sometimes a baby was swaddled onto their backs. Most of the children were alone, without an adult in sight. These were sights we never saw in America. My mind was trying to absorb it. There were so many children. I wondered if these were some of the millions of orphans that lived in Ethiopia. I was overcome with emotion as I realized the level of need in this country, especially for the children, and the more I saw, the more overwhelmed I felt. How could we help when the need was so great?

Two hours later, we arrived in Ambo at the hotel where we would spend the nights. We were given a key to our room where we quickly freshened up and then loaded onto the bus again. It was mid-afternoon and we hoped to go to the orphanage and still have time to get back to Ambo before dark since it wasn't safe to travel at night.

Twenty minutes later, our bus pulled into a fenced area at the orphanage. As we pulled up, we saw them...beautiful little black children lined up waiting for us. As the bus doors popped open, we could hear them singing. Their voices were clear as they sang out a chorus in English, "We are happy to see you again." I was overcome with emotion as one by one they made their way to us, gave us a flower, and hugged us. In that moment, I felt as if God had spread his arms wide and said, "You always wanted more children. Well here are 40 of mine who need to be loved. Choose as many as you'd like."

That was the beginning. My heart and life would be forever changed by these darlings on the other side of the world. Despite having nothing, they were genuinely happy. They wore smiles that lit up the room and were content with something as simple as a stick to play with. The gifts we brought of soccer balls, yo-yos, and pictures were met with delight and joy. You never saw them squabbling over them but, instead, they generously shared with one other.

When one thinks of a third-world orphanage, the images that come to mind are often crammed rooms with crying babies, sadness, and hardship. But this orphanage was made up of children from the ages of 4 - 18, none of whom were available for adoption. In Africa, if an orphanage is adopting out children, the government is more involved. Suleiman, the founder of the orphanage, had also been raised in an orphanage and he wanted to provide a safe place to help the children where they could learn about Jesus and grow up to help other orphans, perhaps even becoming future leaders in their own country. The children all had one thing in common: They had lost one or both of their parents or lived in such extreme poverty that their family couldn't provide for them. As such, they created their own large, extended family who cared for and loved each other.

The small campus was made up of a cook's kitchen that was more of a small shack with wood cooking stoves, a small dorm where the children slept, a water tower that had been built by our church and volunteers, and a large school building. Children from the community came to the school as well as the children from the orphanage. One of the first things they learned about was Jesus and His love.

Although we did not speak the same language, the children were anxious to learn English and would patiently try to teach us Amharic. Even getting the pronunciation of their names correct was a challenge. We learned basic things like how to say I love you, thank you, and Jesus loves you. Mostly though, we communicated through hugs, smiles, tears, laughter, and gentle touches, universal to every language.

Our days started with breakfast at the hotel at the big table in the dining room, followed by morning devotions, prayers, and personal testimonies. Then we'd head out to the orphanage. Our project was to build steel stairs up the water tower so that the top floor could be accessed and completed for a future library. The children had school during the morning so we got more work done then. Once school was dismissed, they were eager to help us. One day, while painting the stairs with paint that was more like turpentine mixed with a little bit of color, the little boys grabbed paint brushes and began vigorously helping. I was under the stairs painting the bottom side and before the hour was over, I was covered head to toe with red paint. But the children were learning new skills and were thrilled to help.

Every day we ate lunch at the orphanage which consisted of cabbage, potatoes, beets, bananas, bread, and beans. There was also plenty of injera, the local flatbread made of a grain called teff, which was their source of protein. Once a month, their diet included meat which was a special treat for our meal the last day of our stay. We didn't have utensils so used our hands and the bread to eat. All the water we drank was bottled since the local water could make us very sick. After lunch we went back to work, but we all took turns playing with the children or just sitting quietly with them. Then as evening approached, we'd hug and kiss the children good-bye and as we did they would say, in their broken English, "Tomorrow come?"

"Yes," we'd say. "Tomorrow we will come back."

Back at the hotel's green garden, we would gather and sit in a circle. We took turns buying bottled soda and then shared our highlight or "sparkle" of the day.

Often they were things the children said or did. It was amazing to witness their lives and be a part of their day.

With each passing day, we got to know the children better: Fasige, who was smart and loving. Birqi, who was so painfully shy she wouldn't even lift her head to meet your eyes. Gadise, who was spunky; Lello, who was learning English and thus eager to help us communicate despite our language barriers. The love they showed to one another and to each of us was amazing. I thought I was coming to show them love and instead, I was overwhelmed by their love.

They had so little and yet they gave what they had with such joy. They shared clothing, having none that was really theirs, slept two or three to a twin bed, and had no certainty of their future yet were happy. And when they sang during church services, they were passionate and enthused. Their love for the Lord was obvious and overflowing with genuine enthusiasm. I thought of the children in America who had so much and yet complained. And I couldn't help but wonder what Christianity in America would look like if churches had this level of energy and enthusiasm for the Lord.

Probably most fun though was watching Kassi as she interacted with the children. As usual, Kassi was a kid magnet. The children were constantly hanging onto her, walking with her, and holding her hand. They braided her hair in corn rows just like theirs. Kassi loved the food and was willing to try anything. She also picked up the language quickly and worked hard to talk to them in their language. It gave me such joy to watch Kassi as she seemed to blossom in this environment. She was carefree and happy as she enjoyed the children and this strange, new culture.

Since Kassi was my roommate, we had some quiet time together at night. Our rooms were small but adequate and certainly more than I expected. There was an instant hot water heater and running water, although we couldn't drink it or even brush our teeth with it. With erratic availability of electricity, water was unpredictable so there was no guarantee of a shower let alone a hot shower.

I was glad we were rooming together, especially at night, when Kassi's relaxed nature was often replaced with fear. The night sounds were so different from Montana. We would hear violent dog and cat fights, shouting and horrific cries of people, and donkeys running in the streets, which actually sounded like rain. Kassi would occasionally climb into bed with me, shaking with fright. In the morning she was often covered with little bites from the bed bugs. I rarely had any bites so she must have been sweeter! But for the most part, we felt safe as we lived life among the amazing people in Ethiopia.

But I couldn't help but think, as my daughter quivered with fright in the night, how blessed we were. I thought of the many times when I tucked my children into bed and prayed that they would have a good rest with no bad dreams, that their friends wouldn't bully them, that they would be safe in the days ahead. How different our prayers were than the ones the children at the orphanage prayed. They prayed for food, for literal protection, for the chance to finish school, for dying relatives. Their prayers couldn't be a rote, recited prayer of "Now I Lay Me Down to Sleep". Theirs were prayers of survival filled with passion. What a different world we lived in.

One day at the orphanage, a grandmother came with her two grandchildren. The children had witnessed their father murder their mother and, since he was now in prison, the children and their siblings were living with their grandmother. She could not afford to care for them so asked the government to place them in an orphanage. The children were extremely malnourished, small for their age with skinny arms and legs. They had spent some time at the orphanage to get used to it, but on that day, they were to stay. As the grandmother said goodbye, the children began sobbing for her not to go. The house mother and older children gathered around the two little ones and tried to comfort them, but the four-year-old boy could not be comforted. He broke away from the group and ran down the road chasing his grandmother, sobbing and begging her to stay. She paused at the top of the road and sat with him a little longer. Then the older boys helped him back to the dorm. I don't think I had ever witnessed anything so heart-breaking in all my life. All I remember thinking is, *Oh, Lord for the day when we're in heaven and little children will not have to say good-bye to the people they love.*

As the days passed, I marveled at how well the two new children were adjusting. The older children hugged on and carried them around, including them and tenderly caring for them. The children knew better than anyone what these little ones were going through. They had been in their exact place, scared and unsure of their futures but then rescued and brought to the orphanage. In only a few short days, the two children looked healthier and, although quiet, they seemed to sense that they were safe and cared for.

But theirs weren't the only lives changed. Ours were too and I felt a love for the children like a parent loves their child. It is hard to summarize all that happened in the 10 days we were there except to say it passed too quickly. Although we had labored to complete projects, what we really had done was fall in love with these amazing young people. I truly felt as if God had given me more children to love and care for, even if we didn't live on the same continent.

The last day arrived and, as we left the hotel for the orphanage, I was filled with dread knowing that today we would have to say good-bye. Arriving at the orphanage, the children too seemed sad. Instead of running out to greet us, they quietly embraced us. Many had tears streaming down their faces. Some of the children had disappeared to a place of solitude to process their grief. We all knew that today would be our last and there would be no "Tomorrow come?"

I went in search of some of the girls I had grown to love. When I found them they had a hard time even accepting my hugs. They had already experienced so much loss and now, they felt the sting of saying good-bye once again. I tried to comfort them and tell them we loved them. They begged me to come back again, but I wasn't sure I could promise that. I knew I wanted to, but whether that was in God's plan was yet to be determined. I'd gone to Africa feeling like I'd be able to check off something on my bucket list, but the children had changed my heart. I knew I would never be the same. I hoped that someday I could return.

That last day seemed to drag as sadness hung heavy in the air. When it was finally time to go, in one last gesture we hugged as many of the children as possible, kissed their sweet faces, told them we loved them, and loaded onto the bus. I cried all the way to town, wondering if I'd ever see them again. I felt as if God had given me these precious children to love so that they would know that they mattered in a huge world where all they had was each other. In silence, I prayed that someday God would allow us to return and show these children that they were not forgotten. And I committed to help these darlings as much as humanly possible. After all, they deserved an education and the chance to live out their dreams as much as my children in America did.

Looking back, I think sweet Fasige is the one who most accurately defined what the mission trip meant. At the end of our last day together, I was sitting on the porch and, without a word, she quietly slipped onto my lap. I was fighting tears, so I tucked her into my arms and began rocking her back and forth. As I was rocking her, I thought, *I wonder if she's ever been rocked?* With that, the lump in my throat grew larger, and I struggled even more to keep from crying. After a few moments, Fasige lifted her head, looked up into my eyes and said, "Don't cry, we'll be together again in heaven!" Well, I lost it. Tears started flowing but through them I assured her that she was absolutely right. For even though we lived on opposite sides of the world and even if years passed before we came back, or even if we never returned, someday, because the children knew Jesus, we would be together again, forever. No more good-byes for us either.

As it turned out, God called us back to Africa two more times and I truly hope there will be another trip in the future. I miss the children, and it grieves me that they are growing up without me. Fortunately though, others have gone. There is now a non-profit organization called Tomorrow Come which was formed by fellow missionaries who felt called to make sure there was higher education for the children at the orphanage as well as in the surrounding community. Tomorrow Come has since built a high school and has paid for teachers to help all the children get a high school education and as a result, the number of children who are getting an education has increased significantly. Tomorrow Come is also working to provide vocational training to the children who do not go to university. For more information about Tomorrow Come check out their website: http://www.tomorrowcome.org.

Thinking back to our trips to Africa, I can't help but think of our amazing God who put dreams of helping children in Africa into the hearts of two little girls, Kassi and Denise, knowing that we would need each other to fulfill His plan. If it had not been for Kassi's desire to tell children in Africa about God, my long-forgotten dream of serving in an orphanage may have never happened. But instead, he placed us in the same family in separate generations so that we could fulfill His purpose together and as a result, our lives and hearts were changed forever.

People have asked, "Why do you go all the way to Africa when there are so many children in need here?" They are right. There are many needs, and I do help on local levels as well. But I also hope that since those people are concerned about the children here, that they will be instruments in helping as well rather than just questioning my actions. God calls us all to different causes because the needs are many. I once heard the phrase; do for one what you'd like to do for many. If we each applied that phrase to our lives, I have a feeling there would be a lot less "many".

For us, His call was to Africa where there is poverty like we have never seen in America. And although I can't help all those children that are orphaned and living on the streets, I can help the children who are part of the orphanage and the ones who will come in the future.

I've also been asked why we spend so much money to travel there when those same funds could support those children for years. Again, that's a valid question but, just like in America, money will never take the place of a hug, a smile, or a simple I love you. Because people have traveled there and shown them love, they also now know the love of Christ. That, quite frankly is priceless and could never have been communicated through a check alone. Someone had to go and show them what the love of Christ looks like for once they know that, they have true hope, hope that only comes in knowing Christ. And if I could give some advice: If ever there is an opportunity to serve on a mission trip, take advantage of it! It is life changing.

On the flip side, the resources given to sponsor children, drill wells, build orphanages, fight diseases, or to the thousands of other worthy causes are also very important. To quote Mother Teresa, "If our poor die of hunger, it is not because God does not care for them. Rather, it is because neither you nor I are generous enough." So for those who cannot travel or aren't called in that way, then give generously. In fact, take it a step further and give **up** generously. Give up a dinner out, a bigger home, an expensive hobby, a night of television, and instead, give more generously in time and resources so that we can impact poverty like never before.

I know our story will never really be complete. God is, after all, still writing our story. But to bring you up to date:

Tucker always had a passion to serve his country and thus enlisted in the US Navy after high school. As I submit this revision, he is currently deployed in Japan but plans to rejoin the civilian world and pursue his interests as an electrician.

Kassi recently graduated from high school and has aspirations of becoming a nurse practitioner or doctor and perhaps doing medical missions. She has a heart for Africa and dreams of adopting an Ethiopian daughter someday.

Josh is completing high school and is still determining his calling in life. He has threatened to buy an Airstream and park it in the driveway, which could have its benefits if my other two children are going to be so far from home! Somehow, I doubt that will really happen. He has a tender heart of concern for others and will use his gifts in his own unique way too.

And the children in Africa? Well, they too are growing up. They, like my American children, have goals for their futures and I am committed to helping as many as possible reach them. For many of the children, their goal is simply to help the orphanage grow so that other children can come and learn about Jesus. They will be the future leaders in Africa who will rescue more orphans and thus spread the Good News of Christ.

When I think back on all that God allowed me to do, it seems surreal. I still can't believe that I got to go to Africa, to walk the dirt roads, and hold the hands of little children who are so desperate for love. I'll never forget the woman who was begging as she extended her fingerless palm, her digits gone from leprosy, or the man who had no legs and thus scooted around on his buttocks. Also imprinted on my mind are the faces of the children as they smiled when there seemed to be nothing to smile about, and Chaltu, the young woman I formed a special bond with while helping to build a church in Ambo. My heart longs to see her again and, although we don't speak the same language, I can't wait to hug her again and let her know I haven't forgotten her. And yes, as Fasige reminded me, someday we'll see them all in heaven where neither language nor distance will be barriers. What a privilege it is to serve the Lord, wherever He calls us to go, if only we make ourselves available to His call.

"For we are God's handiwork, created in Christ Jesus to do good works, which God prepared in advance for us to do," Ephesians 2:10. So whatever it is that God prepared me to do, at the end of my life, I don't want have to missed it, whether it meant going to the other side of the world to love on orphans or serving in a soup kitchen in my own community. God intends for us to serve others. I pray that God wears me out doing good works for Him. That would be a life well-lived.

Epilogue

AFTER BEING PART of the birth of a child, I wonder how anyone could not acknowledge the complete and awesome power of our incredible God. No matter how competent or capable we are as individuals, there is nothing, not even a shred of power or ability that could create the amazing miracle of life. It's humbling to think that God would allow us to be a part of His creation. Each new life is a reminder of God's desire to have ongoing, personal relationships with humankind, with each and every one of us individually.

Ron and I feel very blessed that our family has been made up of biological and adopted children. Regardless of how our children entered the world or our lives, in every way, they are 100% our children. Raising adoptive children is different than raising biological children though because regardless of their environment, biological issues are a part of who they are too. Kassi, for example, always longed to know more about her biological family so, when she was seven, we arranged a meeting with three of her older sisters. Watching them together was amazing. I couldn't believe the number of mannerisms and gestures they shared and yet, they had never spent a day together. Many adoptive children have a sense of abandonment, even in a home where there has always been love and acceptance. Sometimes there is a longing to know someone who looks like them. I am grateful that we maintained communications with some of Kassi and Josh's siblings because now that they are older, they are developing those relationships and it has been a blessing to all of us.

Although our first experience with adoption was tragic, I am so grateful that God gave us the opportunity to adopt again. It has been a huge blessing in our lives and as a result, I am a huge advocate of adoption. I would love to see every Christian family embrace even one child that needed a forever home. The statistics are staggering. According to the Department of Health and Human Services, there are over 400,000 children in foster care in the United States alone. Of those, over 100,000 are waiting to be adopted. Many of these will turn 18 without being adopted. It breaks my heart to think of children who enter adulthood with no family to call their own. I can't imagine not having a family to go home to during the holidays, or no one to call when there is news of an engagement, wedding or baby, or not having a parent who is in your corner through all the ups and downs of life. We could change the world by committing to love one more child who desperately needs a family.

In a perfect world, there would be loving parents for every child. Instead, there are orphans, neglected and abused children, and unwanted children who are killed in abortions. There are parents who desperately want children but cannot conceive and thus seem destined to childlessness. Adoption was created by society as a solution to these inequities.

But adoption really was God's idea. In Ephesians 1:5, "God predestined us to be adopted as his children through Jesus Christ, in accordance with his pleasure and will." When we accept Jesus as our Savior, we become God's legitimate children. He sees us and loves us just like His own son Jesus, just as adoptive parents see and love their adoptive children as their own children. There is no difference. What a wonderful thing, to be loved as a child of the one and only living God. Adopting children has given me an understanding of God's immense love for me as His daughter. He did not adopt me because He was desperate or because it was the right thing to do. He adopted me because He loved me. Adoption, in many ways, is the ultimate love. It's bigger than natural instinct, blood relation, or obligation. It's all about choosing to love unconditionally.

In our culture, adoption and foster care are intended to provide safety for our most vulnerable members: our children. I am grateful to live in a country where children matter and am a strong advocate for protecting children. I have always had the greatest appreciation for the work of Child Protective Services (CPS), who has the task of identifying abused and neglected children. Because of the dedicated staff in this agency, our own children were rescued from highly dysfunctional homes and we have been richly blessed.

But in many states, CPS is a broken system. Sometimes children are removed from dangerous situations but due to a shortage of foster homes, are placed in equally dangerous situations. Sometimes parents are able to play the system and do what they need to do to get their children back without making permanent changes which would ensure the long-term safety of their children. I have seen many cases where children are jerked from biological family to foster family, and back and forth, denied the basic need to bond with anyone, creating life-long damage to the children.

Recently, however, this brokenness in CPS has moved in an entirely different direction, creating an alarming trend. Instead of removing children from dysfunctional homes, CPS is removing children from healthy, solid homes. The reason? Greed. Since funding for CPS is based on the number of children served, in order to maintain funding there needs to be a minimum number of children in the system. So in order to keep the number of children in the system high enough to fund the program, some states are literally recruiting children. This is happening so often around our country that there is even a name for it: Medical Kidnapping.

With my experiences with CPS and my obvious gratitude for their role in expanding our family, I would have never believed this if it weren't for the personal experience of a family friend in Michigan. In early 2014, when Josh and Brenda Burns took their critically ill infant daughter, Naomi, to the ER, instead of getting help, they were accused of child abuse and their daughter was removed from their home. Thus began every parent's worst nightmare.

The words "child abuse" evoke our worst feelings of disdain and disgust. Often we assume guilt and there is no "innocent until proven guilty." As a society there are some crimes that we will tolerate, but child abuse is not one of them. In thinking of my own children, I am grateful they had been rescued from their biological homes where alcohol and drugs were abused, especially since their older siblings had been neglected. I thank God my children were never exposed to that lifestyle.

But my friends in Michigan were nothing like that. They were responsible people with a strong faith and professional careers. They worked hard and made sacrifices in order to be debt-free so that Brenda could be a stay-at-home mom.

In anticipation of their baby, they read books, took classes, and sought advice from other parents. When Naomi was born, her delivery was very complicated which caused medical issues, including failure to thrive. Josh and Brenda took Naomi to the doctor on numerous occasions to seek help for her and never once was child abuse considered. However, when Naomi was 11 weeks old, she became violently ill and an ambulance was called. This trip to the ER changed their lives forever. It was at this hospital, where there was no medical history of Naomi, that Josh and Brenda were accused of child abuse.

Upon hearing of this accusation, I was shocked. This wasn't possible. Josh and Brenda would never hurt their baby. They were thrilled to be parents and loved their daughter as much as any parent could. As details and information began to unfold, I was horrified to learn that in America, many families were living this same nightmare. Children all over our country are being taken from their homes with no solid evidence of abuse and often after a trip to an emergency room. CPS even has contracts with some hospitals in which money is exchanged. Why would hospitals and doctors receive taxpayer funds from the agency that oversees the safety of children and in some case, removes them from their homes after a trip to the ER? One can only imagine but at the very least, it would seem to be a terrific conflict of interest.

As my friends continued through their nightmare, I realized that perhaps I could help raise awareness of this travesty since I had been on many sides of this issue. God had given me the journey of adoptive, foster, and biological mother. I had spent many sleepless nights praying that our foster child would someday be ours. I had also waited for months for the birth of the child that we planned to adopt, only to be forced to relinquish him. I knew what it felt like to wait and hope as well as to love and lose. The thought that CPS, the agency that had blessed my own family, could be causing this sort of devastation and destruction was incomprehensible.

This was America after all, the land of the free where we have the right to raise our own children without government intervention. For many of us, the most involved we get in these social issues is to watch in disgust as the news reports cases of child labor and sex trafficking. Movies like *The Hunger Games* where President Snow snatches children from their families in order to cause suffering and instill fear are just for entertainment. But for many families in America, it's real life and the more they fight to reclaim their families, the more they are spiritually, emotionally, and financially crushed. When families go through this, they are left so broken that many no longer have the ability to fight. As a result, many families are torn apart as they run out of resources to fight against the unlimited funds of the state CPS and prosecutor's office. And in some cases, a parent is forced to serve time in prison or jail for a crime that was never committed.

In the Burns' case, the horror of the situation was compounded by the complete mockery of the justice system. After being charged with child abuse, their case was delayed time and again. It was seven months before it was finally heard; seven months that their daughter was in a foster home, saying her first words, learning to sit, and other milestones that her parents missed out on.

When their case finally went to trial, the prosecutor focused on the results of an MRI done while Naomi was hospitalized. The MRI revealed a chronic subdural hematoma, new bleeding in multiple areas of the head, and retinal bleeding. However, when the MRI was initially done, these issues were so small that they weren't originally identified. It was 10 days later before doctors realized that there had been a misdiagnosis on the MRI and then, without consideration of Naomi's medical history or even the possibility that there could have been other medical issues, the diagnosis of abusive head trauma (AHT) was made. AHT is now the term for what has been referred to as Shaken Baby Syndrome (SBS). Although these injuries can be the result of AHT, they can also be the result of a delivery where suctioning had been used, as was the case with Naomi's delivery. One couldn't help but wonder if the rush to accuse the Burns of abuse didn't help to cover up the hospital's error in not properly diagnosing Naomi to begin with.

Several medical experts, who typically testify for the prosecution, reviewed Naomi's extensive medical history and concluded that there had been NO abuse. Instead, they all agreed that the injuries were a result of the difficult delivery and were the reason for the findings on the MRI. These testimonies would have provided sufficient reasonable doubt to the accusation of child abuse but some of these medical experts weren't allowed to testify. Those that did were frequently interrupted by the prosecutor in what appeared to be a deliberate attempt to make what was already a very complicated medical testimony even more confusing, especially to jurors who didn't have this medical knowledge. Even the second opinion from a prominent specialist, that had been requested by the accusing doctor, was withheld from the jury since it brought into question the abuse accusation. Compounding this, misinformation was also presented by the prosecutor that would negatively impact the jury.

The trial lasted two weeks and in the end, Brenda was exonerated of all charges and Naomi was allowed to return home. At that point, even though Brenda was found innocent, Michigan CPS placed Brenda's name on a state Child Abuse Registry and as a result, she cannot work in her profession as a registered nurse. Furthermore, the state required her to complete a service plan which included weekly visits from CPS contract personnel to supervise her parenting and Naomi's safety. Brenda complied and completed the service plan but even then, Brenda felt harassed and threatened by CPS. Eventually Brenda, out of fear that CPS would once again take Naomi, went into hiding with her daughter.

On the other hand, the prosecutor succeeded in convincing the jury that Josh had intentionally hurt Naomi since there had been a minor accident in the home while Josh was alone with Naomi. As Josh was holding Naomi in his lap, he reached for the phone and she slipped from his knee. As any parent would, he reached to grab her in order to prevent her from hitting her head on a nearby coffee table. Even though Naomi appeared fine, when she became ill the next day, Josh and Brenda took her to the emergency room and shared what had happened. The medical personnel assured Josh that he didn't cause her illness and that it was likely from a gastrointestinal infection and sent her home. It would be two days later, when Naomi took a turn for the worse and an ambulance was called, that their horror began. The jury, however, never got the chance to hear some of the key pieces of testimony and were misled by misinformation and thus, decided to "err on the side of caution" since Naomi couldn't tell them what happened.

I shudder to think of the many times my children were accidentally hurt like the time when my daughter ran up to my exercise bike while I was riding it and unable to stop it fast enough, I caused her to break her toe; or the fingers that she broke when she fell into the creek; or the split open heads and stitches when my children fell against the corners of the furniture. If we were all judged on these matters to the extreme that Josh was, every parent in the world would be accused of child abuse. Whatever happened to common sense?

Once Naomi returned home due to Brenda's exoneration, Josh had to move out since the court wouldn't allow him ANY contact with Naomi. Even convicted criminals are allowed supervised visits, but not Josh. The verdict in the civil trial created momentum for the criminal case to proceed against Josh. In the weeks between the civil trial and the criminal trial, the prosecutor offered Josh a plea agreement but Josh refused because he was innocent. Josh also took two lie detector tests which affirmed his innocence but the prosecutor and the DA wouldn't back down.

Months later, the criminal trial, under the leadership of the same judge as the civil trial, again was riddled with challenges. Critical peer reviewed articles were not allowed. Josh's lie detector tests were not allowed and other key evidence was not allowed leaving the defense with little substance to defend Josh. Meanwhile, the prosecutor presented abuse as the only plausible explanation for Naomi's medical condition and fabricated information to make Josh appear to be a calculating criminal rather than a loving, caring father.

In every sense, Josh was denied a fair trial and was considered guilty first and foremost, contrary to our system which is suppose to assume innocence until proven guilty. In the state of Michigan, there have been many concerns about the judicial system as noted in this link:

http://www.freep.com/story/news/local/michigan/2014/12/07/misbehaving-michigan-judges-disciplined-judicial-tenure-commission/20020833

Josh is currently serving a year sentence in jail. He is still awaiting a termination hearing to determine what, if any parental rights he will have after he is released from jail. Josh is planning to appeal his conviction but he will likely serve his sentence before the appeal will even be heard. Unless he wins an appeal, he will never be allowed to fly as a commercial pilot again so for now, the State of Michigan has not only taken away Brenda's livelihood as a nurse but also Josh's as a pilot. As a result of the terror brought on them by CPS, the Burns family that was once debt-free, ready to buy a home, and live the American dream is now bankrupt with no means to support themselves. This is their punishment for daring to go up against the big hospital and CPS; for daring to fight for their daughter rather than allow her to be used as a pawn in this corrupt system.

Naomi is now a perfectly healthy, happy toddler with no ill effects from her injuries/illness which is generally not the case with children who have survived AHT. Brenda and Josh have both missed out on precious moments of Naomi's life, as have their extended families. Truthfully, the only abuse that occurred in this case was what the state of Michigan did to this family and their child who has been denied a loving father in her life. They destroyed a solid family and, instead of protecting an innocent child, they created chaos, instability, and brokenness.

The bottom line: The hospital and the accusing doctor had too much to lose if either were found in the wrong thus, in order to protect the corrupt and gluttonous system, a mockery was made of justice. If the accusing doctor or the hospital had been found in the wrong, imagine how many other cases might need to be reopened to determine if those families had also been wrongly accused. Or imagine the future cases that would be affected, essentially rewriting law. But perhaps of most value to the system would be the amount of funds that could be scrutinized and stopped had this corruptness finally been exposed. Josh was essentially in a "David and Goliath" situation times 100. There was no way he was going to win his case, even as an innocent man.

Although this case occurred in the state of Michigan, there are many families being violated in similar ways in other states. As I've continued to stay abreast of this issue, more and more stories have come to light. Many who hear about this have expressed horror, disbelief, and outrage. Others have expressed doubt stating, "This can't be true. There must be more to this story that you're not sharing...this wouldn't happen in America." Yes, there is definitely more to this story but the absolute truth is that CPS overstepped its role of protecting this child and violated and exploited this innocent family in order to help fund this massive and growing government program.

For Josh, it's nothing short of a modern day Joseph, wrongly accused and imprisoned for a crime he didn't commit. And like Job in the Old Testament, he has had everything stripped from him: his wife, his daughter, his career, his home, and perhaps most tragic, valuable time to raise his daughter. He is a great husband and father but CPS, the hospital, the accusing doctor, and the judicial system had way too much to lose by admitting they made a mistake. The truth simply wasn't as important as winning.

Due to my own positive experiences with CPS, I could never have imagined myself pointing an accusatory finger at this agency. Their role as protector of our children is important and I am grateful there is someone to help those who are abused or neglected. Absolutely no child should have to endure this. But neither should a parent be serving time in jail for a crime that wasn't committed nor wonderful families be torn apart and not allowed to raise their own children. The price for saving abused children cannot be the destruction of families. That is completely counterintuitive to the role and purpose of CPS because children need good families to thrive.

Our taxpayer funds should be used to support legitimate cases of abuse rather than being used as unlimited resources to financially rape innocent families. Josh and Brenda have spent over $200,000 fighting for their daughter. I wonder how many families have had to give up their children simply because they didn't have the resources or support system to fight a lengthy legal battle. Children are not property of the state to be manipulated in order to fund government programs. This is still a country where we should be innocent until proven guilty and where justice should be about right and wrong. It is a country where parents should be able to take their children to the emergency room without fearing that they will be used as pawns to financially benefit hospitals or doctors.

Throughout this tragedy, the Burns family has clung to their faith. Josh entered jail with his head held high because he knows that he is an innocent man, especially in the eyes of God. God will use even this situation for His purpose and plan. Perhaps this will be the beginning of an awakening in our country and, as Americans, we will beat the drums of justice and demand that this be stopped.

This is a massive problem. It is going to take the voices of many to bring about change. Please do not allow yourself to be complacent. We are, after all, reaping the benefits of our ancestors who risked their lives to make a better life for their families by crossing oceans, venturing to unsettled lands to start homesteads, standing for religious freedoms and voting rights, or fighting to free slaves. They gave their blood, sweat, and tears. Many even gave their lives to ensure these freedoms.

Now it's our turn as a generation, to take a stand and protect our children and to honor our ancestors for the sacrifices they made. We, as United States citizens, cannot allow this horror to continue, left under the radar and with no consequence. We cannot allow elected politicians or unelected officials to take away our basic right to raise our children without government intervention. If we do, we are just as guilty as the corrupt government bureaucracy and justice system for violating the rights of American children and families.

Please take a stand and contact your congressmen, senators, governors and state leaders. The next family to be violated and trampled upon could be yours, your children's, or grandchildren's. God is very clear about how we should respond when we are the benefactors of so much: "For everyone to whom much is given, of him shall much be **required**, and of him to whom men entrust much, they will **require** and demand all the more." Luke 12:48

We are a nation to whom much has been given. Now it is time to give back, to fight back, and to take back what is ours...our children and our families. God doesn't suggest it. He REQUIRES it. And when Josh is released and exonerated of this injustice, God will have the glory! This story is not over. God is still writing it and you could be one of those He uses to finish it.

For more information on this precious family, you can go to their website: **www.tornfamily.com**. Their story was also featured on the Dr. Phil show on April 27, 2015. Additional resources and links are listed at the back of the book.

As this long project of writing and rewriting this book has come to an end, I cannot help but look back and feel gratitude for what has come of this experience. Around me are the reams of paper from the hundreds of rewrites, the notes, and mementos to remind me of my treasured children. Reflecting back to where this all began, I am amazed that this book has finally reached a conclusion. Every time I sat down to write, I would pray that God would provide the right words to express what needed to be said. Now that I am done, I am certain it is a project I could never do again primarily because I feel as if God was the true author. He pulled at my heart, bringing out painful and sometimes even shameful moments. He did not allow me to sugarcoat it or take the innocent bystander position. The journey I took while writing the book was emotionally draining and yet very healing. As a result, I feel like I am a better person having survived. God grew me in the process and my faith is stronger and more alive than it has ever been.

As you've read this book, my hope is that you've seen the power of God at work. This is after all, His story, His testimony of love worked through our lives. If He could fill our lives and make us whole again, He can do the same for you. You see, God knew from the beginning of time that we would go through these experiences. Because He is able to see all time—past, present, and future, He knew that it would cause us to draw closer to him. However, the choice was always ours to turn to God in our time of struggle or turn away from Him. I will be forever grateful that we turned to Him.

We would not have healed if it had not been for our faith in God. He was so faithful to us. Through it all, He provided for us by enveloping us in His love. We are grateful that He allowed us to have more children but even if He hadn't, He is still faithful. Through all the difficulties, He never let go of us or turned his back. He stood by us and loved us through it.

Although I would never wish to relive these experiences, I am grateful for what God has allowed because of them. I have gained more than I lost. In fact, I am not sure I really lost anything because through it all, God gave me five beautiful children that I will cherish and love for all eternity.

God strengthened our marriage and our love and sealed us with a passion for loving Him. He gave us compassion for others who suffer the loss of a child and has provided some amazing opportunities to minister to others. Most importantly, we learned that this present life is not just about this life. It's about the next and, having suffered in this life, we look eagerly to the next life when such suffering will never be again.

As we continue our journey in this life, my desire is to finish well. With each new day, I pray for an opportunity to serve God and to touch someone for Him. Then when given that opportunity, I pray that God will allow me to forget it so I do not become proud or boastful. In all that I do, including this book, my deepest prayer is that God will be honored and glorified.

Oh, how I love my wonderful husband and precious children but now, I love my God even more. I know that He will see us through any circumstance or challenge. I also know that no matter what happens, I will come out a better person because I trust God with the outcome.

> **"For I know the plans I have for you," declares the Lord, "plans to prosper you and not to harm you, plans to give you hope and a future." Jeremiah 29:11**

Additional Resources And Links

The book *Edges of Truth...the Mary Weaver Story*

The movie *An Unreal Dream: The Michael Morton Story* on Netflix or at this link: www.anunrealdream.com/.

The movie *The Syndrome* that can be followed at this link: http://www.resetfilms.com/

The tornfamily.com website has numerous other related links.

Additional sites regarding other families who have been wrongly accused as well as articles of concern about CPS:

http://fixcps.com/

http://www.theatlantic.com/health/archive/2014/11/how-can-doctors-be-sure-a-babys-been-shaken/382632/?utm_source=btn-facebook-ctrl2

http://medicalkidnap.com/2014/12/30/medical-kidnapping-billion-dollar-adoption-business/#sthash.q3UHPp12

http://www.myfoxhouston.com/story/28987791/cps-takes-custody-of-19-month-old-accuses-parents-of-medical-neglect

http://reason.com/blog/2015/01/14/cops-and-cps-threaten-parents-whose-kids

http://calcoastnews.com/2014/12/cps-sued-kidnaping-children/

http://www.familiesandchildrenjustice.com/

http://www.familydefensecenter.net/

http://donnellyjustice.me/2012/09/25/cps-is-breaking-the-law-and-kidnapping-children-here-are-the-facts/

http://www.bostonglobe.com/metro/2013/12/15/justina/vnwzbbNdiodSD7WDTh6xZI/story.html

http://www.youcaring.com/medical-fundraiser/the-medical-misdiagnosis-of-shaken-baby-syndrome/316031#.VPdnOQ3OETQ.facebook

http://m.clickondetroit.com/news/parents-fight-to-reunite-family/32990850

http://medicalkidnap.com/2015/05/06/report-exposes-why-corrupt-cps-agencies-seldom-place-foster-children-with-family-members/

http://apps.americanbar.org/litigation/committees/childrights/content/articles/spring2015-0315-welfare-attorneys-shaken-baby-syndrome.html

Denise Johnson is a passionate advocate for children. She volunteers with children's ministry at her church and coordinates the sponsorship program for New Hope Center, a center for orphaned and handicapped children in Ethiopia. She also has a heart for women's ministries and serves as a ladies Bible study leader. Denise owns her own business and enjoys time with her husband, children, extended family, and friends. She and her husband, Ron, live in beautiful Montana with their growing family.

Visit: www.DeniseEJohnson.com

Made in the USA
Middletown, DE
13 August 2015